# THE TRUTH CHRONICLES
## BOOK I

Secrets of the Soul

Danny Searle

# DEDICATION

To all those seeking the truth and enlightenment.
Never give up your quest. Never give up hope.
You are never alone.

# NOTES

# ACKNOWLEDGMENTS

I owe a great deal of gratitude to my brother David for editing this lengthy tome. Also my parents, Margaret and Trevor, for their constant love and support, in all my ventures. My two boys, Thomas and Jack, who give me focus and meaning. Finally, the one person that found me at the right time, and gave me the impetus, support, and Love to complete this project – my Twin Soul, Adina.

# CONTENTS PART 1

# CONTENTS PART 2

## Appendices

EACH MORNING WE
ARE BORN AGAIN.
WHAT WE DO
TODAY IS WHAT
MATTERS MOST.

*Buddah*

# 0

## INTRODUCTION

*"This is my simple religion. There is no need for temples; no need for complicated philosophy. Our own brain, our own heart is our temple; the philosophy is kindness. (Dalai Lama)*

STARTED THIS book way back in 2004, and finished this part, Book 1 of 3, in late 2014! Yes, a long time, and many things "distracted" me through that time, but also many "new" things came to light. But everything happens exactly when it is meant to happen. In this case, I believe that to be true. I think if I had of published this book 10 years ago, it may not have reached that many people, and many hidden truths would not have been shared. However, since the massive consciousness Shift of 2012, a lot more people are open to this information.

My original plan was to write 1 book. However, over the years, more and more pieces of the puzzle fell into place, and the topics I wanted to include got bigger and bigger. It was my father, ever the pragmatist, that suggested that I split the book up into smaller chunks – in his words *"Why don't you serialised it?"* It was a revelation and a huge weight off my mind. The way I was going, I would never have finished one, giant, single book. But by breaking it up into 3, it became much more manageable. So no, it was not some cynical attempt to force people to buy 3 books instead of 1!

I was presenting a lot of this information in 2 day seminars, however in 2012, I was feeling pressured to get the book finished. But not having the time, it was my dear friend Amber that suggested "why not make some videos and put them on YouTube?" So I did. Much to my amazement, the videos went viral. So while the videos were spreading my message, I had time to finish the book, and here I am!

Make no mistakes, this book is not for everyone, but it is very important for the right people. I hope you will find the answers that the main stream have failed, or are unwilling to answer. It is not my desire to convert the masses, or to put myself out there as some expert or guru. I was given this information, so I am passing it on, just as I promised I would.

I have had a very special relationship with Spirit since I was a child. By age 6, I was seeing and hearing "ghosts", or as I call them, Earth-bound Spirits. By 14, I had had my first (remembered) out of body experience. I was taken into the Astral Plane, and I can assure you I did not want to come back. Then at 22, my life changed forever. My main Spirit Guide, Michael, woke me at 3:33AM. A glowing man was standing at the end of my bed – smiling. He held out his hand and said *"Come on, it is time to go to work..."* I was overwhelmed by a sense of Love, Peace, and Compassion that radiated from this being. I knew I was not dead, and I felt no fear, so I reached for his hand. I thought I sat up, but when I looked back, I saw my physical body still lying on the bed, peacefully asleep.

For the next 2 years and 8 months, I was taken. Sometimes every night, sometimes only a few times per week. But it was always at least once a week, during this intense period of my life. I was taken to every level of the Spirit World. From the arrivals, to the different levels within levels, and to the final departure area. I witnessed hundreds of deaths from the Astral Plane. I personally counselled dozens of Souls that were lost, confused or afraid. In fact, all of the "Spiritual" knowledge I impart in this book, either came from my time back in Spirit, or in direct meetings with my Guide. Yes, that is right – direct. I do not "channel" anything. In fact, I do not put much credence in any source that is channelled. That is only because, the powers that be, can beam thoughts directly into your head...well now I am getting off topic – I will cover that in Book II (hahaha).

Getting back to my meetings. I would sit, stand or whatever directly opposite my manifested Guide. He would appear almost solid. I could not touch him, but I could certainly feel his energy. In these meetings I would ask questions, and he would try and answer them the best he could (or was allowed to). Quite often, he would point me in the right direction as to where I may find out more. The easiest way to explain how Guides give you information is an inverted pyramid – a very broad, and general amount, getting more and more to the point. This may take days, or it may take years. Depends on how hard you want to work, and, how quickly you leave your pre-conceived (Ego) ideals out of it. So there is the other reason why this book took so long to write. I had a lot of research to do!

My friends and family could always tell when I had been in contact with my Guide. They would always comment how bright my eyes were, how radiant I was – *"What have you been doing? You look fantastic"* they would say.

I try very hard to back up any claim I make, because in my experience, there is always someone trying to knock you down. So the best way to fight a narrow mind, is with FACTS. Undeniable facts – even though they will still deny them! Part 1 of this book will answer why they do that.

Part 2 is more to do with my Guides pointing me into a direction, and then, me finding out what I can about it. They will confirm, or say, "Try a different approach" until I reach the desired outcome.

As I said, this book is not for everyone, but I do believe at this time in human's evolution, it is an important tool for those who are willing to open their minds. Also, I would implore you to research these topics for yourself. I am the biggest sceptic going, so I do not expect you to just believe everything, because it is in print. This book is an introduction, not a full exposé. So treat it as such, and you will be well served.

I would like to tell a little story about science, and why you should be careful about closing your mind.

In 1912, Alfred Wegener, a meteorologist, came up with the theory of Plate Tectonics. This theory says that the earth's crust is broken up into "plates", and they move around by themselves, slowly over time.  So originally, all of the Earth's landmass was all joined together, called "Pangaea".  Pangaea broke up and drifted apart, giving us the continents we all know today.

Since his ideas challenged scientists in geology, geophysics, zoogeography and palaeontology, it demonstrates the reactions of different communities of scientists. The reactions from the different disciplines was so negative, that serious discussion of the concept stopped. He was told to go back to weather prediction and leave the real science, to real scientists!

It was not until the 1970's when scientists started to map the surface of the oceans, that they realised Wegener was right.  Unfortunately this was 50 years after his death. Wegener dies in 1930 - in Greenland, still trying to prove he was right.  He never gave up.

One cannot underestimate the effect of a radical new viewpoint on those established in a discipline. The "authorities" in these fields are authorities, because of their knowledge of the **current view** of their discipline. A radical new view on their discipline, could be a threat to their own authority.

One of Alfred Wegener's critics, the geologist R. Thomas Chamberlain, could not have summarized this threat any better:

*"If we are to believe in Wegener's hypothesis, we must forget everything which has been learned in the past 70 years, and start all over again."*

He was right!

---

# 1

## REINCARNATION, KARMA & SOUL AGES

---

*"There is nothing either good or bad, but only thinking makes it so..." (William Shakespeare from the play Hamlet, 1603)*

---

*H*AVE YOU EVER wondered why some people act the way they do? For example, let's say there are five children in a moderate, middle class family that were all brought up on good values and morals. All the children received equal love from their parents and never really wanted for anything. Out of these five children, four of them go on to complete college degrees and become successful professionals in their respective fields.

The other child however ends up in a life of drug abuse, crime, and jail. The parents are left wondering what they did wrong, never fully understanding why this child went off the rails. To make matters worse, it does not matter what support is offered by the parents or siblings, because no one seems to be able to get through to them. More often than not, the troubled child will usually suicide or die from an overdose. People tend to make up all sorts of reasons for why this all too familiar story unfolds, but at the end of the day, it comes down to one thing - Soul Age. Soul age is the major contributing factor for all human behaviour, be it good or bad.

In fact, Soul Age determines how a person navigates their life. To fully understand Soul Ages, we must first understand where the concept comes from.

## Re-incarnation

The word reincarnation literally means to *"come again in the flesh."* Most believe that the process of reincarnation includes continual rebirths in human bodies, which continues until the soul has reached a state of perfection and merges back with the Source (God or the 'Universal Soul').

However, it must be understood that reincarnation is not merely the act of repeated Earth lives, but is part of a much grander plan, as we will discover. Till now, if one was posed the question: *"What is the meaning of reincarnation?"* undoubtedly the response would be: *"We return again and again in new embodiments in order to learn lessons and to thus perfect our souls to a state of Divine enlightenment"*. This answer would not be incorrect; however it still represents a rather broad and abstract opinion.

Reincarnation is the process of dying in one physical body, and after a certain time, being born back into a new physical body. However, contrary to popular belief, once you live and die as a human, you will always be reborn into a human body. Souls never de-evolve by taking on animal or insect lives.

On average, a soul reincarnates 500-600 times before it ceases to incarnate. But soul age does not refer to how many times a soul has incarnated. It refers to the lessons they have learnt in the lives they have lived. You see, the purpose of reincarnation is to learn and ultimately evolve to a higher state of awareness. All souls start off on the same level called Infant Souls, then move up to Child Souls, then Young Souls, Mature Souls and finally, Old Souls.

There are 7 levels within each Soul Age (Fig. 1). So someone may be a Young Soul at the 7th level, therefore they will behave and think differently to someone who is a Young Soul 1st level. In fact, as we will see, there are marked differences the further two ages are from one another.

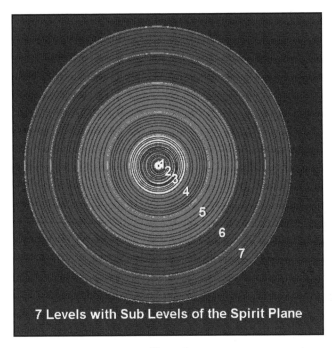

**7 Levels with Sub Levels of the Spirit Plane**

*Figure 1*

Soul Age also determines where you end up when you die and go back to the Spirit Plane. The Spirit Plane is also divided up into different levels. Each level is a higher vibration, or frequency than the one below it. Like Soul Ages, there are 7 levels in the Spirit Plane, each divided again into 7 sub-planes.

The lowest, and therefore the densest (Number 1 in the diagram), sits just above the 3rd dimension or physical plane where you are right now. This is known as the Astral Plane, and all manner or disembodied spirits (ghosts), deva, nature sprites and demons exist there. It is possible to visit the Astral Plane while still alive. This is known as Astral Projection, however it usually takes considerable training before one can consciously travel there at will. Above that is level 2. If there really was a place called hell, then this level may resemble it best. But there is no fire and no devil, only psychological self-entrapment and torment.

The person's own guilt, lack of empathy or hatred keeps them trapped there. A really good illustration of this level can be seen in the movie "*Astral City: A Spiritual Journey*" (2010). This is where the main character André goes to when he first dies. Only when he truly repents for his negative human ways is he taken into the next and much more comfortable 3rd level of the spirit plane. This movie is based on the Portuguese book *Nosso Lar* ("Our Home" in Portuguese) by the Spirit André Luiz channeled through Francisco Cândido Xavier. It was translated into English and renamed "Astral City: A Spiritual Journey" (Astral City: A Spiritual Journey, 2010). This is an excellent book/movie for understanding the lower levels of the Spirit Plane where the majority of people go.

Another excellent book is called *Life in the World Unseen* by Anthony Borgia (Borgia, 1997). This book has a slightly more advanced soul travel back to the Spirit Plane after death, but this time to the 4th level with some sneak peeks into the 5th and higher. I will discuss the Spirit World in more depth in Chapter 10.

For more advanced Older Souls the uncomfortable or unpleasant feeling lasts right up to about the 3rd level. That is why Old Souls rarely "hang out" in the lower planes. On the other extreme is the 7th level and this is beyond any human understanding. It is known as the Mental Plane and it is here where souls merge into one huge super consciousness. These Super Souls work on planetary and dimensional projects.

Eventually, the Super Soul is assimilated back into the Source (God) and all of the information that has been accumulated over the eons is downloaded and shared. It literally takes millions of years between a Soul being born and finally assimilating back with the Source.

We have all heard people say they are in 7th Heaven, but I don't think they are referring to this place! Indeed, what many people believe to be the heaven of the Bible is located around the fifth sub plane of the 3rd level (3.5). Souls generally stop incarnating once they reach the Level 5.5. That is, around the 5th Sub plane of the 5th Spirit Plane.

This is where all full time Spirit Guides reside, all the way up to Level 6. Other souls who are not Guides also reside on those levels. Level 6 is where all new creation takes place, so many advanced souls dwell there. You may ask, why bother to incarnate on Earth at all? Why don't we just stay in the Spirit Plane? Another question I hear a lot is what about children that die very young – what was the point of that? What about people born with disabilities or disfigurement?

Quite simply, the Earth Plane was created to accelerate soul's advancement. On the Spirit Plane there is no negative energy what so ever. Since Souls want to learn about all aspects of creation, they must also experience the negative. After all, you cannot have light without dark, so to be truly balanced and thus 'enlightened' one must walk both paths. Indeed, there is no "right" or "wrong", just choices and experiences.

So imagine for a second you want to be an ice-cream expert! Yum right? Not a bad way to earn a living. The problem is that you have only ever sampled vanilla ice-cream. You have tried every variation and now you can tell where it came from just from the texture and taste. Then you find out that in another country they have a flavour called 'chocolate'. What do you think your initial impulse would be? I know if it was me, I would be on an airplane and heading straight for the chocolate ice-cream country! After all, to be considered an expert in ice-cream, I would need to be at least familiar with both flavours.

Therefore, I would set myself up in the new country and learn everything there is to know about chocolate ice-cream. Furthermore, I would also like to teach the denizens of this country the wonderful attributes of my beloved vanilla ice-cream! And then when everyone in the world knows everything about both vanilla and chocolate ice-cream along comes 'strawberry' flavour. But that is in the future... So you see, vanilla is not better than chocolate or vice versa. They are just different types of the same basic ingredient – but in life, the base ingredient is energy, and the flavours are light and dark. Energy on its own is neutral. It is our "intent" that influences how energy will flow around us. Thus, if you feel you are surrounded by negative energy, you can simply change it to positive energy.

Another problem with experiencing the negative aspects of a situation in a place that does not contain negative energy, is it is not very productive. It's like trying to learn how to swim in the middle of a desert. While you can imagine the feeling of water, and imagine the sensation of swimming, you will never really understand it until you go into the water!

Indeed, if you have always lived in extreme heat, how could you truly imagine extreme cold? You can read all the books you like and attend all the workshops in the world but without a reference point to start from, you have very little chance of fully grasping a concept.

So in reality, a child growing up in a war torn country who has only ever known hunger, fear and hardship, who dies at 12 years old, has a soul that will learn more in that short life compared to a Soul that stayed in Spirit. To give you an idea, hypothetically, the negative trait of abandonment could take a soul about 10,000,000 earth years to 'intellectually' understand what it feels like to be abandoned by your parents as a child.

On the other hand, a life as a girl in rural India could knock that one on the head in under a decade! So you see, the earth offers souls a chance to fast track their learning and progress at a rapid pace.

On the points of brain damaged children or severely deformed individuals, this is often a two-fold situation. On the one hand, the Soul that is in the handicapped body usually wants a break. They need to incarnate, but they don't want to have to deal with all the usual emotional dramas and stresses of everyday life.

So they offer their service as it were to souls that want to learn about the Carer Role. Part of Soul's learning, particularly in the Mature Soul level, is the carer role. This is where they will care or look after someone or many people as in the case of doctors and nurses.

This shouldn't be misunderstood with Child Souls who will care for a family member. They do this more out of obligation or more appropriately, because it is the right thing to do. The Mature Soul will actively seek out people to help and draw great satisfaction from this type of work.

The soul that offers their Earth life for the service of other Soul's experience as a carer will in itself gain great positive Karma for the giver, so this is also another reason why some souls will "donate" their life. They may need to catch up on Karma and this is a great way to do it. That said, there will be at least 1 life for every soul that finds them in a handicapped body. When people die unexpectedly, there is a good chance it was not unexpected from that person's soul. When the soul had learnt or experienced what it came here to do, it went straight back home!

## The Story of an Old Soul - Ryan White

A very good example of an Old Soul coming to Earth not for their own Karma, but to help all of humanity, is the life of Ryan White. In 1985, the HIV AIDS virus had reached epidemic proportions around the world and was widely considered a 'homosexual' disease. As such, no politicians gave it much thought, yet alone offered funding for a cure. In fact, the Child Souls were having a field day claiming it was a curse from God for being homosexuals! That was all until Ryan came along.

Ryan White was a 13 year old, haemophiliac who acquired HIV AIDS from blood products (Factor 8) he was given to make his own blood clot. People at that time 'assumed' he had been doing something wrong and therefore he deserved to die. Mainly due to ignorance about how AIDS can be spread, both students and teachers at his school protested and demand that he leave.

Ryan, a 13 year old gave this response, *"I don't want nobody [sic] else to get it, and I can see why they are worried. But I mean, if my doctors says it's ok to go back I can't see any reason why I can't..."* It goes to court. Local so-called doctors give evidence saying they would not treat him, nor would they let their kids go to his school. Eventually the court decides in favour of Ryan and he is allowed to return to school.

After a local 'citizens group' got involved, he only went back to school for a few hours before they filed for an injunction. That is when it got really ugly, but on a higher level – that is when the national media jumped on it.

Ryan's family had rubbished dumped on their front lawn all the time. They got threats in the mail and finally after a bullet went through their dining room window while they were eating, they decided to leave town.

The new town they went to was (thank the Universe) much more open hearted. They welcomed Ryan to their school where he attended proms and dances and said *"You know mom, for the first time in my life I feel like I am not fighting this disease on my own."*

Ryan's struggle turned people's fear into sympathy. Ryan's story attracts powerful friends including Charlie Sheen, Cher, Elizabeth Taylor, Dionne Warwick and Michael Jackson to name but a few. In the UK the AIDS campaign was about to get some very high profile support from Princess Diana. In 1987, Princess Diana visits a HIV AIDS ward in a hospital and the people see her holding hands and comforting the patients. This had a profound effect on the people's views about AIDS (I love it when Old Souls team up!!!) In 1989 Diana opens "The Landmark" for people with HIV and AIDS.

Back in the USA, Ryan White uses every bit of his short life to promote education about AIDS. Ryan would often state that he felt it was his mission to educate people. Ryan White died on April 8 1990 aged just 18. Four months later under immense public pressure, President George W. Bush signs the "Ryan White Care Act". It creates the first government funded program for HIV and AIDS sufferers. To date, the fund is still the largest government care provider for people with HIV and AIDS providing new drugs that give back sufferers an almost normal life (The Ryan White Story, 1989).

This is a typical story of a very Old Soul coming to earth purely to help. When his mission was complete, he went home. As I just alluded to, that on top of the basic factors of reincarnation, there is a more complex system to integrate – Karma.

## Karma

The Universal English dictionary defines karma as: *"An act considered in its causal relation to a person's fate or destiny"*. In Buddhist philosophy it means: *the sum of a man's acts, words and deeds which decides his fate in each stage of existence*. Sometimes the word karma is used as a synonym for fate or destiny. In Spirit, it simply means the total of a person's actions or deeds, which means both positive and negative. People often say when something bad happens that it was 'Karma'. However, I have never heard anyone say when someone has a win fall that it was Karma. They usually say "That was lucky". As we will see, there is no such thing as good luck or bad luck – there is just a state of mind that at its core is the Law of Karma.

I am as guilty as anyone when I often refer to Karma as "lessons". We usually say we return to earth to learn new lessons. But in reality, life is not a series of lessons - Life is experiences. Moreover, as well as experiences, it is your perception of these experiences that determine the cause and effect in your life. For many, as soon as something goes wrong, or, if their life seems to be on a downer all the time, they blame fate or worse, blame someone else for their difficulties. The most fundamental and simple ideal that everyone should understand is like attracts like.

If you perceive life as a series of lessons to be endured, then it will be. It takes a brave person to go beyond the conditioning and restrictions that we at times seem to be surrounded by. Indeed, question and keep questioning until the answers come... *"Seek and you shall find..."* Furthermore, if you always adopt a 'victim' role whenever something bad happens, you are negating the experience, and will relive it in another variation, until your Soul is satisfied that it has dealt with it in such a way, that Karma is balanced. So rather than adopt the 'woe is me' attitude, start asking "why has this just happen?" Maybe there is a lesson in there somewhere and by identifying the issue will help put you half way to solving it.

The law of cause and effect states that for every action there is an equal and opposite reaction. So imagine if instead of getting stressed and having an emotional meltdown or angry outburst you sat quietly, centred yourself, breathe deeply and just thought about why this may have occurred. Is it something you have created? Were your actions responsible for this situation? Be honest with yourself. Finally, when you are settled, the solution may just come. Remember, nothing you encounter in this life will ever be 'unfixable' – it is all a state of mind!

The reaction may not be the same as the action because time may elapse before the law takes effect. This was purposely built into the Earth plane experiment. If cause and effect were instantaneous one can only imagine what a chaotic and horrendous world we would incarnate into. Just pause for a moment and look at your own life. I am sure you can find at least one time when you were so insulted, slighted or hurt that your immediate thought was for justice and retribution.

But having to wait for a period of days, months or years your resolve was more subdued and even a change in heart may have occurred. This is precisely what we were talking about before – that Karma is your life experiences and your perception of these experiences that determine the cause and effect of your life!

Thus, your reaction will be in kind, but exactly what that kind will be is not for me to say. Be advised that it does balance eventually and we are only responsible for every word, thought and deed committed in this life. We do not have karmic debts to pay from previous lives, how could we? How can anyone be made to pay for some deed committed in another time? This is yet another fallacy of the New Age movement.

Think of it in terms of a financial debt. If, on your first life you borrowed $100. By the end of that life, you still owed $60. So for your next life, instead of starting with $100, you start with $40 (because you have to pay back the outstanding $60 from the previous life).

So automatically you are behind the eight ball. Now you are expected to live on a $100 life with only $40! As we have already stated, the average soul reincarnates 500-600 times before it ceases to incarnate. So just after 3 or 4 lives your karmic debt will be in the minus, which no soul would be able to contend with! No!! YOU are responsible for the life you are living right now. As you will see later, during the review process immediately after each death, you have to experience every emotion you caused to others. By doing this process, it cancels out your previous life's Karma.

Progress is open to all! The idea that one would 'have to pay' for acts committed in another time is tantamount to saying that one will be punished for the rest of your incarnations before they even start! There can be no wrong because of the law of cause and effect. Conversely there is no right.

As William Shakespeare so eloquently wrote in Hamlet: *"There is nothing either good or bad, but only thinking makes it so."*

It means that there is nothing right or wrong, good or bad, only our values determine whether or not we think a certain action is good or bad. For example, the majority of people in the world can agree that torturing children is a bad thing. Why? Well because children are deemed innocent, so if someone is hurting them physically and mentally, it offends our sense of right and wrong. However, for the person that's responsible for torturing the children, in their perspective, they don't find it a bad thing at all. Pol Pot killed 1.7 million Cambodians and let his people live in extreme poverty. Hitler murdered over 6 million people. Joseph Stalin is responsible for the deaths of over 20 million during the same period.

In their perspective, what they did was not 'bad', it was just a means to an end. Not everyone in the world thinks the same way; someone can think something is immoral, while someone else can think something is moral. It doesn't have to be something as extreme as torture...just something like abortion or sex before marriage or not washing your hands before you eat.

Like in the case of the handicapped life, offering the opportunity for others to learn, do you think the Hitler consciousness taught others compassion? Maybe Stalin taught some caring, and Pol Pot forgiveness and acceptance. I am not condoning the actions of these men; however I am trying to get you to see that things are not black and white. The Law of Karma is not about right and wrong – it is about cause and effect.

Reincarnation is not a difficult term to come to grips with. Many believe that the spirit has many different lives and this belief is not restricted to any creed or dogma. Simply stated, a vehicle is created, (the body), and a spirit is assigned the 'life'. Naturally there are many that do not believe in reincarnation, but they still say it's 'their karma' if anything goes wrong for them. I guess there's nothing like having a bet each way!

It's this mixing of ideas and terms that create confusion. How many times have you met someone who admits that they have no belief in religion or are not religious and yet they will not eat meat on Good Friday? The thing that makes each person's life unique is the way each handles the ups and downs that they encounter. I realise that it is not easy and I am not saying that it is, for there is always a new experience to be faced and handled with the amount of experience each has. But rest assured, you are never given a challenge that your Soul cannot overcome.

The development of an individual's consciousness is subject to variables, like the country of birth, social status, gender etc. To understand cause and effect is to give one the knowledge to face 'life's little tests' with confidence and balance. This then, is the role of the 'vehicle'.

The Soul's role is slightly different, for it experiences the energy that is generated by the 'life' and it is by this energy that it learns to evolve its consciousness. Life is a series of experiences for the body, and the Soul being the sum total of all experiences, in all life times. Hence, the doctrine of reincarnation and karma.

## What Determines My Soul Age?

As stated earlier, Soul Age is determined by how many lessons or experiences a soul has had. By learning a particular lesson, a soul automatically moves a little bit higher up their evolutionary path. By a rough rule of thumb, a soul progresses from 1 level to the next every 25 – 30 lives.

So in other words, to go from Infant Soul to Child Soul takes about 25-30 life times. Unfortunately, most souls become distracted or jaded and can wallow on the same level for hundreds of lives. This is because they fail to learn a particular lesson or accept and embrace an experience and will continually, life after life, retreat to their "safe-zone" of familiarity, even if it is not good for them. For example, it is common for some women to be continuously attracted to the 'wrong' type of man who may beat and mistreat them. Some men continually turn to alcohol rather than accept responsibility for their mistakes.

This can be extrapolated to the Soul's journey. For example, a soul may want to learn forgiveness, so it sets up circumstances where they are cheated on, lied to, betrayed etc. If for just one instance in one life they can forgive the transgressor, they would move past that experience and evolve. However, it is more common for a Soul to fall back into safety zone of a previous Soul Age and seek revenge or self-harm.

These safe zones usually revolve around substance abuse, greed, power, lust, sexual hedonism and depravity. That is because those traits were mastered in the very early lives and are now easy to perform. It should be remembered that about 60% of all the experiences you come to earth to learn are about overcoming some fear based emotion. Some of the most common Fear based emotions include anger, greed, jealousy, self-loathing and self-harm and so on.

It is easy to tell if you have already learnt a lesson in a previous life. Just ask yourself a series of questions like:

- Is it ok to kill someone out of greed, anger or passion?
- It's ok to kill someone who abused my child or loved one?
- Would I steal from a friend or family member – even if they wouldn't miss it?
- It's ok to steal from a family member or friend if they wronged me in the past.
- Would I assault a stranger for pleasure or satisfaction?
- Can I forgive someone that has lied or cheated me?
- I believe in an eye-for-an-eye punishment.
- Pay back feels so good!
- Salvation can only be found through accepting Jesus as my own personal saviour.

Be honest with yourself. You will usually feel a sensation like heaviness in your solar plexus if you have not truly learnt a lesson. There is no shame in admitting the truth. In fact, once you realise there are lessons you have not yet learnt, gives you a perfect opportunity in this life to address them.

A good lesson to start with is forgiveness. Forgive yourself, your parents, siblings, and friends in fact anyone, anything as in an institution/government/school you feel has slighted you. This could even include your country! Eventually you will work it out that everyone in your life is doing exactly what you asked them to do before you got here! But more about that in Chapter 11. And don't forget yourself. Start by forgiving yourself if you feel inclined to.

Anyway, some souls choose to accelerate their learning even faster, by choosing particularly difficult lives.

Maybe it's because they wasted a few lives being famous, being ridiculously rich, or because they didn't learn a lesson, or maybe they just want to get it all over and done with!

Usually they will choose a life without much money, or lots of illness and/or loneliness. Other times they will incarnate into a country that is predominately a younger soul group than they are. That's right, countries have a predominance of Soul Ages in them as we will find out! By understanding Soul Age, it helps you to better understand human behaviour. It also explains why the world is in the state it is in, and why things are changing so rapidly. The Earth is in a constant state of flux. In the past, the Earth was predominantly inhabited by Mature and Old Souls.

But after the **Fall of Atlantis**, about 3,100 years ago, most of the Mature & Old Souls left the Earth, and the Infant/Child/Young Souls took over; and they have been dominating the planet ever since!

Indeed, as I have stated, the Earth is very rarely stagnant, so the upcoming **Age of Aquarius** will once again see a predominance of Mature and Old Souls populate the planet. By now you are probably thinking 1 of 3 things:

1.  What Soul age am I or my friends/family?
2.  Or...I already know I am an Old Soul so I don't really need to read the rest of this book. (Well, chances are you are a younger soul, however I think if you keep reading you will learn more about your true soul age.)
3.  Or...Jesus is my own personal saviour and this mumbo jumbo will get me burnt – I am out of here! (No worries, I probably couldn't help you anyway...but please donate this book to someone else!!)

In the next few chapters we will examine each Soul Age and break down the typical personality traits associated with them. First up we will exam the **Infant Soul**...

---

# References:

*Astral City: A Spiritual Journey.* (2010). [film] Brazil: Director: Wagner de Assis, Writers: Laura Malin (contributing writer), Wagner de Assis.

Borgia, A. (1997). *Life in the world unseen.* 1st ed. [S.l.]: "Two Worlds".

*The Ryan White Story.* (1989). [film] USA: Directed by John Herzfeld, Writing Credits (WGA) Phil Penningroth (story & teleplay), John Herzfeld (teleplay).

# 2

## THE INFANT SOUL

---

*"Let's not do it"*

---

here are 2 parts to the human consciousness – **Ego** and **Soul**. Ego refers to the self, that human part of you responsible for survival, procreation and of course, fear – which can be handy when you are in a tight spot! Think of it as your primiordal urges and instincts. The Soul on the other hand brings a belief in an afterlife; it creates beautiful art, music, literature, a search for higher knowledge and spirituality. In each person there is a constant balancing act between Ego and Soul. I often view the Ego as a school bully, always wanting things done their way. So in a very young and inexperienced Soul, the Ego will always call the shots and have the last say. In very Old and experienced Souls, they have learnt a few tricks to put the Ego in its place. In simplistic terms, Younger Souls are dominated by the human Ego, and in Older Souls, the Soul dominates the Ego. So with this in mind, we will examine the youngest souls of all – Infant Souls.

Because there is a marked difference in traits within the 7 levels of any Soul Age, I will describe a typical Soul trait from ages 1-4, then 4-7. And yes, I repeat level 4 because it usually overlaps.

## Infant Soul Ages 1 – 4

The early Infant Soul is raw, without experience, undisciplined, unpractised, unseasoned, unskilled, untaught, untrained, untried, unversed and very young! Thus their main motivation in life is survival. Being unfamiliar with the Earth Plane they are usually in a constant state of fear. Imagine how you feel when you go to a new school, new job or your partner's parents' house for the first time. Well, these Soul are landing on Earth, many for the first time!

For the early Infant Souls, it is all about the basics of survival – finding food, shelter and staying alive. To older souls, their lives look extremely hard and short lived. They regularly experience famine, disease, drought, flooding, natural disasters, wild animals and war along with every other survival threat imaginable!

The reason for this, is they need to experience as many lessons as they can, as quickly as they can. However, the human mind and body can only take so much, so these lives are often short lived. However, the emotional experiences they can cram in are amazing. Being so fresh from Spirit, Infant Souls can often have a mystical essence about them, and be profoundly connected to the earth. They resonate closely with nature and rarely feel on an individual level, but rather, they feel a great oneness with everyone in their family or tribe. They can be intuitive in a simple, unquestioning way, similar to the way animals have a 6th sense for predicting natural disasters. Again like animals, they live in the moment, which can be very adventitious, and something older Souls have all but forgotten.

## A note on the Psychic Phenomena

Just a side note at this point, you do not need to be an Old Soul, or even spiritual for that matter to be psychic. There is a (New Age movement) myth that people who are psychic are highly spiritual individuals. Nothing could be further from the truth! Infant Souls can display profound psychic abilities. This is because they are not long out of the Spirit world and have not been conditioned by society to say it is all mumbo jumbo. So you see, it has nothing to do with being spiritual or an Old Soul. That said, living a spiritual life will automatically awaken your dormant psychic skills – so start practising now!

Getting back to Infant Souls, their intellectual centre is not yet fully developed in this phase, so they do not have any real sense of ethics or personal morality. Indeed, early Infant Soul have to learn what is right and wrong, just as a child learns from its elders. Some early Infant Souls can be highly intelligent but they still come across as simple or dull. This is because they have not learnt how to apply intelligence to everyday life. In a psychological sense, Infant souls are new to the world, and consequently they do not know very much about what is going on, nor do they care about worldly events. They are weak on savvy and common sense which is often mistaken for lack of intelligence, but the two deficiencies should not be confused. It should not be thought that Infant souls are intellectually dull. Intelligence is a factor completely separate from Soul Age. There are bright and stupid people in all Ages. Each Infant Soul absorbs the culture and knowledge of their society very well. The hardware of their brains is functioning fine. The thing that distinguishes them psychologically is that their perceptions are shallow and simplistic. For example, cooking and eating are strictly exercises in survival, not even close to being opportunities for optimising pleasure. It is very common for at least one older Soul (usually late Young/Early Mature occasionally Old) to incarnate as a leader or Sharman/Wise man/woman of a tribe, to try and lead and teach by example.

Infant Souls from levels 1-4 tend to cluster around the equator due to the constant climate. This makes some aspects of survival simpler. Outback and Northern Australia, Rural Guatemala, El Salvador, Honduras, Sri Lanka, Borneo, New Guinea, the Amazon basin and much of Ethiopia and Sudan and pockets of Mexico and South America are areas with predominantly Infant Souls; Iraq and Iran have had them in large numbers 100 years ago, but are declining in numbers now as the Child and Young Souls take over.

Modern, western society is ordinarily too perplexing and complex in its demands to be a place for early Infant Souls. When found in modern western countries, which is rare, they will generally gravitate towards less populated, 'backwoods' areas. Infant Souls are not usually involved in regular employment because it is too complicated and overwhelming for their simplistic views. Living on the fringes of society, they are often unfairly branded by the rest of the population as being lazy, stupid and out of tune.

Early Infant Souls are not yet a part of societal institutions. They are not yet part of the greater culture of a nation or country. Just like new born babies, early Infant souls are more deeply in the grasp of the species, so they show more "animal" behaviours and responses.

## Infant Souls Ages 4-7

At this level Infant Souls start to incarnate into more westernised, modern countries that have a mix of shanty towns and large cities particularly South Africa, North America, Northern Australia, New Zealand and Indonesia to name but a few. Here they can begin to learn higher lessons, usually taught by older souls who live in the same town. Like children, later Infant souls lack understanding, and they are often in need of guidance.

Imagine a child learning to walk. They may knock things over and stumble into walls with the odd fall. They do not know the value of things they encounter and may break them. They often hurt themselves with their clumsiness and ignorance. So it is with Infant souls in their attempts to cope in a complex world. But children grow up and usually learn to handle the situations of life, whereas Infant souls do not: they are immature all their lives.

Infant Souls rarely come into the spotlight except through notoriety brought about by heavy karma-creating lifetime, usually in phases 4-7. Typical Infant Souls don't yet feel regret; and when they show up in a court of law, their lack of conscience stands out. It is often mistaken for cold, callous evil, but ironically it is only older souls that can focus their energies in that way.

Even in the later ages of the Infant Soul they are still like children in as far as they are not well socialised. In the worse instances, they can be uncouth and lacking in social grace. They are lacking in "taste" and "class" and often lack sophistication in dress and manner. If you think about how little girls dress up in their mother's clothes and clumsily apply her (expensive) make-up. They are trying their best to look good, and in their own mind they think they look great. But to the adult, or older souls they look comical. The child, and indeed the Infant Soul does not understand why you would think them funny. However, at their very best, they are innocent and simple, even as children are.

Later Infant souls only make up about 7% of the world population, but that said, I have actually worked with one typical, later Infant Soul! I would equate these people as being like spoilt brats. When they don't get their way they throw a tantrum, or if you pick them up on a mistake they lash out aggressively. These behaviours are typical Fear based behaviours.

Infant Souls don't fit in very well with the mainstream of society which is predominantly Young and Mature Souls at this stage in history.

Everyone that has to work or be around a later Infant Soul is forever telling them to: "grow up", "quit being silly", "stop being foolish", and "stop being childish".

Infant souls are naïve when it comes to dealing with the modern, complex society. The older souls (Young and Mature) who dominate world events are involved with issues and experiences totally beyond the capacity of the Infant soul to comprehend. And if you don't really understand what is going on, why pursue it right? So they rarely if ever get involved in, or show an interest in, the wider and more complex aspects of life, such as politics, religion, humanitarian causes, the arts and sciences. They dabble in the limited, elementary, and simple things of life — home and family, or a routine job, or odd jobs working for someone else. Often they do not even pursue a lifetime career, preferring to go from one menial job to another. They tend to live in the moment and rarely plan for the future so they are not good with money.

Infant souls do not have very much inherent knowledge. By this I mean, they do not have extensive, experiential background stored in their subconscious memories. Infant souls simply believe what they are told: they absorb a lot of information just as children in their early years accumulate an enormous amount of basic information, and they readily adopt the teachings of their parents and society — but without modification, because they do not have the breadth of perception to know otherwise. Their concepts are not well founded. Sometimes Infant souls latch onto some pretty "kooky" notions because of their simplistic worldview, and lack of experience. They are gullible because they do not have enough depth of personality to recognise a silly idea or suggestion. They are easily fooled, and some older souls who are not very morally advanced themselves, may enjoy playing tricks on them and making fun of them for their simple ways.

My description so far should not be construed as condemnation or judgment of Infant souls. It is just that they are primitive, even as children are. At their best, Infant souls have a childlike innocence and naiveté about them that can be charming (but most people do not find this childishness charming in adults like they do in children). The best thing about them is that they are usually genuine. Like children, they do not have enough savvy about things in general to pretend to be anything other than exactly what they really are. Their range of experience is too narrow for them to respond outside their own natures. They do not believe in things they have not personally experienced.

Young children have to be socialized over a period of many years — which often means being taught to pretend to be this way or that way in order to get along with others, even when you don't really mean it. Infant souls, especially in the early Levels, are at a stage where they have not been fully socialised in order to be civilised. Therefore, they do not know how to be phony. This also means they are tactless. In these later Levels, they can be taught the ways of civilisation, but it is still not truly a part of their nature. Older souls, Young and later, are inherently civilised.

## Motto: "Let's not do it"

They do not know how to confront the world effectively. They also have a strong fear-based mentality, so it is better to do nothing, than to risk something bad happening.

## Outlook on Life

Infant souls often find the whole business of living to be fearful, since so many things happen which are beyond their comprehension and control. They also possess of a lot of foolishness as in "fools rush in, where angels fear to tread". Infant souls typically have a very narrow range of responses to life. If they are confronted by something they do not understand (which happens quite often), they usually exhibit two types of reaction. One is, that they will withdraw: run away and hide in fear and bewilderment. The other is, that they might launch a blind, savage attack on the confronter or the confronting situation. Both of these are appropriately primitive response patterns, not unlike that of animals. Infant souls are dealing with survival issues, and most of the Infant souls on the planet are members of primitive tribes where these issues are being dealt with on a daily basis.

## Social Media

It is highly unlikely that early Infant Souls would even know about social media yet alone use it. It is far too technical. Furthermore, they are not really interested in dealing with anyone outside of their family/ tribe group. However, later Infant Souls may dabble in social media like dipping a toe into the water. They would use Facebook more for playing games than for making friends.

## Relationships

Infant souls perceive themselves as "me" and others as "not me". They treat other people as objects, not as people like themselves. Therefore, they may not see anything wrong in lying, stealing, cheating, and murdering, if it seems superficially to further their personal circumstances. They are clannish about their families, since dealing with strangers is often too much of a challenge for them to cope with.

## Sexuality & Love

There is rarely any sexual activity in phases 1-3. By level 4 they begin their sexual experience as simple, animal lust, driven by instinct, without the complications of higher meaning present in older souls. They lack finesse, variety, and subtlety in lovemaking, as with everything else. Infant Souls do not know anything about, or participate in oral sex or foreplay. Men use sex as a mark of ownership over a woman, and women use sex as a submissive act to curry favour or protection. At this level there is absolutely no concept of 'love'. They may express a fondness for someone or something, but that is all it is – a fondness.

## Spiritual Outlook/Religion

In religion, as in everything else, Infant souls typically believe whatever their parents teach them, not having the capacity to believe otherwise, or to think outside the box. Whatever religion, if any, was traditional in the family is carried on. They rarely depart from parental instruction even when they are grown and their lives are usually dominated by superstitious belief. Infant souls are easily "programmed" by authority figures or life experiences. Also, they are easily manipulated by unscrupulous individuals. That is why so many Infant Soul cultures were "won over" by the Christian ministers and preachers. But true to Infant Soul thinking, they include parts of the old faith with parts of the new faith. A typical well know Infant Soul religious practise would be Voodoo which incorporates Catholicism and ancient African magic rituals. In New Guinea mountain tribes, they follow and pray to Jesus, the "pig" of god! That is because they did not know what a lamb was, and pigs are highly prized in their culture.

## How They Relate to Other Soul Ages

Infant souls have a very simplistic interpretation of life. If they are intelligent and knowledgeable (in an educational sense), they think they have things figured out pretty well, and are amazed that other people (older souls) make things so complex. Older souls (Young and Mature especially) are deeply involved in more subtle and complex issues, and they marvel that Infant souls have such a shallow and superficial understanding of the issues.

Because of the upcoming Ascension, Planet Earth is close to the time when the last Infant Soul will incarnate.

In the next chapter...**The Child Soul Age** – fire and brimstone, patriotism, and Obsessive Compulsive Disorder!

## References:

*Idi Amin: Monster in Disguise.* (2000). [film] USA: Biography A&E Channel.

*The Man Who Ate His Archbishop's Liver...?.* (2004). [film] UK: Director & Writer: Elizabeth C. Jones.

*The Man Who Stole Uganda.* (1971). [film] UK: Alex Mitchell Investigation (voice).

A good example of a later Infant Soul was Idi Amin. Idi Amin Dada was the third president of Uganda, from 1971 to 1979, who seized power through a Coup d'état. He broke promises, ruled with extreme violence, murder and thuggery, yet had a very childlike demeanour to the outside world. Indeed, popular media outside of Uganda often portrayed him as an essentially comic and eccentric figure. In a 1977 assessment typical of the time, a Time Magazine article described him as a "killer and clown, big-hearted buffoon and strutting martinet". Other commentators even suggested that Amin had deliberately cultivated his eccentric reputation in the foreign media as an easily parodied buffoon in order to defuse international concern over his administration of Uganda. He gave himself the official title *"His Excellency, President for Life, Field Marshal Al Hadji Doctor Idi Amin Dada, VC, DSO, MC, Lord of All the Beasts of the Earth and Fishes of the Seas and Conqueror of the British Empire in Africa in General and Uganda in Particular"*, in addition to his officially stated claim of being the uncrowned King of Scotland.

Just for the record, he was not a recipient of a Distinguished Service Order (DSO) or a Military Cross (MC). He conferred a doctorate of Law on himself from Makerere University, as well as the Victorious Cross (VC), a medal made to emulate the British Victoria Cross.

During his lifetime, there were many rumours that Amin practised ritualistic cannibalism, believing that if he ate the heart or liver of his victim, it would give him their power and strength, as well as stopping their "spirit" haunting him. Countries like the Soviet Union and Israel, were more than happy to sell and supply Amin with arms. East Germany was heavily involved with the running of the General Service Unit and the State Research Bureau, the two agencies which were most notorious for terror.

## My Wish...

MY WISH FOR YOU IS THAT YOU CONTINUE. CONTINUE TO BE WHO AND HOW YOU ARE, TO ASTONISH A MEAN WORLD WITH YOUR ACTS OF KINDNESS. CONTINUE TO ALLOW HUMOR TO LIGHTEN THE BURDEN OF YOUR TENDER HEART.

Maya Angelou

# 3

## THE CHILD SOUL

---

*"Do it right or not at all"*

---

*A*S WE HAVE already seen, there are 7 levels between each Soul Age. It can take an Infant Soul anywhere from 25 to 30 lifetimes to complete, but in reality, most have averaged 50-100 lives to reach the next level. At this point, they are ready to start exploring the Child Soul phase.

### Child Soul Ages 1 – 4

By now, the soul has had a little bit of experience on the Earth Plane, so there is less fear and more focus on becoming civilised and sophisticated (in a Childlike way). The outside world is still a scary place, but survival has been worked out, so now they want to prove they can 'do it right!'

Child souls have more advanced perceptions than Infant souls, but less understanding than Young souls. Much that can be said about the Child soul is what would be said about toddlers and pre-teens. They are in a stage before teenage years when they still fear punishment from adults for not doing the right thing. They still look to please authority figures with their 'good' behaviour. Like persons in the first decade of life, Child souls are going through a lot of changes in the growing-up process. Child souls are like children: eager to go here, go there, and do this, do that. They are no longer like mere infants, but there is still a lack of understanding and they have an immature perspective. And just like pre-teens, they know everything, you just ask them!

The Child Soul not only craves structure, but they need it. They want to be told what to do; they want to know what the rules are, and they want to show you that they can follow the rules. But they will also expect reward for their good behaviour just as a child does. Child Souls live by popular stereotypes and standard clichés and have very little sense of humour.

They will occasionally seek out discipline from the prison system time after time in a way to civilise themselves. That is why prisons are at bursting point in most 3rd world countries. This soul age will hold traditional religious leaders in esteem, turn doctors into gods, and likely feel their country, their army, and their politicians, can do no wrong. The USA was dominated by Child Souls during the first and second world wars. That is why the Allies seem to have had an endless stream of young men ready to sacrifice their lives for God and Country. By the 1960's the Young and Mature Souls began to outnumber the Child Souls for the first time in that country's history. Thus the Vietnam protests and hippy movement would dominate over patriotism and infallible politicians, but left the returning Child Souls bewildered.

Traditions, rituals, and law and order provide a welcome sense of security. *"That's the rule and that's what we'll do!"* is typical thinking. They make sure your car is not parked in front of their house, or their neighbour's trees don't hang over their fence. Their lawn is mowed and sprinkled to perfection, and the inside of the house is spotless. They may even leave the plastic on the new sofa to protect it so it lasts longer! In a dogmatic, black-and-white way, they know right from wrong and are usually conscientiously good citizens. They are the sort of people that be counted on to do the "right" thing. This is also the soul age with the greatest propensity to long-term grudge holding. Certain organisations will have a predominance of a particular Soul Age as memberships and ideals are almost exclusively of that Soul Age. There are also positive and negative poles to each group. Therefore, a Child Soul organisation in a negative pole would be a group like the Ku Klux Klan. Organisations in a more positive pole of expression include many service organisations like the Rotary Club. Fire-and-brimstone preachers, Hillsong Church (Sydney, Australia), Anti-abortion and right-to-life organisations all arise from Child Soul consciousness and ideals.

## Child Soul Ages 4 – 7

Child Souls are often found in small communities where life is a little simpler, preferring to be big fish in small ponds. They are nearly always involved with some type of service like local police, governmental, local school or hospital bureaucracies as they love law and order and making the rules. For this reason they will often be pillars of the community, staunch, upright and unshakable in their beliefs. Child Souls are so sure they are right that they have difficulty comprehending opposition. When their beliefs are opposed, they will become inwardly and outwardly bewildered.

The Child Soul age is not a self-reflective age like the Mature Soul, therefore when they are perplexed or frustrated, or just plain thwarted. They are more likely to show an outward display of belligerence than to see your point of view. A fantastic example of the Child Soul vs the late Young Soul was an interview between the famous evolutionary biologist Dr. Richard Dawkins and Young Earth Creationist Wendy Wright. After watching this interview you can see firsthand a typical reaction by a Child Soul (Wendy) to the facts and rational points made by Dawkins. Wendy cannot accept or believe any fact Dawkins puts forward in a calm, rational manner.

In fact, she is openly in a state of disbelief that he could even offer a different opinion to her own. Then, when she knows she is beaten, she accuses Dawkins of being belligerent. This is a common ploy by younger souls – turn defence into attack. Be warned, if you decide to watch this interview, it is extremely hard to get through – this women would try the patients of a saint! But that said, it is a very good, text-book example of a later Child Soul in action. See link below in the reference section.

Child Souls are the most likely of all the ages to develop Obsessive Compulsive Disorder (OCD), particularly in relation to cleanliness, neatness, and keeping germs at bay. The Stepford Wives is also a very good example of the typical, female Child Soul. TV Evangelist preachers are a good example of male Child Souls. When it comes to their health however, they are unable to make the connection between long term negative emotions or attitudes causing physical and psychological problems. To them it is all 'hog-wash' to believe that their angry feelings become gallstones, or fear turns into kidney, bladder or back trouble and their negative resentment manifests physically as cancer.

Child Souls opt for conventional medicine and health care. They are strong believers in health insurance and will always be paid up to date. Looking for the root of a problem or using alternative therapies does not make any sense to them at all. Perhaps the hard core Pentecostal church goers would consider faith healing, but these are more likely to be very early Child Souls. As far as psychology or psychiatry go, they will display outward fear. Even being seen in the street next to a mental health practitioner will leave them frantic. If someone they know was to see them, they would die of embarrassment. They view Psychologist/Psychiatrist as witch-doctors and avoid them like the plague. But in reality they fear being branded 'crazy'.

In appearance, if they are well bred, Child souls will try to always look neat and tidy — well dressed, hair fixed, cleanly groomed — in a childlike, innocent way. If they are not well bred, then they will make crude attempts to look respectable. In either case, they lack the capacity for true polish and classy sophistication such as is inherent to older souls.

Child Souls don't often look for a big stage, so they only rarely come into prominence. They lack the resourcefulness or experience to handle fame, but occasionally some 7th level Child Souls make the big time. Usually they are involved in fundamentalist Christianity or Islam with unyielding political or religious beliefs. TV preachers like Jerry Falwell, Jimmy Swaggart and Jim and Tammy Bakker (before their scandalous demise). Politicians like George W. Bush (the younger), Australian Prime Minister Tony Abbott, Texas governor Rick Perry and the President of the Democratic People's Republic of Korea, Kim Jong-un. There has been a sudden influx of TV shows in 2012/13 featuring Child Souls. Some of the more famous are the Robinson boys (except Willy who is a Young Soul) from **Duck Commander**. The people in **Swamp People** and my favourite – Turtle Man! from **"Call of the Wildman."** The 7th level of any soul age can be a time of smug complacency, because everything at that soul age has been handled. However, it can also be a time for them to give a little back by leading their group by example.

Child Soul countries often have an austere leaning, usually divided against themselves or a close neighbour. Countries with a predominate Child Soul outlook include, but not limited to, North Korea, Israel, Iraq, as well as most of the strict Muslim countries. China, much of both Central and South America, parts of North India and Pakistan. Northern Ireland is still firmly entrenched in the Child Soul cycle however their neighbours in the southern Republic of Ireland have already moved into the Young Soul phase. Russia moved out of Child perspective around 1984 which culminated in the fall of the Berlin Wall in 1989. Since then they have moved full forward into the Young Soul phase.

## Motto: "Do it right or not at all".

The Child Soul is so excited to prove they have advanced and for the first time know between right and wrong. If you can't do it right from the start, then why bother at all is their mind set.

## Outlook on Life

Child souls are typically ideal students, because this is part of doing what should be done. When they grow up and get a job, they do fine as dedicated employees in follower positions in occupations that are not overly demanding. They do not typically desire a lifelong career as such, but prefer to do a good job for someone else who will take the responsibility and make the big decisions. Although they have a high opinion of themselves, the big, bad world is under the sway of the devil, so it is something they avoid. To try to succeed in the cutthroat, dog-eat-dog business world would be too worldly. This kind of activity is left mostly to the Young Souls, as we shall see.

## Social Media

Child Souls use social media to stay in touch with existing family and friends. They will often play games like 'FarmVille' on Facebook at least weekly – maybe on the weekend. They share pictures on Facebook, Twitter and Instagram because it is expected – ie. The latest weddings photos, family vacation pictures or pictures from the latest war zone they are involved with. They will use a flag or patriotic icon as their profile picture. They rarely have a photo of themselves as they are too shy, or they like to hide behind a cartoon character. Child Souls will usually have a small amount of friends on their lists, mostly made up of family members, unless they are part of some group like an Army unit or church group. They don't get too stressed if they don't check their Facebook page daily and it is unlikely they would even notice if someone dropped off the friend list.

## Relationships

A Child soul sees itself as "me" and other people as "many other mes". The meaning of this, is that they expect others to be like themself, and they are surprised and bewildered when this proves to be incorrect. They do not know how to deal with the differences in other people. Therefore, they becomes cliquish. Child Souls avoid people not of their race, nation, tribe, culture, religion, socioeconomic status, political party, special interest group, etc.

Child souls, of all the soul ages, feel most comfortable with their own kind, whatever they perceive that to be. Their sense of identity is reinforced by the groups they belong to. They perceive the differences in others as evil, and shun them for it. However they identify strongly with family and raising children. They enjoy the traditional 'family' celebrations like Christmas, family BBQ's, and even church outings when the whole family attends. These social 'rituals' help them to feel like they are a good, upstanding member of their community. Unfortunately they are the first to go to the recruitment office and volunteer in times of war.

## Sexuality & Love

When dealing with sexual matters, Child Souls are completely out of their depth. They approach these things with a healthy dose of guilt and shame. You can forget hot tub entertaining – they like to hide their body, make love in the dark and probably with their pyjamas still on, without any sensuality. Child Souls have strong feelings about remaining a virgin until they are married. After sex, they will often pretend like nothing happened, being too embarrassed to acknowledge what just occurred. As far as teaching their children about sex – forget it! That is why they convinced the Young Soul government law makers to include sex-ed in schools. That way, the teacher has to deal with it and not them! Whilst they are very loyal to a husband or wife it is more of a companionship rather than unconditional love. In fact, it is not until the Mature Soul level that Souls even know what true love is. They stay with an abusive husband or dominating wife because it is the right thing to do in society's eyes, and they enjoy playing the "martyr role". The one thing they despise is a scandal in their own life. They would rather be vilifying someone else for not sticking to the rules. But that said, later Child Souls have a strong reputation for secretly breaking the rules. The more famous Child Souls are notorious for having sexual affairs, dodgy deals and con man status. That is because they are preparing to move into the Young Soul phase. Child soul single people would do well to seek mates in evangelical or fundamentalist churches. At least then they may start with some basic commonalities.

## Spiritual Outlook / Religion

They borrow simple concepts of right and wrong from the rules of society, or better yet, what they perceive to be the laws of God. Then they stick doggedly to them all their lives. In regard to religion, Child Souls tend toward fundamentalism or an evangelical sects. Belief in the personification of the deity is more natural to this Age than any other. To them, God seems like one of them, but more knowledgeable and powerful, but still just a glorified human being. That is why many fundamentalist Christian groups worship Jesus rather than God. This is because it is easy for them to view Jesus as a super hero, than it is to imagine an invisible God.

They believe in the forces of evil, and these forces are also typically personified in an anthropomorphic "Satan" or Devil figure. The 'Word of God' — the Bible, is interpreted literally and the supposed battle between good and evil, right and wrong, darkness and light, is a big issue with Child Souls. In religious philosophy, Child Souls live by external regulations, having a list of do's and don'ts, rather than going by their own internal moral standards — they are too young in terms of soul age to have profound ethical principles inherent in their consciences. Having a somewhat undeveloped conscience, they tend to be inherently self-righteous. They truly believe in salvation and damnation, and for the most part, they feel they work for salvation or for good.

## How They Relate to Other Soul Ages

The Child Soul Age is like the typical teenage, know-it-all stage. In their simple understanding, they think their elders who speak of complex issues are irrational and crazy. In their lack of understanding they cannot comprehend what their parents mean, so they dismiss it as unreasonable or arbitrary. This is very similar to the way Child souls regard the ideas of older souls.

Child souls are '"uptight' about life in general. Who wouldn't be under the stress of always having to find the correct way to do things? They tend to avoid eye contact with others — or any other kind of contact. They do not feel comfortable with physical closeness or affection. They make and follow rules of etiquette and courtesy: to keep people at a reasonable distance for one thing, and to keep their own behaviour in check. Child souls cannot easily deal with conduct outside their own narrow channel. They are unwavering patriots, hard workers and generally good, upstanding members of any community. In fact, they are often horrified by the "decedent" behaviour of the older, **Young Souls**, which we will look at next.

# References:

Anderson, H. (2012). *Duck Punt: How Phil Robertson found stardom after giving up football.* [online] SI.com. Available at: http://www.si.com/college-football/campus-union/2012/03/22/duck-punt-how-phil-robertson-found-stardom-after-giving-up-football [Accessed 25 Jul. 2012].

Copeland, S. (2013). *Duck Dynasty, How It Almost Never Happened.* [online] Sportsspectrum.com. Available at: http://www.sportsspectrum.com/articles/2013/03/23/Duck-Dynasty-how-it-almost-never-happened/ [Accessed 25 Jul. 2013].

Ford, D. (2013). *'Duck Dynasty' star suspended for anti-gay remarks.* [online] CNN. Available at: http://edition.cnn.com/2013/12/18/showbiz/duck-dynasty-suspension/ [Accessed 25 Jul. 2013].

Gostin, N. (2013). *'Duck Dynasty' star Phil Robertson talks values, family in new book.* [online] Fox News. Available at: http://www.foxnews.com/entertainment/2013/05/07/duck-dynasty-star-phil-robertson-talks-values-family-in-new-book/ [Accessed 25 Jul. 2013].

O'Connell, M. (2013). *A&E Welcomes Phil Robertson Back to 'Duck Dynasty'.* [online] The Hollywood Reporter. Available at: http://www.hollywoodreporter.com/live-feed/a-e-welcomes-phil-robertson-667647 [Accessed 25 Jul. 2013].

Sports Spectrum Magazine, (2013). *Willie & Phil Robertson talk about fake bleeps and praying in Jesus' name.* [online] YouTube. Available at: https://www.youtube.com/watch?v=Y_0XS1vaX-M [Accessed 25 Jul. 2013].

Staff, S. (2013). *Duck Dynasty's Phil Robertson had impoverished childhood with no running water or electricity -* starcasm.net. [online] Starcasm.net. Available at: http://starcasm.net/archives/218207 [Accessed 25 Jul. 2013].

YouTube, (2013). *Richard Dawkins Interviews Creationist Wendy Wright* (Complete). [online] Available at: http://www.youtube.com/watch?v=-AS6rQtiEh8 [Accessed 25 Jul. 2014].

## CHILD SOUL PROFILE - Phil Robertson

Phil Alexander Robertson was born April 24, 1946 in Vivian, Louisiana USA. He was the fifth of seven children. The family lived in abject poverty having no electricity, toilet or bathtub. They rarely went into town and instead lived off of the fruits and vegetables they grew in their garden; the meat from deer, squirrels, fish and other game, they hunted and fished; and the pigs, chickens and cattle they raised.

In his book, "Happy, Happy, Happy", Robertson recalls that *"It was the 1950s when I was a young boy, but we lived like it was the 1850s... but we were always happy, happy, happy no matter the circumstances."*

As an athlete in high school, Robertson was all-state in football, baseball, and track, which afforded him the opportunity to attend Louisiana Tech in Ruston on a football scholarship in the late 1960s.

Robertson was made an offer to play professionally for the Washington Redskins, but he declined because football conflicted with his hunting. He went on to patent a duck call that led to his first company Duck Commander. Today, Duck Commander is a multi-million dollar business, headed by his son, Willie Robertson.

The cable TV channel A&E produce a reality TV series about Duck Commander (called Duck Dynasty) and the Robertson family. Robertson is a devout, fundamentalist Christian, and is outspoken about his beliefs. He had various personal problems in his 20's, including excessive alcohol drinking, causing a separation in the marriage for a period and he credits a subsequent religious awakening for being able to overcome the problems.

His strong religious outlook has caused several clashes with A&E, which came to a head during in 2013. During an interview with GQ magazine, Robertson was asked what he thought about same sex marriage. He said *"Start with homosexual behaviour and just morph out from there. Bestiality, sleeping around with this woman and that woman and that woman and those men."* He paraphrased a Biblical passage from First Corinthians saying *"Don't be deceived. Neither the adulterers, the idolaters, the male prostitutes, the homosexual offenders, the greedy, the drunkards, the slanderers, the swindlers—they won't inherit the kingdom of God. Don't deceive yourself. It's not right."* Robertson also questioned the appeal of same-sex relationships saying that a vagina is more appealing to a man.

This sparked a massive controversy in the United States and A&E announced the indefinite suspension of Robertson from the network. However, after a strong backlash from supporters, including a Facebook page that accumulated 1.5 million likes, A&E lifted the suspension before any episode was affected. Robertson opposes abortion and has called it a violation of the *Declaration of Independence*. He frequently speaks about the issue during public appearances.

# Give yourself
# Permission

# 4

# THE YOUNG SOUL

---

*"Do it my way!"*

---

NOW THE SOUL has mastered the issues of survival, discipline and order, it is ready to see how powerful it can become. Much that can be said about the Young Soul is what would be said about a young person prior to age 30. They are cocky, all knowing and 'bullet' proof. It's all about keeping up with your friends. Make no mistake, this is the most competitive phase of all soul ages and can take a long time to get through!

## Young Souls Ages 1-4

Still coming to terms with their emotions, most early Young Souls express a lot of anger. They can be domineering and very cautious about strangers or the unfamiliar. At this level there is a strong attraction to gangs. This is a hangover from the Infant and Child Ages of tribal instincts, however, now they have a deeper insight, so they are looking to fill certain gaps. Usually their family ties are not strong so they will gravitate toward others like themselves. In fact, at this stage, it is quite usual to incarnate with parents either the same Soul Age or slightly younger. This accounts for many broken homes and financially poor families and areas that they grow up with. It is for this reason that most city prisons are full of Young Souls.

They can still be dogmatic like the Child Soul, however, unlike the Child Soul, they prefer to be in control and exert authority. They want to control others and will do this effectively through the use of fear and dogma.

By level 4, they begin to emerge as the typical Mafia type. Driven by greed, they will become ruthless in their quest for money, which in their mindset equals power. Life is cheap to early Young Souls. They continually measure their own life against others – who has the biggest car, the hottest investments, the most famous friends, the most extravagant parties, the most lavish house...the perfect boobs and hips, the perfect lips, the tummy tuck and nose job.

## Young Souls Ages 5-7

At level 5, they will almost universally withdraw. Because of the excess and base behaviours of the previous 4 levels, they are advanced enough by now to realise that living like that is not the way. However, they are still not advanced enough to look introspectively or inward. They know something is not right, but cannot put their finger on it. So as a knee jerk reaction to avoid further mountains of negative Karma, they will choose a life where they live a quiet, almost hermit existence. They do this more because they want to avoid people and therefore, avoid lessons on an emotional level. In fact, they don't like people at all and come across as the classic grumpy old man or crazy bag lady. Believe it or not, the outcome of these lives is a huge jump forward. They perfect their lessons in self-discipline, survival, idea of self and separation.

Now at level 6, the later Young Souls are friendly, and successful. They are your typical yuppie. After so many lives at the 5th Level living alone, they are more than ready to make friends and mix with as many people as they can. They are still attracted to positions of authority, wealth and power, but have managed to temper their anger. Young Souls at this level tend to be focused on physical prowess, so many end up in professional sports, modelling, movie stars, TV personalities and 'get rich quick' gurus. Others on the other hand, will be ambitious nobodies, always striving for recognition and fame, but rarely find it.

An excellent example of this, is in the true life story movie **Pain & Gain (2013)**, where a trio of bodybuilders in Florida get caught up in an extortion ring and a kidnapping scheme that goes terribly wrong.

On the up side, Young Souls are the architects of civilization, the builders of empires, the leaders of business and economics. Their basic motivation is materialism, and they will work tirelessly for their material achievements. They are the most likely of the Ages to be "workaholics", constantly in a state of unrest, seeking their materialistic goals. More than any other Soul Age, Young Souls feel at home in the physical body — the flesh is their playground. They really like it on this planet.

We owe them our efficiency, much of our high technology, military might, and our continual push to make things happen and change. However, with a focus on quantity, rather than quality, something like Genetically Modified Organisms (GMO) agriculture will be valued. For example, it is all about bumper crops, regardless that the chemicals they use may render the soil useless after five years. "We'll just move to a different field right!" The fact that the majority of agricultural areas of the world are now so polluted with nitrates and herbicidal poisons, and that up to 95% of seed types that were available 125 years ago, are now gone, would likely not even raise an eyebrow – after all – it's a bumper crop!

The "yuppie" phenomenon is another making of the Young Soul Age. They attend financial seminars, Donald Trump courses, super-salesman conventions, and the like. They invest in the stock market and horse racing (same thing!). They seek to be 'professionals', and their career is their life.   Indeed, Young Souls at this level define their very existence by their social status.   That is why many will opt for suicide rather than face financial ruin or endure some other scandal.

## And controlling all this power, production and advances are the 7th level Young Souls.

**7th Level Young Souls** - They crave absolute authority and power. They come across as calm, polite, well spoken, superbly dressed and well presented. They are usually born to money and are gifted a plush career. Their authoritative manner, sophistication of dress and decorum is a crude attempt at the Mature Soul level.   But unlike Mature Souls, they lack the compassion and insight that accompanies true authority and sophistication. Even so, they dabble around with esoteric and spiritual work, but more from an academic level. They now know inherently right from wrong, but the Young Soul can convince themselves they are doing nothing wrong, so they will choose to work for the  Light or Dark (from their limited view of Spiritual matters).

For example, the majority of the elites of the world (The Illuminati/ New World Order types), are in this level and like to perform rituals and dark magic, full of child sacrifice and abuse.  They study the dark aspects of occult practise always with the view to empowering themselves further.  They feel no pangs of guilt for their horrific acts because they have convinced themselves that they are special, and the people they hurt are below them, so it doesn't matter!  I will be discussing this group in great detail in Book II – and I will name names! On the other hand, we have the New Age movement with their message of Love and Light, Peace on earth and warm and fuzzy stuff for everybody!  So what's wrong with that you ask?  Nothing, except they manage to commercialise it, package it, post it and make a ton of money to boot!  Typical Young Soul attributes.  Remember the bumper crops – this is the same mentality – mass produce spiritual wisdom and SELL IT to the masses.  That is why a lot of them come across as hokey, air heads, and eccentric tree huggers!  That is also why most New Agers spend years reading every book, going to every workshop and getting every degree, so they can put letters on their business cards and diplomas on the walls or their office. But they rarely put into practice all they have learnt.  On an intellectual level, they do understand Spiritual lessons, but on a Soul level, they lack the ability to put those lessons into real world practice.  Instead, they invent what is supposed to be the Spiritual "normal", and everyone goes along with it, because typical Young Souls want to fit in and be normal!

The reality is, most New Age Gurus and New World Order elites are in the same level – Young Souls.  So contrary to popular belief – they are not Super Gods (as in the New World Order), and they are NOT Old Souls in their last life as in the New Agers.  They are preparing to start a whole new level of understanding in the Mature Soul level.   I know that this reality is going to hurt a lot of feelings, and most will not accept that they are Young Souls, but I am trying to help them make the jump to the next level. Indeed, if you find yourself deeply offended by this, then I really have hit a raw nerve, which usually indicates a truth that you do not want to acknowledge.  Cue meditation music – go within, and be honest with yourself!

There are more Young Souls on this planet than any other Soul Age. Indeed, 41% of the population is Young Souls. The planetary average is Fifth Level Young. Therefore they are the most ordinary and conventional. They form the "Establishment". In fact, Young Souls have somewhat of a hang-up about normalcy. They want very much to be considered 'normal' themselves, and they want everybody else to be what they consider normal.

That is why, if you show an interest in something that they do not consider normal (like this book!), they will tease you, feel sorry for you, or shun you. So now you know why they do it, hopefully you will not feel like you need to hide your true feelings or interests. Moreover, don't feel like you need to win them over, or convince them of anything. As Young Souls, they have every right to be sceptical and unreasonable, and for that reason, you will never convince them of your Spiritual Truths. It is like trying to teach year 12 Math to year 6 kids – they will never get it, and it's not their fault.

Countries that have a predominance of Young Soul perspective, tend to be the more technologically advanced places with strong economies. Hong Kong, South Korea, Japan, Germany, Australia, Canada, the majority of the United States, Israel, Syria, Saudi Arabia, Great Britain to name but a few. Like with all Soul Ages, there are many countries that will have pockets of one soul age or another. Some countries that have pockets of Young Souls are South Africa (the majority being Infant and Child), Russia, Taiwan and India. Interestingly, Ancient India was an Old Soul country, but has done a complete cycle. As of 2013, it is edging from late Child into Young Soul phase. Most of the Eastern European Bloc countries moved into the Young Soul phase in the mid to late 1980's.

If they don't conquer you in the business or economic world, Young Souls will conquer you in the military. Young Soul American leadership wants to make the world safe for its ideology — 'democracy'. American democracy has become a euphemism for bomb, invade and take over a country, then put in puppet governments that answer only to the USA! They call it the struggle to maintain freedom and liberty. But what Young Souls really mean by this, is that they don't want others telling them what to do — you do it MY way instead. Since they want this liberty for themselves, they champion it for others. On the other hand, Young Soul Russian leadership wants to bring the whole world around to its socialistic point of view, professedly for their own good. Really, both these supposedly noble ideologies are just excuses for "do it my way" taken to the extreme.

While Young Souls are productive, industrious and goal oriented, their vision extends only so far, and they are not likely to question their motives or ethics.

## Motto: "Do it my way!"

The Young Soul desperately seeks to fit in and be seen as "normal", so the best way to fit in is to get everyone else to do things their way!

## Outlook on Life

Young Souls do not age gracefully. They are so focused on their body and physical prowess that it has been the Young Souls that have spawned and continued to finance the billion dollar health and beauty industry. After spending their youth in pursuit of "things", when they reach middle age, they try to hang on to their youthful appearance with health regimens such as diet, exercise, vitamins, and spas. It is important to them to remain youngish looking. This is why we have plastic surgery for noses and breasts; tummy tucks, fake tans and a booming multi-billion dollar industry devoted to beauty products for both men and women.

While a Mature Soul is interested in personal appearance and healthy living, it is for completely different reason. Young Souls begin experimenting with creativity during these cycles and perfect it in the Mature phase. However, there are still many, many people who find fame and fortune in acting, TV personalities, singers, comedians, movie stars, movie directors/producers, politicians, executives, religious leaders, scientists, authors, New Age Gurus or even very Young Souls like Paris Hilton who are famous just for being rich and doing nothing. In movies, the typical Hollywood action movie heroes and directors are usually Young Souls. The 1987 ilm, *Wall Street*, is a movie that portrays the classic Young Soul persona – ironically directed and acted by a Mature Soul. A more recent take on the 'greed is good' theme is *The Wolf of Wall Street*. If you really want to learn more about Young Souls, then just watch these movies!

In the next chapter we will look at the Mature Soul – this is where the big psychological issues begin, but it is also the time for the soul to finally learn what real, emotional love is!

## Social Media

Young Souls more or less invented social media. The original proto-type of Facebook was called "Facemash". The website allowed visitors to compare two student pictures side-by-side and let them choose who was 'hot' and who was 'not'. This is typical Young Soul, so-called humour. Young Souls like to make fun of people in a harsh and derogatory way. In fact, Mark Zuckerberg, the alleged founder of Facemash, and later Facebook, wrote on the Facemash page: *"...some of these people have pretty horrendous facebook pics. I almost want to put some of these faces next to pictures of some farm animals and have people vote on which is more attractive."* .

He was mainly referring to female students. I am sure you can appreciate how these girls felt, considering all of this was viewable by everyone on the college campus. Thus, Young Souls use social media for completely different reasons to everybody else.

Of course, their main reason for signing up is to make business networks, be trendy, have the most friends on their list, and post the 'coolest' stuff. They also like to use it to meet new people that they can have extramarital affairs with. They do use it for some of the usual reasons, like posting pictures, but these are usually pictures making them look good or to show off. Many Young Souls will become Facebook or Twitter addicts rarely being able to go more than one day without logging in. They are motivated by how much people like them, or what their friends are doing so they can keep up with them. It is not common for them to have family members on their friend list. Beware the person that 'unfriends' them. Young Souls consider this a personal attack and will plot to return it in kind, with interest.

They really like secrecy and a certain amount of anonymity. The classic story of an over-weight, balding middle-age man passing himself off as a buff, 20 something year old to younger woman online, is inevitably a Young Soul. When it comes to profile pictures, older women tend to use a picture of themselves when they were much younger, when they think they looked their best. Men on the other hand, will choose a show off pose, or a 'cool' look pose. Others will use what they think is a cool car, motorbike or boat, or some other extreme sport vehicle.

It should also be remembered that it was Young Souls that created the original secret societies that are really the precursors to online social networking.

## Relationships

Although more advanced than Child and Infant Souls, Young Souls still have fairly simple perceptions about life. In fact, they are not emotionally open at all, so they rarely get introspective enough about themselves to question their motivations. Since they value material success so much, they usually ignore emotional, psychological, and spiritual considerations within and without themselves.

The desire here is to win other people over to one's own point of view, or make them over in their own image. The Young Soul perceives "me" and "you", and wants to change "you" into "me".

The Young Soul wants to organise people into a society, a civilization, or a company. They believe every person should know his place in the rank and file of the culture. A classic example of this mentality, is in the novel *Brave New World*, written in 1931 by Aldous Huxley. It was made into a movie in 1980. Huxley was part of the New World Order / Illuminati and it was his vision of the future.

Set in the year AD 2540, people are "grown" in test tubes and are strictly limited to worker drones with (chemically induced) low intelligence and 2 other classes, each a little more intelligent, then finally, the elites which are enhanced to be super humans with high IQ's and perfect bodies which never age beyond 30 years old. They rule over everyone in this so-called "Utopian" society. Each class wears a particular uniform and everybody is brainwashed to love their own class. This is a Young Soul's societal dream come true!

They believe in this sort of thing so much, that they are willing to fight for it to convince others to do it their way. Wars are mostly a Young Soul phenomena. Nationalism and imperialism are rampant in this stage of maturation. Just on wars, I often think of it like this: Young Souls wage war, Child Souls fight the war, Infant Souls get swept away by the war, Mature Souls protest the war, and Old Souls shake their heads and lament the war, wondering when they will learn their lesson.

Their inability to understand unconditional love also affects their relationships with their children. Therefore, they do not make very good parents from an emotionally supportive point of view, but they will buy their children everything money can buy! They do this more for status – you know, the typical yuppie baby in designer label cloths. They then raise their children as mini versions of themselves, or they live their life vicariously through their children. These are the parents that push their kids into sport or child modelling and stand on the sideline screaming advice. In fact, in later life, the children will be pushed to excel in high school, college, marriage and career. Of course, the one thing they do not push their children to do is to express their feelings or to follow their heart. This they would have no idea how to deal with.

## Sexuality & Love

Young Souls tend not to be very good with romantic relationships; however they excel at physically based, sexual relationships (friends with benefits). They find it difficult to commit to long term relationships and will often cheat on their partners, because they are always looking for something better or a new challenge. They will spend a lot of time and money on making themselves beautiful and surrounding themselves with beautiful things. A typical scenario is when you find the 21 year old super model marrying the 80 year old billionaire. In their mind, and that of their friends, there is absolutely nothing wrong with this arrangement.

As far as sensuality in the bedroom goes, their sexuality is still driven by lust and adventure, so most perversions stem from this Age. They do not understand what unconditional love is. They learn most about what they know about sex from watching pornography and imitating what they see. In fact, the whole porn industry is a Young Soul phenomenon. While they make great lovers from a technique point of view, you will never find passion or a deep connection. A Young Soul woman I once knew told me that "...*sex is a sport*". To me, that sums up their perspective in a nutshell!

## Spiritual Outlook / Religion

As discussed, Young Souls are obsessed with being normal, therefore they will usually attend mainstream Churches as in Catholic, Anglican and Uniting Church in Western Countries, and the mainstream religions like Islam, Hinduism and Buddhism in the remainder. Young Souls are what are considered to be the 'moderates' in radicalised religions like Islam (it is Child Souls that are the majority of Jihad / suicide bombers). In fact, they are the moderates in all religions showing far less zeal and dedication than the Child Souls. Indeed, the Young Soul is more likely to go to church to network or promote their latest business venture rather than push dogma.

Going to church each Sunday would be seen as an inconvenient necessity. You will see them dressed in their Sunday best, checking their email on their Smartphone during a lull in the services. It is not surprising, given that their so-called leaders like the Pope and his Cardinals are all from this Soul Age. Indeed, the Catholic Church is a typical example of corporate greed, corruption and forcing people to do things their way, which is the hall mark of the Young Soul. Finally, an odd thing I have noticed with a lot of Young Souls, is they are universally superstitious. I would expect this more from younger souls, but it seems to carry through. The fact they make fun of psychics, is because deep down they fear them.

## How They Relate to Other Soul Ages

Young Souls do not appreciate Infant and Old Souls especially, because these are at the extremes. This is just another "do it my way" manifestation. Young Soul humour is to make fun of people who are different. There is some repressed hostility in this, and a lack of understanding. They tend to adhere to all social institutions and cultural norms, such as marriage, religion, law, politics, education, and family. Young Souls find it distressing when Infant Souls or Old Souls do not follow society's rules. They particularly resent Old Souls who may try to advise them. On some level, they sense the Old Soul is Older and this makes them feel threatened. So they will always twist it around to make it look like the Old Soul is trying to manipulate or control them. They will show outward belligerence and even violence toward Old Souls who they know are correct, but are not willing to accept responsibility for their actions. It is a cornered animal response. It is best to leave them be. After all, they seem to want to learn the hard way.

# References:

Huxley, A. (1946). *Brave new world*. 1st ed. New York: Harper & Bros.

March Against Monsanto, (2014). *MARCH AGAINST MONSANTO*. [online] Available at: http://www.march-against-monsanto.com/ [Accessed 18 Aug. 2014].

The New Indian Express, (2014). *Failure of Monsanto Bt Cotton*. [online] Available at: http://www.newindianexpress.com/columns/Failure-of-Monsanto-Bt-Cotton/2013/12/06/ article1930013.ece [Accessed 18 Aug. 2014].

Wikipedia, (2014). *History of Facebook*. [online] Available at: http://en.wikipedia.org/wiki/ History_of_Facebook [Accessed 18 Aug. 2014].

Wikipedia, (2014). *Madonna* (entertainer). [online] Available at: http://en.wikipedia.org/wiki/ Madonna_(entertainer) [Accessed 18 Aug. 2014].

Wikipedia, (2014). *Monsanto*. [online] Available at: http://en.wikipedia.org/wiki/Monsanto [Accessed 18 Aug. 2014].

YouTube, (2014). *WTF! Bill Gates Depopulation Plans Caught On Camera MONSANTO, FOOD RIOTS, EUGENICS*. [online] Available at: http://www.youtube.com/watch?v=3TyAJZVARPw [Accessed 18 Aug. 2014].

Monsanto is a publicly traded American, multinational chemical, and agricultural biotechnology corporation headquartered in Creve Coeur, Missouri.

It is the leading producer of genetically engineered (GE) seed and of the herbicide *glyphosate*, which it markets under the *Roundup* brand. Founded in 1901 by John Francis Queeny, by the 1940's Monsanto was a major producer of plastics, including polystyrene and synthetic fibres. Monsanto was the first company to mass-produce light emitting diodes (LEDs). The company also manufactures controversial products such as the insecticide DDT, PCBs, Agent Orange, and recombinant bovine somatotropin (a.k.a. bovine growth hormone).
Monsanto began aggressively selling genetically modified cotton seeds, known as Bt cotton, to Indian farmers with the claim that the seeds produced insecticides and led to higher yields. The GM seed was up to 10 times more expensive than regular seed, but with the promise of bumper crops the farmers signed

up. It cost the farmers the equivalent of half their yearly income. After the first year, all Bt cotton failed, and the farmers were desperate and in debt.

They were told by Monsanto that the seed was engineered to only work with the Monsanto patented fertiliser. So the farmers mortgaged their farms and homes (that had been in the family for 10 generations), to buy more seed and the magic potion fertiliser. That year they had the promised bumper crops.

Unfortunately, they all had bumper crops and the price of cotton plummeted. So now the farmers had no way to pay off their debts. Monsanto offered to clear the debt if the farmer signed over their farm to Monsanto. The farmers had no option. This sparked mass suicides and it is said that a farmer in India commits suicide every 30 minutes, crushed by debt, and the destructive policies associated with the introduction of GM cotton seed by Monsanto. Then on top of this, in November 2009, Monsanto's scientists detected unusual survival of the dreaded pink bollworm (*Pectinophora gossypiella*) in Bt cotton fields. After extensive studies, Monsanto admitted that their Bt cotton resistance to pink bollworm only lasted 8 years and a new strain of the Bt cotton will be required – at a greater cost. It is thought that only 5% of natural cotton exists in India today, and Monsanto is aggressively pursuing these farmers to force them off their land.

Madonna Louise Ciccone was born August 16, 1958 and is an American singer-songwriter, actress, author, director, entrepreneur and philanthropist and member of the Illuminati. Born in Bay City, Michigan, she moved to New York City, where she lives. Madonna is known for continuously reinventing both her music and image, and for retaining a standard of autonomy within the recording industry (only because she is a big wig in the Illuminati.) Critics have praised her diverse musical productions which have also been known to induce controversy. Her music and style has influenced numerous artists around the world. Madonna is considered by Forbes as a cultural icon and she is often referred to by the international media as the "Queen of Pop". She has been recognized as an acclaimed businesswoman, involving herself in fashion design, writing children's books, and film directing and producing.

Madonna has sold more than 300 million records worldwide and is recognized as the best-selling female recording artist of all time by Guinness World Records. *Time Magazine* included her in its list of the "25 Most Powerful Women of the Past Century" due to her major influence in contemporary music. Madonna is the best-selling female rock artist of the 20th century and the second bestselling female artist in the United States, with 64.5 million certified albums sold. In 2008, *Billboard* ranked her at number two, behind only The Beatles, on the "Billboard Hot 100 All-Time Top Artists", making her the most successful solo artist in the history of the chart.

Madonna became attracted to the teachings of the Kabbalah Centre in the 1990s and her family learn and practice at the Los Angeles Kabbalah Centre, where she became connected to Rabbi Philip Berg who became her personal instructor. Madonna often wears a red string bracelet, said to deflect the evil eye. She does not give concerts on Friday night, because of Shabbat and she wears special ritual objects. She has also tried to spread her faith to other entertainers, such as Demi Moore. In recent years, the IRS has looked into tax evasion by the Kabbalah Centre in Los Angeles and financial mismanagement of two Madonna-linked charities run by former Kabbalah Centre development director Phillipe van den Bossche.

## Love and Affection

You can explore the
Universe looking for
somebody who is more
deserving of your love
and affection than you
are yourself, and you
will not find that
person anywhere

UNKNOWN

# 5

## THE MATURE SOUL

---

*"I know how you feel"*

---

B Y THE END of the Young Soul phase, something doesn't feel quite right. All the wealth, power and praise aren't quite enough anymore; profits and winning no longer have any real value or meaning. It is now, that the Mature Soul period begins. No longer worried about competing with other people and what they think about you status wise, the Mature Soul begins asking questions like "Who am I? Why am I here?" with regular frequency.

Mature Souls are akin to people in middle age. That is, they have more experience and depths of subconscious lessons not present in younger souls. Therefore, their awareness is a lot more advanced. Rather than look forward and outward like younger souls, they look backward and inward.

This is the most emotionally intense level of all the Ages. This is when emotions finally open up and when 'real', meaningful relationships start. The boundaries younger souls impose around themselves now begin to break down. Seeing another person's point of view becomes possible as Mature Souls become deeply immersed in relationship issues.

They constantly evaluate whether their life goals are being achieved, and what they would do differently if they could start again. They have a strong tendency to be introspective. However, this incessant self-evaluation can and does lead to psychological issues. There is more emotional centring here, more intensity, more angst, more addictions, more pain, more schizophrenia, more suicide, more love, and more sensuality then in any other Soul Age.

Mature Souls are in the "mid-life crisis", so to speak, of the maturation cycle, so they make a lot of adjustments along the way in their lives. One of the reasons why Young Souls are able to direct so much energy towards success, is that their inner lives aren't calling for attention. This allows their energy to flow easily after externals. Not so in the Mature Age.

The musician Kurt Cobain, before his apparent suicide said, *"Wanting to be someone else is a waste of the person you are."* This is typical Mature Soul ideology, realising that you need to be yourself and not try and be somebody else (like Young Souls do). Then later he said,*"A friend is nothing but a known enemy."* Again, this bemoans the angst of the Mature Soul and both embody the typical Mature Soul intensification of feeling.

## About Love

Another important shift happens at the advent of the Mature Soul phase. Love! True, Unconditional Love is experienced for the first time. In the previous Soul Ages, "true love" is a foreign concept. The Infants experience raw lust and an urge to procreate the species. Men treat women worse than some animals. Infant women are completely driven by their hormones. The Child Soul experiences a deep fondness, but more like the love for a puppy or a kind grandparent.

Child Souls are also naturally loyal, so some mistake loyalty for love. Young Souls are the most perplexed about True Love, and will even at times ponder the question – "what is love?" For the Young Soul, a partner is selected for looks, money, status or convenience. A man will view his pretty young wife in the same way he views his sexy new sports car. They are both possessions that enhance his status. So when his wife starts to look old, just like his car, he will "upgrade" to that latest model. Young Soul woman tend to get bored easy and will happily go from one man to another as long as he can support the materialistic lifestyle she yearns for. If both male and female are Young Souls and share a love of money, power and greed, they mistake their mutual lusts for love. But make no mistake, a Young Soul has no qualms about breaking off a relationship he/she believes it will be beneficial to them in some way. Mature Souls regularly incarnate and partner up with Young Souls (levels 5,6,7) to try and teach them about unconditional love.

I am sure you have heard of stories about a devout, loving wife that cared for her husband through sickness and in health. After 20 years of marriage, the husband wins the lottery, or finds celebrity, or a new, higher status, and suddenly leaves his wife and takes up with a much younger women. On the flip side, I knew of a couple where the male nursed his sick wife through 2 bouts of cancer over several years. Later in life, the man contracted testicular cancer. The short story is the women left within a week of his prognosis. Her reason was that she wanted children and time was running out (due to age), so she wanted to find a healthy man that could give her children. This behaviour may seem shocking to the Mature or Old Soul, but to a Young Soul, this is very logical and makes complete sense. I will talk more about Unconditional Love later.

## Mature Souls Ages 1-4

It's time to let your creative juices flow! All forms of art, music, literature and philosophy are eagerly pursued. It is not only for their intrinsic value, it is also because Mature Souls have a vivacious appetite for learning all things new. There is very little that escapes their attention. Even early in life, the Mature Soul will seek knowledge in libraries, universities and nature. They are great believers in education and knowledge. They go to school for a different reason than Young Souls. Whereas Young Souls get educated to further their careers, most Mature Souls seek knowledge for its own sake. They truly want to understand. It may not always be in a formal or institutional setting, since this can seem too structured and limiting or too Young-soulish for them.

They often pursue knowledge on their own, reading widely or taking night-school classes on whatever subject is of interest to them. This they often do rather than seeking a formal degree. The courses that Mature Souls take are less likely to involve occupation, and more likely to be for personal improvement. Mature Souls care more about what they are learning than about the grades they make in learning it.

That said, as consciousness has expanded over the last 20 years, it is almost commonplace now to see someone with a Diploma in Homeopathy, or a PhD in Naturopathy etc. These people are usually Mature Souls (1-4). They still have the hang-over of the Young Soul need for letters after their name and a certificate on the wall, even though their ambitions are very different.

Mature Souls are often viewed by Child and Young Souls as being disturbed, weird, or "airy-fairy". That is only because these younger groups do not understand the intense emotional dramas Mature Souls go through on an almost daily occurrence. Therefore, Mature Souls tend to seek out others like themselves or even communities of Mature Souls, where they can be understood. Sedona, Arizona in the United States and Glastonbury in the UK are two well-known Mature Soul cities, as is Amsterdam in Holland.

Mature Souls are in a searching mode all their lives. There is an itch to "find themselves" and "express themselves". Personal fulfilment is their constant quest. This they never quite achieve to their own satisfaction. The problem is that Mature Souls are complex — the most complex of the entire Soul Age cycle. There is so much going on in their psyche, which other people cannot fathom, and they themselves do not understand, which can lead to them becoming agitated, over sensitive, and touchy.

Because of their psychological sensitivity and complexity, early Mature Souls often exhibit a lot of confusion in their lives. For this reason they are often considered neurotic, probably because of all the psychological garbage they have kept churning around in their heads. The Mature Soul's main learning in these lives is largely concerned with feelings. They are working through emotional blocks. They are the most likely of the ages to need and seek psychological counselling for their emotional difficulties. The majority of people who go to psychologists for counselling are Mature Souls, and the majority of psychologists are themselves Mature Souls — and they probably have a lot of psychological churning that they themselves are working through.

Many psychological issues come to the surface in the Mature Soul Age which have to be dealt with on a conscious level. If it cannot be dealt with, the person may turn to alcoholism or drug abuse as an escape. These methods of numbing ones emotions are more prevalent in this Age than any other. Mature Souls will not often let themselves do actual physical harm to other people, like younger souls might, so they turn their frustrations concerning others upon themselves. Jim Morrison is a perfect example of a Mature Soul tormented by his own thoughts and feelings. Amy Winehouse, the young singer that died from an overdose in 2001, was a text book version of a 2nd Level Mature Soul.

## Mature Souls Ages 4 – 7

In the later Levels of the Mature Age, the person almost always seeks answers to the big questions of life in a way that few people in the earlier cycles do. This often means involvement in metaphysical endeavours, practice, or knowledge. By metaphysical I mean everything from psychology to religion to the psychic. Mind-Body-Spirit. This is not the "New-Age" movement as such – that is a 7th Level Young Soul phenomena.

Concepts and issues which younger souls would pass over as meaningless are very important to Mature Souls. For instance, the Young Soul is somewhat anti-psychological — he finds fulfilment in material things. The Child Soul is downright afraid of Psychologists! He rarely questions his own motivations, or that of others. But the Mature Souls looks for a larger meaning in life. They want to understand the significance of everything, and the motivations for why people do things. More than a person of any other Age, the Mature Soul cares — cares about the problems of the planet and wants to correct  them. They care about other people and wants to help them. They care about their own well-being and want to improve it. Mature Souls are open to all experiences, and are prone to try pragmatic solutions to their difficulties, rather than using canned Establishment (Young Soul) solutions.

In fact, the one thing that typifies Mature Souls to me, is they are nearly always fighting for some cause, or are certainly passionate about injustice.  Animal rights, volunteering for work in 3rd world countries, freedom for enslaved peoples. They really do want to save the world! In 2013, I was driving along and noticed the car in front of me.  It was an old, but loved, VW Kombi van painted in rainbow colours and murals.  On its back window were no less than 9 bumper stickers, all of which were save this, support that.  I had to laugh to myself, because I would have bet a house this driver or owner of the car was a text book Mature Soul!

Since Mature Souls are relatively evolved in their consciousness, their behaviour is very ethical. They are working on the finer points of human relationships. They value the feelings and opinions of other people. It hurts them when others do not think well of them. While it is true they can be somewhat nonconformist and even a little bit rebellious in their nature, nevertheless Mature Souls are not completely detached from a sense of social obligation and law and order. Unlike Child Souls who are afraid to break the law, Mature Souls just don't want to rock the boat. They would prefer to abide by the law of the land rather than make a fuss. That is until a law does not make sense to them or it impinges on their rights as a human. They will be the first arrested for defending an injustice.

Though relationships, knowledge and emotions are their primary concerns, Mature Souls do work for a living, but it is not with the gusto of a Young Soul. There is not the willingness to put everything into a career and rise to the top, and family, friends and health nearly always come first over their career.

Countries with Mature Soul attributes may tend to put more attention on social relationships than on material goods or efficiency. Examples are Italy, Greece, Spain, Egypt and Mexico. Italy has had about 50 post-war cabinet crises. This is typical Mature Soul thinking – death by committee, never wanting to hurt anyone's feelings, but never being able to come to a compromise in case it may harm some members of their community. They really do try and please everyone, and in a Young Soul world, this is not seen as very productive.

England, even with its stolid roots, is a little off balance due to its entry into the Mature phase. With the advent of socialism, which aims for a more equal distribution of wealth, the average Briton is suddenly more focused on internals, than on the never-ending struggle to maintain a power position in the world. People are less interested in nose-to-the-grindstone hard work, but not just because their basic survival is supported by the socialistic system. They have changed on an inner level. An interesting example of this is the decline of the British Empire in the last 20 years. Most modern historians now agree, that the British Empire is finished, which highlights the shift from Young Soul to Mature Soul.

Around mid-1987, many Young Soul countries, like Holland and France started nosing into a Mature consciousness. This happened because, suddenly their populations had more Mature Souls than Young, and the old balance started changing. Those countries will still feel primarily Young Soul in ambiance and action for some time to come, but you'll notice within them, that the desire to make sure everyone is taken care of crops up to a greater and greater extent.

Mature Souls are starting to realise that everything is connected. Therefore, they will support animal rights, save the whales, the dolphins, the rare and endangered. They will protest against live animal testing in cosmetic laboratories as well as the fur trade used for clothing. People for the Ethical Treatment of Animals (PETA) are a typical Mature Soul organisation, so too is Green Peace. Unfortunately, both these organisations were co-opted by Young Souls and are now just money making organisations. On a slightly different note, it was Mature Souls that started pet cemeteries and who patronise them.

Poland and Russia are countries brimming with Mature Souls, where strong agreements exist for assets to be divided fairly, for everyone to have equal shares of the wealth. Marxist theory is very much Mature Soul in flavour and this is why Young Souls demonise it. An interesting development in 2013, saw the President of Russia Vladimir Putin put the US Government in its place, when it was threating to invade Syria. Putin offered to go into Syria and remove its stockpile of chemical weapons. The US on the other hand want to bomb Syria! Putin displayed a calm, rational Mature Soul approach, where the US are still pushing the "might is right" ideology (a Child/Young Soul view).

The US, Australia, New Zealand and several other countries have ever increasing pockets of Mature Souls growing every year, but their current leaders are still Child/Young Souls.

## Motto: "I know how you feel"

For the first time out of the Soul Ages the Mature Soul can empathise with other people and actually care deeply how other people feel.

## Outlook on Life

Mature Souls are very much involved in the affairs of the world, but they have a great need for a quite refuge to which they can retreat to in times of stress. They like to have a cabin in the woods or by a lake or near the sea, where they can take a vacation from the rat race. They do not seek material things or have a second home for status, like a Young Soul, but for an escape or sanctuary. Mature Souls seek less tangible things than material possessions. While they can naturally appreciate the beautiful, material things in life, like nice houses, a new car or fine dining, they rarely yearn for these things.

Mature Souls are the avant-garde of society. It is they who make the genuinely novel contributions to the advancement of culture.

They are the inspired visionaries. Whatever field of endeavour you might name — whether scientific, religious, political, technological, artistic, philosophical, humanitarian, or economic — it is the Mature Souls who are in the forefront, at the leading edge, on the frontiers.

Mature Souls often campaign for reforms in society. They form the core of the environmentalist movement, the antinuclear energy movement, the anti-genetically modified crops, anti chemtrails and other such improve-the-world endeavours. They are beyond the Young Soul in perception of the value of the spiritual aspects of life. However, they are nevertheless entangled with the affairs of the world to such an extent, that they think the planet is worth the trouble of making it a better place.

## Social Media

Mature Souls use social media to make friends and keep in contact with existing friends.  They also love to share and gather information. They will always be clicking 'Causes' and 'Like' buttons on Facebook almost daily. In fact, it is very hard for Mature Souls not to check their Facebook page at least once per day, but more typically several times a day. They are the employees most likely to be on Facebook during work hours. If they lose a friend off their list, even if they didn't really have much to do with them, they take it personally, and will want to know why the person de-friended them.  They also love to share pictures on Facebook, Twitter and Instagram. They will often update their profile picture just so people will leave them nice comments about it. They usually do this when they are feeling down.  Mature Souls will usually have a moderate amount of friends on their lists. This is because they would rather have 100 people they communicate with regularly (thus develop meaningful relationships), than have 1000 strangers on their list (like Young Souls do).

## Relationships

Mature Souls are very relationship-oriented and they seek the camaraderie of like-minded companions. In contrast to Young Souls, who tend to regard their career as paramount, Mature Souls often value their relationships as the most important thing in their lives. They build their lives around social contacts and friends who have similar interests. Family members, in the sense of blood relatives, which are very important to the three younger soul Ages, are not as important to Mature Souls as good companions are. Many tortured artists and drama queens are Mature Souls, but so too are many health professionals and social service workers.

## Sexuality & Love

While Young Souls seek mates for status and pure lust driven sex; Mature Souls do so for love. It is unusual for a person younger than Mature to experience true love for their mate. Mature Souls want someone to whom they can relate meaningfully, rather than just someone to fulfil the stereotypical role of a mate ordained by Young-soul society. A good place for Mature Souls to meet others for companionship or romance, is in school or at the library. Second choice would be informal and loosely organised singles groups, where they can get to know others as friends before they become lovers. The bar scene does not appeal to them at all. Mature Souls want to mate for life, or at least a long term relationship – preferably no one night stands here. For the first time, Souls can explore true passion and sensuality during sex and you can bet they know a bit about Tantric sex and the Karma Sutra! And yep, unlike the Child Souls, the candles are lit, the warm massage oil is out, and prolonged exploration of each other begins!

### Spiritual Outlook / Religion

Mature Souls that seek out religion tend to frequent liberal churches, rather than the mainstream churches. If they go for organised religion at all, it is the undogmatic and quiet faiths such as Unitarianism and Unity Churches. In their quest for truth, at the extreme, the Mature Soul may experiment with more unorthodox or offbeat brands or New Age sects, Neo-Paganism and Eastern philosophies like Buddhism. Mature Souls have a strong sense of morality and ethics, but it is of the situational ethics and moral relativism variety. This disgusts younger souls, particularly Child Souls.

In political philosophy, the Mature Souls is liberal — "left-wing" — perhaps even to the point of being socialistic. The idealistic hippie era of the 1960's was a Mature Soul phenomenon. Often they lived in communes or shared homes. Mature Souls are reluctant to fight in wars, because they regard all of humankind as their brethren. For this reason, they also tend to be pacifistic — and not in a militant way like a Young Soul might be. Even though they love freedom, they usually prefer to submit to domination rather than fight for that freedom. A clear example of this, is in America today where the Mature Souls form a majority of the populace in many areas. They submit to the domineering Child/Young Souls who control almost all levels of the government.

## How They Relate to Other Soul Ages

Mature Souls enjoy the company of other Mature Souls for their emotional potency, as well as for the kindred spirit kind of feeling. They appreciate Old Souls for their information and guidance, while Young Souls are enjoyed for their reminders of how to push forward in the world and get things done.

Mature Souls have a highly developed sense of humour and they laugh easily. The type of humour they prefer, is "situation comedy" involving social relationships. An excellent example of a Mature Soul film director is Anne Fontaine.

Anne's movies explore deep emotional issues and 'taboos' that Young Soul directors wouldn't touch with a ten foot pole! Mature Souls like to tease and joke with their friends, but their teasing is rarely hostile or denigrating like it can be with Young Souls. The type of movies they prefer are the award-winners with depth, meaning, and originality, usually produced by Mature Souls — not the shallow, action or adventure type produced by Young Souls.

That is why in 2010, the Mature level movie Avatar and its Mature Soul director James Cameron, were dumped by the Young Soul Academy Awards in favour of a badly produced "war film" in The Hurt Locker. It's moments like these, the older souls just have to shrug their shoulders and shake their heads.

# THERE ARE NO COINCIDENCES. THE SOUL SEEKS ITS OWN PATH.

ANGELA GWINNER

## MATURE SOUL PROFILE - Fred Hollows

Fred Cossom Hollows, AC (9 April 1929 – 10 February 1993) was a New Zealand and Australian ophthalmologist who became known for his work in restoring eyesight for countless thousands of people in Australia and many other countries. It has been estimated that more than one million people in the world can see today because of initiatives instigated by Hollows, the most notable example being The Fred Hollows Foundation.

Hollows received his BA degree from Victoria University of Wellington. He briefly studied at a seminary, but decided against a life in the clergy. After observing the doctors at a mental hospital during some charity work, he instead enrolled at Otago Medical School. Hollows was a member of the Communist Party of New Zealand during the 1950s and 1960s.

In 1961, he went to Moorfields Eye Hospital in England to study ophthalmology. He then did post-graduate work in Wales before moving to Australia in 1965, where he became associate professor of ophthalmology at the University of New South Wales in Sydney. From 1965–1992, he chaired the ophthalmology division overseeing the teaching departments at the University of New South Wales, and the Prince of Wales and Prince Henry Hospitals.    Hollows was married twice: in 1958 to Mary Skiller, who died in 1975, and in 1980 to Gabi O'Sullivan.  Hollows was originally a New Zealand citizen. He declined the award of honorary Officer of the Order of Australia in 1985. He adopted Australian citizenship in 1989 and was named Australian of the Year in 1990. He accepted the substantive award of Companion of the Order of Australia in 1991.

Upon his death, the Chief Minister of the ACT Australia, Rosemary Follett, described Hollows to her parliamentary colleagues as *"an egalitarian and a self-named anarcho-syndicalist, who wanted to see an end to the economic disparity which exists between the First and Third Worlds and who believed in no power higher than the best expressions of the human spirit found in personal and social relationships."*

Fred Hollows once said: *"To my mind, having a care and concern for others is the highest of the human qualities."*

Catherine Élise "Cate" Blanchett was born 14 May 1969, and is an Australian actress of screen and stage. She is widely considered one of the best actors of her generation, and has received critical acclaim and many accolades, including two Academy Awards, three Screen Actors Guild Awards, three Golden Globe Awards and three BAFTA Awards. She was appointed Chevalier of the Order of Arts and Letters by the French government in 2012.

Blanchett made Brighton, England, the family home for much of the early 2000s.  However, she and her husband returned to their native Australia in November 2006, because they wanted a permanent home for her children, and to be closer to her family.  She also wanted to have a sense of belonging to the Australian (theatrical) community. She and her family live in Bulwarra, an 1877 sandstone mansion once owned by Halse Rogers Arnott, in the harbour side Sydney suburb of Hunters Hill. It was purchased for in 2004 and underwent extensive renovations in 2007 to be made more "eco-friendly".

In 2007, Blanchett became the ambassador for the Australian Conservation Foundation's online campaign – trying to persuade Australians to express their concerns about climate change. She is also the Patron of the development charity SolarAid. Opening the 2008 9th World Congress of Metropolis in Sydney, Blanchett said: *"The one thing that all great cities have in common is that they are all different."*

At the beginning of 2011, Blanchett lent her support for a Carbon Tax. She received some criticism for this, especially from conservatives. Blanchett has spoken passionately about feminism and politics, telling Sky News in 2013 that she was concerned that *"a wave of conservatism sweeping the globe was threatening women's rights."*

She has also commented on the pressures women in Hollywood face now: *"Honestly, I think about my appearance less than I did ten years ago. People talk about the golden age of Hollywood because of how women were lit then. You could be Joan Crawford and Bette Davis and work well into your 50's, because you were lit and made into a goddess. Now, with everything being sort of gritty, women have this sense of their use-by date."* In January 2014, Blanchett took part in the Green Carpet Challenge, an initiative to raise the public profile of sustainable fashion, founded by Livia Firth of Eco-Age.

# References:

*How Putin Saved Obama, Congress and the European Union from Further Embarrassing themselves on Syria,* http://www.juancole.com/2013/09/congress-embarrassing-themselves.html

*Barack Obama's Faustian pact with Vladimir Putin over Syrian chemical weapons brings despair to allies,* http://www.telegraph.co.uk/news/worldnews/middleeast/syria/10309943/Barack-Obamas-Faustian-pact-with-Vladimir-Putin-over-Syrian-chemical-weapons-brings-despair-to-allies.html

*Australian of the Year Government Site*

*"Fact Sheet Fred Hollows".* The Fred Hollows Foundation. Retrieved 18 November 2009.

*Fred Hollows Foundation,* Our Network Fred Hollows Foundation International Website. Accessed 10 February 2014

*Cate Blanchett:* http://en.wikipedia.org/wiki/Cate_Blanchett

# 6

## THE OLD SOUL

---

*"You do what you want, and I'll do what I want"*

---

*A*WARE OF THE big picture from very early on, Old Souls recognise the interrelatedness existing among all life on Earth. They naturally perceive that everyone is connected on some level and as such, they do their best to live and let live and to not harm or judge others.

Old Souls have moved away from the high drama and intense emotional ways of the Mature Soul to allow themselves to view life's ups and downs more objectively. There is a strong urge to be impeccable and to maintain personal integrity in all transactions.

Much that can be said about an Old Soul is what would be said about an old person. Usually old people have travelled to many places and done many things. They are a storehouse of wisdom and understanding because of this range of experience. Because of the age of the body, there is often a tiredness about them that prevents much expenditure of effort. They are quieter than younger people, have a more relaxed lifestyle, and are more subdued in their manner of expression. They have mellowed out considerably compared to their younger days. The energy and excitement of youth is mostly gone. It is very similar with Old Souls.

## Old Soul Ages 1 – 4

After hundreds of lives, in dozens of cultures, they have also been in both genders many times, so it is not surprising that it is difficult for the Old Soul to get caught up in the right-and-wrong, us-and-them games people and countries both play. Having played the hero and the villain in many past lives, they can now see the big picture, as well as both sides to any argument, so they tend to be calmer, peaceful and centred.

They have access through the subconscious to a great wealth of experience, so they tend to be teachers of teachers. They are a storehouse of knowledge and wisdom, but they will limit the number of students they pass it on to. In fact, there is little desire to release their understanding into the world in general. Indeed, Old Souls can be so world-weary that they are ready to just lie down and die. Like a person in the last decade of life, the Old Soul is "winding down" so to speak, or "in retirement", preparing for death, settling the estate, and tying up loose ends. In terms of reincarnation, the Old Soul is clearing the way for the final break with the physical plane once and for all. So for that reason, they see little reason to try and 'save' the world.

Even from a very early earth age, Old Souls will be noticed for their odd behaviours, or what quiet babies they are. As toddlers, it will become apparent to their parents that they step to a different beat (in a Young Soul culture). By their teen and young adult years, they are often guiding or counselling their younger soul parents! However, Old Souls do not generally grow into their full Old Soul age until about 30-35 years of age.

But as stated, even from a young age, others want to be near them and follow them - and they don't really know why. Younger souls are drawn to Old Souls much like a child is drawn to kind, elderly people or a grandparent. It is because of the calming energies that they naturally exude. You certainly know when you are in their presence! They are often driven by an insatiable appetite for spiritual growth and as such, have very little time for developing political or material punch. This also means that they rarely do anything they don't want to do. When it comes to work or making a living, they would rather do things in their own 'unconventional' way and follow a path of least resistance. This is so they can free up their time and energy to work on spiritual development. Because of their vast experience of many life-times, they are extremely competent in a wide range of skills, but hardly ever take up anything one thing as a career. A jack of all trades, master of none is a fitting statement. They will try to find work that supports their personal growth: counselling, teaching, music, writing, gardening and carpentry being some favourites. Indeed, many are drawn to philosophy, art and music. In fact, we can thank the Old Soul musicians, like the late Tony O'Connor, that compose and record all of the beautiful meditation music we all enjoy. If their work requires them to undergo higher education, like the Mature Soul, they will opt for less orthodox schools.

## Old Soul Ages 4 -7

Not unlike the Infant Soul, but for different reasons, it is rare for an Old Soul to make a great contribution to society or culture. The reason for this, is that they have largely given up on the world. It just does not seem worth the trouble to spend a lot of energy for things that do not last. Material things just decay anyway, so why invest in that? A fancy house or car, or impressive clothes and jewellery aren't too high on an Old Soul's priority list. Neither is a nine-to-five job.

The other problem is that they are advanced in their perceptions to such an extent, that the genius of their contributions would go unappreciated by the great majority of people, i.e.: the Establishment. Old Souls know this and do not even try to get them to see or understand their often brilliant ideas. Younger souls, who largely control the course of society, cannot understand Old Souls, and regard them and their notions as eccentric. Old Souls are perceived to be "far out", or "cranks", or "crack-pots" if they do make themselves noticed. Younger souls are often too busy to stop and really listen to the wisdom of Old Souls anyway.

It is for this reason, the Old Souls often have difficulty with self-esteem, because their perceptions and values are not shared by the rest of society. Indeed, this proves to be a major stumbling block for the Old Soul cycle. No Soul is complete until they love themselves and have learnt forgiveness of themselves and those in their life. As mentioned previously, Old Souls deal with many self-esteem issues because they live in a world that does not value their contributions. To the Old Soul, many solutions seem obvious to them. But when they try and enlighten their Younger Soul administrators, they are met with scorn and ridicule. No wonder the give up right!

Old Souls rarely display arrogance or cockiness, because they innately understand what a small part they play in a vast and expanding, multi-dimensional Universe. In fact, Old Souls tend to be experts at beating themselves up, and this is probably why they only come into their full Old Soul awareness about one-third of the time.

Old Souls have very few psychological problems to deal with. Presumably, these have been worked out in previous lifetimes. Their subconscious access to depths of experience means that there is very little they do not understand about what is going on, both out in the world, and within themselves. However Old Souls do have one significant psychological issue, and that is they are subject to clinical depression. All the soul ages can suffer from depression to some extent, but it is especially acute in Old Souls. The reason for this, is that to them, life seems heavy and boring — "life is a drag".

They perceive that it is all a game, a contrived situation, and they no longer want to play. They feel like they have seen it all, so what is there left to live for? The material pursuits of Young Souls seem quite futile to them, so what is there to get interested in? Even the Mature Soul's excitement about newfound truth seems passé to Old Souls. Underpinning all this, is the fact that many have conscious memory, if only abstract, of the Spirit World, and quite simply they miss home. This nonchalant attitude and home sickness can severely limit an Old Soul's happiness and well-being. It can also be a source of misunderstanding for younger souls who are enjoying life. Whether he understands it consciously or not in terms of reincarnation, the Old Soul simply wants to graduate from the physical plane, and go on to new and better things in the higher planes.

Old Souls do have one advantage with the material world though: as they begin to seek and understand, they use the laws of the physical universe to their advantage, so goals can be attained with less effort. Thus, there is an outer, as well as an inner draw to understand the universal laws distilled in astrology, metaphysics, the tarot and other ancient teachings.

The Old Soul is in the process of removing itself from entanglement with the usual affairs of life. Thus, they do not have a strong sense of attachment or kinship with the world, such as is possessed by younger souls. They want to purge and purify themselves of materialistic connections. Therefore, their primary motivation becomes the pursuit of some specific life task, or perhaps spiritual refinement.

Because of their advanced perceptions, Old Souls are inherently ethical in behaviour, feeling, and thought. They do not have to be taught right and wrong by parents or society. There is some socialising to be done when they are children of course, but the programming for decency, honesty, and integrity is innate. It is as if they are grown-up even when they are children. They obey the rules of their culture, only in what is required to get by without causing trouble.

They are not usually jealous, envious, possessive, competitive or pushy — any one of a number of things which involve attachment to other people or things. When Old Souls are dealing with these ethical issues, it is with their subtle aspects. They are gentle toward the faults of others. The harsh perceptions often present in younger souls are absent here. They rarely perceive actions as being truly evil. Rather, they regard things that cause suffering as foolish and primitive, and they seek to cure the cause of the problem by imparting wise knowledge and understanding.

Old Souls try to maintain neutrality in time of war. It is part of their non-attachment and seeing the "big picture". There are certain nations primarily populated by Old Souls, such as Norway, Holland, and Iceland, who value their independence and neutrality in political issues. If Old Souls care anything for politics, it is that they are pacifists. Most often they are simply apolitical — they rarely get involved with it at all. But even Old Souls can only be pushed so far, so occasionally they will rally the oppressed through inspiring speeches and literature.

In 2008, the Old Soul citizens in Iceland rose up at Parliament and succeeded in forcing the resignation of both the incompetent Prime Minister and his corrupt government. New elections were held and leaders of the up rise were voted in by a landslide. Their next mission was to kick out the greedy and corrupt bankers from their country. They succeeded, and since then, they have left the Euro and their economy had grown by 7% by 2012. To give you an idea, countries still in the Euro system that grow by 2.5-3% are considered to be economic powerhouses. Younger souls will often perceive Old Souls as weak or soft, but the reality is, an Old Soul can call on powerful 'warrior' energies from hundreds of life- times. So the moral of the story is, let sleeping lions lie!

## Motto: "Live and Let Live"

Old Souls are individualistic — they believe that people should basically do whatever they want to do, so long as it doesn't hurt anyone else. The motto of the Old Soul is, "Live and let live", because they rarely campaign for anything and they do not want to change the world — they just let it be.

## Outlook on Life

The Old Soul is likely to sense his or her differentness. They may even think perhaps they do not belong on this planet. Robbie Williams, a 4th Level Mature Soul, summed up the Old Soul outlook in the lyrics for his song "Feel" when he says: *"I don't want to die, but I ain't keen on living either..."*

Another major Old Soul trait, is that they love being on planet Earth! Manifesting sufficient mastery that you have enough of what you want to make it pleasurable, is all part of the fun (and challenge). And just a note on that - it is never your last life, until you like being here; your Higher Self would never let you off the hook before then! One last thing, a soul can never compete the cycles of death and rebirth, until they have shared everything they have learnt with at least one other soul. Namaste!

## Social Media

Some Old Souls use social media while other Old Souls don't even own a computer, nor know how to turn one on! It is not because they don't have the intellect, it is simply because they have no need, or will to own a computer or any technology for that matter. Again, it has to do with their non-attachment to the world.

However, for those Old Souls in a heavy teaching life (6th level mostly) will embrace any media that allows them to spread their spiritual message or teachings to as many people as possible who want to learn. Therefore, they tend to use social media to spread a message or try and 'wake' people up. Unfortunately, many of their 'friends' are younger souls who miss the messages all together. Unlike Young or Mature Souls, they never become addicted to Facebook or Twitter. For them it is just another way to spread their wisdom - a means to an end.

Their friend list will be made up of a huge cross section of society. They do not wish to hurt anyone's feelings so they accept everyone! But they do not suffer fools or crass behaviour and will have no hesitation in 'unfriending' certain people. They do not care if they have 2 friends or 2000 friends on their list.

## Relationships

In their social lives, Old Souls are often loners. They go their own way, caring little for societal norms. They are a rare breed, comprising about 8% of the total global population, spread thinly and never forming communities. They have very little attachment to encounters of a casual nature, such as co-workers and neighbours. Even their sense of connection to blood relatives is not very strong. They generally shun heavy entanglements with other people. When they do get involved, it is because there is a strong spiritual bond. By this, I mean that there is either a karmic attachment (past-life association), or an 'agreement' — i.e. contracts made between lifetimes to conduct a relationship, usually for mutual benefit. On rare occasions, they will meet their Twin Flame or Twin Soul and the bonds are indestructible, but more on that in Book III.

When Old Souls do seek companionship, they often do so in metaphysical groups, astrology and tarot classes, psychic development, meditation circles and so on. Here they will be most likely to meet those with whom they have spiritual connections. They seek out the few others who are like themselves (but rarely finding them), and form networks of people with similar interests. This is not usually for the purpose of business advancements like Young Souls, or for psychological comfort like Mature Souls, but just to share being with other Old Souls. When Old Souls "party", they usually just sit around and talk! Indeed, conversations with or between Old Souls can cause time warps – that is, it seems like you were talking for 30 minutes, but the clock says it was 4 hours!

## Sexuality & Love

When it comes to dating situations, they do not need to go anywhere, like to a movie or dinner, or do the typical societal norm as a means of developing social intimacy. Their first date could easily be meeting in a park with a coffee or fresh juice and talk for hours. If the basis for psychological intimacy is not quickly apparent to the Old Soul, he or she will not put themselves through much trouble to develop it. Indeed, it if is not happening in their head, it will not happen in the genitals! It is difficult for Old Souls to make strong bonds with people that they have not been together with in numerous past lifetimes.

Old Souls have spent countless lives in both male and female bodies therefore they have very little issue with a person's homosexuality or lack of femininity.  In fact, Old Souls can sometimes come across as androgynous, as they can easily blend male and female energies into a third gender – the Old Soul!   The type of sex most preferred, is when they can blend their energies and Chakras with their partner, taking on a cosmic experience and their passion is legendary.    There are not too many Old Souls that are not aware of Tantric sex, however, this type of sex is all but impossible if their partner is less than 5th level Mature.

But at the end of the day, sex is not highly prized by the Old Soul, especially in a casual sense.  They are usually competent therein, but lack interest.  This can be disconcerting to younger souls who still prize sex highly. What the Old Soul seeks in romantic relationships, is a "soul mate" — someone to whom they relate to on all levels. This is usually someone with whom they have spent many lifetimes with, so the drive to find this person is so strong that it could be described as a compulsion.  It is not like they have any trouble attracting potential partners, but unfortunately, they can remain doggedly single for many, many years – refusing to get involved with anyone that is not potentially 'the one'.  This can quite often be to their own detriment.

## Spiritual Outlook/Religion:

Old Souls may explore many religions and teachings, being most drawn to those emphasising love and forgiveness to those they've resonated with closely in past lives. But being rule-bound, or as orthodox as some disciplines require, does not usually last long. They rarely, if ever, get involved with mainstream religions. Unique, personal spiritual practices, like a beach ritual at sunrise to mark a birthday, are often developed and used.

Child Souls and even some Mature Souls will go to great lengths to show their devotion, or how spiritual they are.  The Old Soul usually comes across as a very down to earth, non-committed (in a religious sense) person.  That is because their beliefs and Spirituality are very much a personal and therefore private affair.  You will never find them preaching or trying to convince others of their beliefs.  They will happily share knowledge when the right question is asked, but they really don't care if people believe what they believe or not.

Even though the Old Soul is non-religious, they will always be naturally respectful toward other religions.  In the event they are invited into a church or mosque for a ceremony, like a wedding, they will show the same respect as any follower of that religion does. Old Souls are very tolerant of all religions and points of view.

## How They Relate to Other Soul Ages

Old Souls are very capable of unconditional love, and many consciously work on not ever judging other people. For this very reason, some Old Souls appear to be annoyingly remote. This is usually a soul who has previously handled many emotional issues and comes to the planet intent on examining intellectual, philosophical and spiritual issues, period. There is however a strong sense of service to others and they will bend over backwards at times to help any Soul Age individual.

There is not much in an Old Soul that can offend a younger soul, though there is much that can be misunderstood by them. To some, it may seem that Old Souls do not care. It is more accurate to say that they are non-attached. They do not make much investment in what is going on around them, and do not have strong expectations for any particular outcome. Whatever will be, will be, so why fight it? Old Souls inherently see the bigger picture. They see that the world rolls on, day after day, year after year, millennium after millennium, with the same basic stories being told, time after time with minor variations. Old Souls know the big lesson of the whole Maturation cycle, and that is non-judgmental acceptance of anything and everything. What little they cannot abide, they simply avoid.

Rarely do they seek to change things. They rarely organize into social clubs which have a hierarchical structure of leaders and followers, or join organisations which promote some cause. Rather, they form loose networks of friends and associates having common interests. As far as being competitive, forget it!

Old Souls can have a bawdy and somewhat cheeky sense of humour at times, because they lack the hang-ups of younger souls. Child Souls, in particular, can find this unnerving because they are not sure how to deal with it. In fact, younger souls in general can down right detest the presence of an Old Soul. This is because the younger soul feels threatened by them, or feel they need to raise to their level even though the Old Soul asks for nothing! It is literally like an obnoxious teenager dealing with an old person. They will throw abuse like *"get out of here you stupid old codger..."* Again, because something about the old person reminds the teenage how they should be acting, even though the old person said nothing. Younger Souls are sometimes angry, bitter and frustrated with the world, so when they see a caring, smiling, loving Old Soul, it is too much for them to bear.

---

# References:

crazyemailsandbackstories, (2012). *Iceland's Amazing Peaceful Revolution - Still Not in the News (backstory).* [online] Available at: http://crazyemailsandbackstories. wordpress.com/2012/05/12/icelands-amazing-peaceful-revolution-still-not-in-the-news-backstory/ [Accessed 2 Aug. 2014].

Dobrev, D. (2014). *Dobri Dobrev. [online]* Wikipedia. Available at: http://en.wikipedia.org/ wiki/Dobri_Dobrev [Accessed 2 Aug. 2014].

Elder Dobri Dobrev of Baylovo, B. and Sanidopoulos, J. (2010). *MYSTAGOGY: Elder Dobri Dobrev of Baylovo, Bulgaria.* [online] Johnsanidopoulos.com. Available at: http://www.johnsanidopoulos.com/2010/08/elder-dobri-dobrev-of-baylovo-bulgaria. html?m=1 [Accessed 2 Aug. 2014].

Greene, A. (2013). *Rodriguez: 10 Things You Don't Know About the 'Searching for Sugar Man' Star.* [online] Rolling Stone. Available at: http://www.rollingstone.com/music/news/ rodriguez-10-things-you-dont-know-about-the-searching-for-sugar-man-star-20130328 [Accessed 2 Aug. 2014].

MaranAta0, (2009). *Elder Dobri from Baylovo - Bulgaria.* [online] YouTube. Available at: http://youtu.be/vaau8iT0D0o [Accessed 2 Aug. 2014].

Pope, J. (1992). *The World According to Michael.* 1st ed. Fayetteville, AR: Emerald Wave.

Rodriguez, (2014). *Sixto Rodriguez.* [online] Wikipedia. Available at: http://en.wikipedia.org/ wiki/Sixto_Rodriguez [Accessed 2 Aug. 2014].

VOAvideo, (2012). *Iceland Turns Away From EU Membership as Economy Recovers.* [online] YouTube. Available at: http://youtu.be/rsAMYWyJnLc [Accessed 2 Aug. 2014].

## OLD SOUL PROFILE - Sixto Rodriguez

Sixto Diaz Rodriguez (also known just as "Rodríguez" or as Jesús Rodríguez; born July 10, 1942) is an American folk musician based in Detroit, Michigan. His career initially proved short lived, with two little-sold albums in the early 1970s and two Australian concert tours.

Unbeknownst to him, however, his work became extremely successful and influential in South Africa and at one point in time, more famous than Elvis Presley. Ironically, it was mistakenly rumoured in South Africa that Rodriguez committed suicide on stage no less! Rodriguez's fame in South Africa had remained completely unknown to him until 1997, when his eldest daughter came across a website dedicated to him.

After coming into contact with the authors of the website and learning of his long-standing fame in the country, Rodriguez went on his first South African tour, playing 6 sold out concerts in front of thousands of fans.

Rodriguez's albums "ColdFact" and "Coming from Reality" were re-released by Light in the Attic Records in 2009. The Rodriguez story is told in the 2012 Academy Award–winning documentary film, "Searching for Sugar Man", which has also helped give Rodriguez a measure of fame in his native country.

Rodriguez earned a Bachelor of Philosophy from Wayne State University's Monteith College in 1981, and on May 9, 2013, Rodriguez received an honorary Doctorate. A Doctor of Humane Letters degree, from his alma mater, Wayne State University (WSU) in Detroit, Michigan.

Despite the magnitude of his success abroad, Rodriguez has lived in the same modest Detroit house for over 40 years. He has no car, computer or even a television. His daughter Regan forced him to get a cell phone a few years ago, because she grew weary of driving around the neighbourhood trying to track him down. *"He lives a very Spartan life,"* says Regan. *"I almost want to call it Amish. He once told me there's three basic needs – food, clothing and shelter. Once you get down to that level, everything else is icing."*

He plans on giving much of his money to his three daughters and some old friends. *"That's his philosophy,"* says Regan. *"He takes great pleasure in giving it away, especially to people that supported him when he wasn't a big commercial success. I do really wish he'd spend some of the money on himself, though".*

## OLD SOUL PROFILE - Elder Dobri Dobrev

Bulgarian Elder Dobri, is considered a holy man of God. Born on 20 July 1914 in the village of Baylovo. His father died in World War I and his mother raised her children alone. In one of the bombings of Sofia during Second World War, a shell fell near him and he lost almost all his hearing.

For those that have met him, they all remark on his innocent kindness and simplicity. People from Sofia know him as Elder Dobri Dobrev, from the village of Baylovo. He is a 99 year old elder who could often be seen standing in front of the church St. Alexander Nevsky or St. Methodius and Cyril and their five disciples with his metal cashbox, begging for money. He donates everything he has collected back to the church for refurbishing of monasteries or he gives the money directly to the to poor.

Maran Ata met Elder Dobri at the Church of St. Kyriaki, when he was attending the Holy Liturgy which was led by several bishops, in the presence of the graceful relics of St. Stephen Milutin, the King. Ata says, *"Simply, he entered through the church gate, stood in front of the relics and, as a young boy, made a few deep bows (prostrations). That was an amazing scene, especially because of the feeling of unworthiness when God crosses our life-path with one of His righteous men."* Over the years, elder Dobrev separated from the materialistic aspects of life and devoted himself entirely to the spiritual world.

Around year 2000, he decided to donate all his belongings to the church and now he lives very modestly in a small extension to the church "St. Cyril and Methodius" in his native village of Baylovo.

About that time he initiated his mission to raise funds for the restoration of churches and monasteries in Bulgaria. It is this new direction in life and the example he gives with his asceticism that led many to call him "The Saint of Baylovo". As of 2013, he is 99 years old.

(At the time of finishing this book in September 2014, Elder Dobri was still alive and well!)

Kind eyes, pleasant smile, humble look... all that makes him bright in the eyes of those who have met him and without hesitation hurry to get a blessing from this sagacious elder. He wears traditional shoes from raw hide and he never uses modern transport vehicles. Simply, he says he loves the aesthetic walk - several kilometres every day. He eats whatever the good people give him and he never complains or shows any malcontent for his condition. His face shines with heavenly light which at one point of the moment makes people unconsciously to understand that he really is like someone out of the Bible.

Quote form Elder Dobri *"We must love each other as God loves us..."*

# 7

# WHAT SOUL AGE AM I?

*"Older is not better!"*

AS MENTIONED, EACH soul age has seven distinct stages, so that an individual can be referred to as a fourth level Old Soul or a seventh level Young Soul. Every soul age level gives a distinct flavour to the lifetimes spent within its arena. Each level can take anywhere from 25 to 200 lifetimes to complete, though some souls speed through faster, while others enjoy a more thorough, leisurely pace. The sixth level takes the longest to get through and it is not unusual for souls to get stuck on this level and languish for centuries!

## 1. FEELING A LITTLE LOST?

At the first level of any Age there is a sense of uneasiness, and people at this level will usually spend about 70% of their time back in the comfortably familiar level just completed. The first level is like dipping a toe in the water, so it does not give itself to centre stage behaviours. Think of it as getting a feel for the new perspective, the soul is becoming orientated.

## 2.  FEELING FRUSTRATED?

The second level, though cosier, still has much push-pull, drifting between the old perspective and the new. Souls begin to realise they can function best by moving ahead into the new consciousness, however the former perspectives keep them frustrated; yet they aren't sure of their footing within the new level just yet.

## 3.  FEELING A NEED FOR TIME OUT ALONE?

The third level person begins to assimilate the new soul age internally, but has difficulty manifesting it in the world. This person becomes extremely introverted and intellectually introspective while trying to integrate the new awareness into day-to-day life. Third level people do best when they give themselves the space and time to stay home and be alone as much as they want. Respecting their own tastes and loving themselves just the way they are, always smooths the way for more enjoyment of self and life.

## 4.  FEELING CONFIDENT?

Fourth level - bingo! Integrated and consolidated, the assimilation is now both inner and outer. Comfortable and feeling assured while pushing out into the world, fourth level lifetimes are spent in full swing, doing and achieving any number of things - perhaps forming bits of karma along the way.

## 5.  FEELING I AM OVERSTEPPING THE BOUNDARIES!

Fifth level people start pushing on the limits of their reassuring fourth level existences. Believe it or not, humans don't stick with comfort long, especially when it starts impinging on growth. Leaving the beaten path, this level stretches every point and often shows up as pretty eccentric in the process. At fifth level a person may feel out of his element, odd and off-balance socially, and may be seen as less mature than his more secure fourth level friends.

## 6.  FEELING TIME FOR BAD BEHAVIOUR – FEELING TIME FOR MAKING AMENDS

Sixth level lifetimes are all about karma. In Infant, Child and Young lifetimes, you are usually busier creating karmas than paying them back. Every soul plunges in during these early phases and forms the karmas which cause shudders when you sense, from the perspective of later soul ages, what took place and what troubles you caused. Usually, once these karmas have come back in your face, you know you would never act like that again, ever, because you understand all too well what it felt like.

So for example, right here and now, would you go out into the street and kill someone for no good reason? I seriously doubt you would, because you have done that in an earlier life, but you have since learned that lesson, so now it comes across as grotesque and wrong.

In Mature and Old sixth level lifetimes, you piece together the experiences of the prior levels and start handling obligations incurred along the way. This means accumulated karmic debts get paid back through numerous, intense, nearly overfilled sixth level lives. A person will likely have trouble after trouble and hard luck after hard luck. But as I mentioned earlier, there is no such thing as hard luck, bad luck or cursed lives! They are all lessons/experiences your own Soul has set up in order to balance their Karma, or learn new things. Many sixth level lives are catch-up lives, and are difficult and demanding thus will nearly always take longer to complete than any other level. Almost every 6th Level Mature or Old Soul will entertain suicide at least once. However, given their experience and the fact they have already learnt that lesson, they rarely carry it through. This may even incense them even more – "I can't even kill myself I am so useless!!!!"

# STOP! BREATH IN – NOW LAUGH!
# LAUGH! LAUGH!
# IT DOESN'T HAVE TO BE THAT SERIOUS!

You have to admit, when you see it in writing you see how silly it all is. As a 6th level, you are a beautiful being with such love and wisdom. The world needs you, so go to the shelf and get yourself a can of "Harden the F@#$% Up!" But seriously, if you haven't started meditating, then now is a good time. After meditating regularly, life's little downers are almost drowned out. You certainly learn to bounce back quicker. And remember what we said about Karma: "life is experiences and it is your reaction to these experiences that determine the cause and effect to your life."

For Old Souls, these lives are truly the last chance for all karmic completions, some of which have been avoided for dozens upon dozens of lifetimes. So there is no more time to slack off. But it is all worth it...

## 7.  FEELING RELIEVED AND BLISSFUL

Seventh level - Phew! The karma's paid; it's time for some well-earned rest and convalescence. Not too many obstructions or impeding subplots here; seventh level lives usually unfold rather gracefully. Having freshly understood the lessons themselves, individuals are in a good position to teach others - especially those of the soul age just completed. For Mature and Old Souls particularly, there is an urgency to share their profound insight and ways of being with others. Seventh-level lives often have a comfort and flow to them. In fact, I have always thought that the best lives of all are 7th Level Matures.

These are the "charmed" lives. Good looks, good health, usually born to money or come into it early in life. But they are never materialistic, and are usually very charitable and kind. They are always learned and cultured people with an eye for beauty and charming to the last. They probably speak several languages and are well travelled. If they do work for a living, it is always something they are passionate about. I often think of Mr. Brownlow from the Oliver Twist story that adopts Oliver and lives happily ever after...

A typical story would go like this. Two childhood sweethearts have finally got engaged. Their parents are extremely happy and as they are both wealthy, they intend on giving their children a wedding to remember. The male is captain of the football team and dux of the college. The female is head cheerleader, and class valedictorian. They both choose archaeology as their career and go to university together. It is a passion they have shared since childhood when their families would take vacations in the wilderness every year. After their graduation, they wed in the spring. There were hundreds in attendance as they were so liked as a couple. They now spend the next 30 years travelling and working together and raising a family. Both are highly respected academics in their field and are often asked to speak at archaeological conventions the world over. They have four beautiful children who each go on to have successful careers and families of their own. They now have 13 grandchildren and 2 great grandchildren. They live in the house they built high in the mountains, and their grandkids come to visit every vacation time. In their 90's, the male dies. Three months later the female follows him. On her death bed, she whispers "What a wonderful life we had". She closes her eyes and she is gone.

## Age Percentage Population (2013)

There are 35 Levels in all. The average youngest souls on earth are 3rd Level Infant, and the overall average Age is 5th Level Young. The Ages are distributed in a bell curve graph below (Fig. 2):

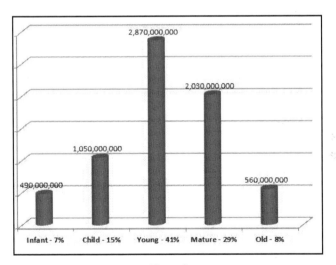

*Figure 2*

- INFANT  7%  = 490 million
- CHILD 15%  = 1.05 billion
- YOUNG 41%  = 2.87 billion
- MATURE 29%  = 2.03 billion
- OLD 8%  = 560 Million

At the moment, 7th Level accounts for about 14% of the population for older ages and 86% of the younger population. It also shows percentages at 10% intervals of completion of the entire cycle. For instance, a 4th Level Mature soul is shown to be 70% of the way through the Maturation scale.

With practice, a person can learn to discern someone's Soul Age readily. Sometimes this can be done from physical appearance and behaviour alone, but it is more easily done by verbal cues which give away the person's insights about life. The eyes are another important clue — the depth of the personality is often displayed here if one knows what to look for. However, there are some potentially misleading factors such as intelligence, education, or socioeconomic status. A wide deviation from average — higher or lower — in these factors might cause one to misjudge their Soul Age.

For instance, many 7th Level Old Souls are vagabonds and nomads, just like the Elder Dobri Dobrev of Baylovo, because their attachment to the physical plane is so tenuous. It is also wise not to be misled about Soul Age, by a person's degree of social status – after all, it is a Young Soul run world. Furthermore, a person's depth of "metaphysical knowledge" does not automatically indicate someone is an Old Soul. Old Souls are more open to mystical and occult knowledge, but this is not always the case by any means.

Reincarnation seems to be a key metaphysical understanding that comes naturally to older souls. I personally have known a few later level Young Souls who were aware of reincarnation. There is also an Infant Soul known to me who is practicing tribal metaphysicians. Usually, it is mid-level Mature and Old Souls who believe in reincarnation. Since there is no strict scientific proof of reincarnation, they come to believe in it, because it seems intuitively obvious to them. Furthermore, the New Age movement is abound with Young Souls who are merely trying to make a buck. They study hard, so their spiritual "knowledge" is good but their metaphysical skills are less impressive.

Indeed, there are several celebrity mediums that "channel" past loved ones live in their show or on TV. The fact is, many of these charlatans have been exposed as hoaxes. They set up microphones near the people lining up to go into the show, they get names and quickly google them before the show starts etc. Then the host is fed this info via a small ear piece. It looks like they are getting "messages" from the other side, but in fact, they are being told the information by the people in the control box. But like I said, they are really only trying to cash in without any real understanding of the Unconditional Love, Older Souls naturally attach to their work.

## Soul age manifestation is sometimes a mixed bag!

A 5th level Old Soul may be manifesting Young in the area of money, for example, Mature in the area of relationships, and Old in most other areas. The energies that these perspectives generate might, combine to form a composite manifested age of 6th level Mature. Since it can be an average, manifested soul age may not always seem to completely fit. Furthermore, most souls only spend between 40% - 60% of the time in their actual true Soul Age. These numbers are much higher in Older Souls on later levels. This is, because when times get tough, souls automatically revert back to old comfort zones of familiarity, which of course, are from soul ages they have already mastered. So a 3rd level Mature Soul may come across as a 5th, 6th or 7th level Young Soul. This is why a lot of souls, a lot of the time, get stuck in a cycle and can literally take hundreds of lives to get through it.

### FEAR – FEAR - FEAR

Fear is the mind killer.  Fear is the emotional killer.  Fear is the body killer.  Humans only experience 2 sets of emotions - Love and Fear.  All other emotions branch directly or indirectly from these two emotions.  When I speak of Fear, I am not really talking about the 'fear' when you see a spider or watch a spooky movie.  The Fear I speak of, is a negative mindset.  Fear-based mindsets include, but are not limited to: Anger; Hate; Jealousy; Greed; Retaliation, Revenge; Vanity; Self-loathing; Addictions; Manipulation; Control; Judgment.  Fear based decisions will ALWAYS be bad decisions and ultimately the WRONG decisions.  No matter how much your Ego tries to justify a fear-based decision, it will never be the correct one.  In fact, you only need to look back through history, or indeed your own life, to see whenever there was a bad outcome to a situation, it always had Fear at its core.  If you can overcome Fear, and allow the Wise Mind to call the shots, then you will be well and truly on your way to Old Soul perspective.

### The Wise Mind

Think of the Wise Mind as a part of you that is the oldest, wisest and most knowledgeable being in the Universe.  It is the part of you that has lived hundreds of lives and assimilated thousands of experiences.

The Wise Mind operates from complete Universal Love, and never allows Fear to enter. The Wise Mind looks at a situation from a complete unbiased and objective view. It would be the same if you were reading about a stranger and were then asked to advise on that situation. You would do so without any emotional attachment or bias. This is how the Wise Mind works.

Therefore, the next time you have a major decision, no matter how hard you think it is, simply calm your mind, and ask "What would the Wise Mind do?"

## Other Beings

The system of soul Age classification is good for application to the general population and most of the people you will meet, but there are exceptions and anomalies. Highly evolved souls from other planes or dimensions, or other planets within the physical plane sometimes incarnate in human form for the value of the experience, or for a special mission. This type of soul has been called a *"wanderer"*, a *"walk in"*, or *"Star Seed"*. These types do not experience the full range of normal human-soul transformation.

Such a one might be an Old Soul in terms of psychic and knowledge maturity, but just a Young Soul in terms of earth-plane understanding. Needless to say, such a discrepancy can cause some psychological conflict within the person. These beings are nothing to fear, they are usually just here to observe or assist and will usually go out of their way to avoid direct contact with anyone that is not part of their agenda.

## Older Is Not Better!

It is well to note that there is no superiority implied in the advancement of Souls. Being an Old Soul is just as limiting in perception as being an Infant Soul, only in different ways. All Ages are necessary in the scheme of things, just as it is necessary to start out as a baby and advance through old age. All Ages have their particular kinds of problems and difficulties in adjusting to the life it has chosen.

It is no better to be an Old Soul than to be Mature or Young, just as it isn't better to be 45 years old than it is to be 35 or 25. A young person may be wise, and an old person foolish. A Child Soul may be loving and an Old Soul bitter. People of every soul age are capable of manifesting their true personality—that is, of acting out of their positive poles, which are motivated by love. Younger souls are simply less experienced than older souls, not having completed as many lessons.

There is a tendency for older souls to have a greater understanding of what the younger soul thinks and feels like, rather than vice-versa. Knowing about soul ages is exceedingly helpful in understanding the way other people think, the way they look at life and in understanding something about their life tasks and motivations.

Each soul age is trying to experience as much as possible within that particular level. It's absolutely to the point for an Infant Soul to be fearfully concerned about basic survival, and for a Child Soul to be requesting law and order. A Young Soul is appropriate when striving for great material wealth, power and acclaim, and a Mature Soul when beginning to feel intensely emotional and ask those deeper questions. It's appropriate for an Old Soul to not meet societal norms, to look and act mildly eccentric, and to be teaching others, even when their own personal life isn't exactly together.

An Old Soul starts each lifetime being born as an infant who experiences Infant Soul consciousness, and gradually grows into prior levels of consciousness. A toddler often perceives through Child Soul consciousness; think about a two year old shrieking because a parent offended thier sense of right and wrong. People vary, but generally reach their competitive, Young Soul consciousness, sometime in their late primary school years. Mature Soul consciousness arrives for many during high school, and is what your up-and-down, full-of-drama, teenager is experiencing. Indeed, the first half of the Mature cycle is akin to teenage angst!

Individuals don't come close to obtaining their true soul awareness roughly one-third of the time. They get stuck. They get lazy. Other times the Soul may find it easier to complete easier lives at earlier, more ambitious, or more emotional soul levels. Most Old Souls (Mature Souls too) will be doing the intense, Mature phase, in their teens and early twenties. An Old Soul is often not consistently acting out of Old Soul awareness until between twenty five to thirty-five years of age, and even then it may only be in some areas of life and not in others. For example, when security buttons get pushed, it is often difficult to remain completely centred in your soul level age. Old Souls will be able to successfully drop some of the Child Soul discipline, Young Soul ambition, and Mature Soul emotionality, only if those qualities are integrated sufficiently into their personality. On the other hand, they have access to those traits when necessary. It does not work to stick your nose in the air (or your head in the sand) in an attempt to avoid lessons and gifts from the other soul ages.

People who come to this information are usually relieved to find out why they are different from mainstream society; they knew they marched to a different step anyway. The purpose of the teaching is understanding, not to allow yourself to be one up.

Younger souls are not less intelligent, less appropriate or wrong. Their lessons are about survival, structure, ambition and success, while Mature and Older lessons are about emotional and universal connections. Younger souls are a natural part of that whole - you know it is all connected, right? So, if you're indulging yourself by feeling superior, aim for mild tolerance as a way to begin clearing up that attitude, which ultimately is a painful, separatist one to carry around.

## Some Tips for Developing an Older Soul

### Practise Unconditional Love!

Unconditional Love means just that – **UNCONDITIONAL**. The Love I am talking about is not the emotional love you are familiar with. The Love I speak of is a Spiritual state of being. To live life in Love, is to live in Spiritual Bliss. To Love your fellow man is to see that we are all connected, and other people are just expressions of the same soul – your soul – my soul – all souls!

So many people who claim to be spiritual or holy have very conditional love for humanity. For example, they love one group, like Christians, but dislike, or even hate another group, like Muslims. The same can be said about race, gender and any number of dichotomies. The Old Soul instinctively sees all humans and life on earth as connected, therefore they love everything equally. However, for younger souls, this can be very challenging. So start off small, and work your way up. Start with yourself, then immediate family and friends and people you come into contact regularly. Be polite, be kind, and be your brother's keeper. Show compassion, express your Love, and most of all FORGIVE! Try to break out of the societal conditioning that you should only care about that group, or that team, or that racial group.

In your personal relationships, where emotional love is involved, you should not have expectations, and you should not have conditions. Things like, *"He is really cute, and I really like him BUT..."* Or *"She is the best girlfriend I have had in a long time HOWEVER..."* and *"I do love my husband and we have been together for a long time BUT..."* It should be, *"I love my partner unconditionally. Even though they* do things I do not like, my love for them is strong enough that we can work through anything". I am not saying just accept anything or anyone, or to put up with inappropriate behaviour.

What I am saying is, if you have an issue or problem with your partner, or potential partner, then you should not be in that relationship if you are not willing to change or adapt. I said it before, and I will keep saying it – there is no such thing as an unfixable problem. It is only your mind that must change.

## Live By 3 Simple Life Lessons

Over my life I have had many experiences that have led me to believe we are all governed by 3 main things. Once you can master these things into your life, then life will get a lot easier:

1. **TIMING:** Everything happens exactly when it is meant to happen. Be patient. Forcing your Will is a one way ticket to hurdles, problems and ultimately failure, and then having to repeat the experience over and over until you get the right outcome. Part of this is letting go and...

2. **ACCEPT & ALLOW:** When you make a choice, accept it and allow it to take its course. There is no point in stressing about it or wondering "what if?". This also goes for when something happens against you. Accept it – allow it. Do not fight it or hold onto it. Holding onto to negative thoughts will manifest into disease and you don't want that.

3. **BALANCE:** It's all about balance! Balance in everything you do, every day, including what you eat, drink, watch, say, do, don't, everything! Balance is the key to health, wealth and happiness!

These chapters on Soul Ages were really just scratching the surface. There is so much more to this topic, however it was my intention to introduce you to Soul Ages in an attempt to help you understand who you are, and why the world is like it is right now. **Annex 1.1.1** and **1.2.1** are charts showing comparision and quick references for Soul Ages.

By understanding your Soul Age, and of those around you, it is my hope that it will assist you on your own personal journey. But above all, try not to judge people, because who knows what lesson they may be trying to learn, or more importantly, what agreement they made with your soul before you both incarnated. Therefore, it is appropriate to find out what happens when you die, spend time in the Spirit World, then come back again. So get ready, because coming up next - **Life Begins at Death!**

---

# 8

# INTO THE LIGHT – LIFE BEGINS AT DEATH

*"In death - no! Even in the grave all is not lost. Else there is no immortality for man. Arousing from the most profound slumbers, we break the gossamer web of some dream. Yet in a second afterward, (so frail may that web have been) we remember not that we have dreamed." (Edgar Allan Poe, The Pit and the Pendulum)"*

Taine Greyman was a 39 year old father of two. He was a shift worker doing 12 hours at a time. This meant that he never really got much time to spend with his family. On this occasion, Taine was driving the usual route to his work place. It was 10:30pm and he was already feeling a little drowsy. His eldest child Emma had come down with the flu, and as his wife Stella had to work during the days to help make ends meet, it was up to Taine to tend to his daughter's needs. He didn't mind one bit because it gave him time to share with Emma. She too was secretly glad that they could spend some extra time together.

Unfortunately, it meant Taine was only getting half the sleep he would normally have before his shift. As he drove, the uncontrollable urge to shut his eyes for just a minute came over him. The car heater was on and the radio droned on in the background. It was so warm and cosy. He started to day dream about how much he really loved his kids and wife and how he would make it up to them, once he had saved enough money and could look for a better job.

It was at this point that he found himself high above the road, looking down onto a scene he did not recognise at first. He saw a car just like his, slowly and gently move onto the other side of the road. He saw the semi-trailer truck bearing down. He heard the driver of the truck blast his horn, then the screech of tyres. But it was too late. The truck collided head on into the drifting car. It was only now that Taine realised that it was his car, and that he was actually floating above the scene, witnessing his own death.

*          *          *

Jane Clovers lay in a hospital bed. At 92 years old, she felt she had lived a good and long life, and was ready to let go. She felt tired of this world and longed to close her eyes and never wake up. As a devout Christian, she was sure she was going to heaven. Her children sat around her bed and prayed for her soul. This comforted her to no end. Suddenly, a young man appeared at the end of her bed.

He was smiling and completely surrounded by a glowing white light. It was not Jesus (who she was expecting), but she felt it must be one of his messengers. This young man radiated such love and peace, she could stay in his presence forever. Then she remembered! It was her backyard neighbour she had such a crush on when she was 12. He was older and had to go away to the war and she never saw him again. They began a conversation and those in the room saw and heard Jane mumbling, and occasionally chuckle. They were amused by this odd behaviour, as she had barely moved in the last 2 days. They could see she was having a great old chat to someone, but to their eyes she was talking to nobody.

Thus, they figured it was just her ailing mind finally breaking down. "Random firing of synapses in a dying brain" is what the doctor said. However, for Jane, it was the most wonderful conversations she had ever had, "Is it true? Ronald is waiting for me? You will take me to see him?" Ronald was Jane's husband of 70 years. He died two winters ago when his lungs finally gave out to his second bout of pneumonia in as many years. Jane had devoted her life to her husband, children and Church. The young man held out his hand and Jane sat up in bed. Rising to her feet she felt incredibly light. In fact, she felt like a healthy young women again. She looked at herself in disbelief – she was a young woman again! She let the kind and smiling gent take her by the hand and followed him into the Light.

*     *     *

Kevin Stye had been a tyrant and a bully. He had amassed a huge fortune in his short 57 years of life, and no one was going to get their hands on it. He had taken so much from so many, but felt it was his right to do so. After all, he had worked his bum off for it, and if other people are too weak, then that was their problem. He had managed to fend off 2 ex-wife alimony law suits, not to mention the two children he had – 1 from each wife. He despised them also. They never loved him, they just wanted his money,or so he told himself. When they reached 21 they tried to sue him. He had to laugh when his daughter tried to tell him it was not about the money, they just wanted him to love them. Love them? What the hell was she on about? Luckily he could afford some pretty ruthless attorneys and he was able to outsmart their claim. Lawyers were blood suckers as well, but at least they served a purpose.

Kevin was now lying in bed in a private hospital, the best money could buy. He was dying from an aggressive form of bowel cancer. Once a stout and heavy man, well obese really, he was now a stick figure, with no hair, and barely the strength to scratch his nose. All he could do was think - think incessantly about all the people he knew, that would be circling like vultures ready to get their hands on his wealth. "I won't let them!" he raged in his own mind. Overcome by the rage he started to cough. Cough, cough, cough! He couldn't stop coughing. His face glowed red and his body heaved. Then it came, the stabbing pain in his chest. Immediately he knew the stents in his heart (that he paid a fortune for), had finally collapsed, and his heart was going into arrest. There was a blinding flash, suddenly the pain stopped, and everything went black.

*     *     *

## The Process of Death

Every one dies. Let's face it; it is about the only thing you can guarantee in life, right! But does that mean it is the same for everyone? Simple answer is no. In the previous three scenarios, each person will have a different experience at the time of their death. That is because death is a very unique experience for every person on the planet. There is a basic framework for death that each person will experience as in, leaving their body, but the actual manner in what they see, feel or experience is unique.

Humans have had an expectation of an afterlife for hundreds of thousands of years. Intentional burial, particularly with grave goods, is one of the earliest detectable forms of religious practice. Philip Lieberman suggests it may signify a "...concern for the dead that transcends daily life" (Lieberman, 1991). Though disputed, evidence suggests that the Neanderthals were the first human species to intentionally bury their dead, doing so in shallow graves along with stone tools and animal bones.

However, the earliest undisputed human burial discovered so far, dates back 100,000 years to remains found at Skhul cave at Qafzeh, Israel. Human skeletal remains stained with red ochre and grave tools and trinkets were discovered in there (Gargett, 1999). Although our burial practices may have changed and different cultures view death in very many different ways, the ultimate transition from this life to the next has never really changed. Indeed, when it is all said and done, death is the same for everyone. It is a transition from one state of existence to another.

Imagine you are swimming in a pool. After a while you get out of the pool, dry yourself, and lay on a sun lounge to warm up a bit. You have just transitioned from one state of existence to another. In the first world, you were in water, which had its own set of rules. You couldn't run very easily, but you could float. You couldn't breathe under the water, but you could still see. Then, when you got out, you could no longer float, but you could run.

But best of all, you can now see more clearly, taste, smell and breathe with ease! Even though you went from one unique environment to another, your consciousness did not change. The environment changed, and the laws which dictates life in each environment changed, but your consciousness did not. Death is exactly the same. You transfer from one state of existence to another.

Your environment will change, but your consciousness will remain the same – for the time being.

## Death Process Stage 1 – Leaving the Body

The first thing you can expect is to be floating outside your body. You will notice how light you feel. You are so used to the weight of your body that you don't really notice it. But if you take a moment to concentrate on your shoulders, chest and head area you will find that they are quite heavy. Then you feel your lower back and legs. So it is no surprise that when you first leave your body you will notice the lack of weight. Of course, the most obvious thing is you are floating! Not exactly something you have ever experienced in the physical world. Even though, it will feel very natural. There will be no fear, only a curiosity. Everything looks a little different – surreal in a way, and the colours look more vivid.

In the case of Taine Greyman, he watched while his car was pulverised by a large truck. This is a very common phenomenon. It is extremely rare for a person to feel the actual impact, or bullet, or stabbing etc. of any sudden, violent death. Just prior to the fatal blow, the Soul leaves the body and observes. Of course, in the case where a person is injured, and it takes time for their body to die, it is actually part of that particular Soul's experience. Yes, they want to experience the sensation of a dying body. Taine's Soul is a 2nd Level Mature which is not really that experienced, but also not a beginner, and most of the fear is gone. Indeed, depending on the age of the Soul will greatly influence the type of death experience you will have.

As he rises up, the idea that he has just died begins to take root. However, he does not panic.

It should be noted at this point, that you do not suddenly have all the knowledge of the Universe at your disposal. You do not become all knowing just yet. You are psychologically the exact same person you were one minute before you died. The only difference now, is you have a calm acceptance, that comes from an inner knowing that this is a perfectly natural process.

Taine's main thoughts are now with his wife and children. Actually, as soon as he concentrates on them he finds himself in a room filled with people. His wife and two daughters are in a corner, still sobbing and hugging each other. It is his wake. He notes the other people there, and even wonders why some people are there and others are not. But again, this does not upset him anymore. When he was a younger soul it would have, and may have, even caused him to hang around longer. Taine now exists in the **Astral Plane**, or as some people call it, the Earth Plane. The Earth Plane is an exact analogue or copy of the Physical Plane that you are in right now. The main difference is there is a lot more soft light, and a bluish hue surrounding everything. Of course you can float, and you can move through walls! But the walls are not really physical, but I digress...

Since Time is a construct of the Physical Plane, it does not apply on any other level. Therefore, to the discarnate Soul, time no longer exists. So to Taine, it felt like he just witnessed his death, then in an instant he was at the funeral wake. At this point, Souls will normally feel a sense of frustration. They want to tell their loved ones that they are ok. They feel no pain and in fact they feel great. But as much as they may jump up and down and yell, they are not heard.

More advanced Soul's know that yelling won't help, so they employ a technique where they insert comforting thoughts into the minds of their grieving friends and family members. Many people experience this as a sudden calmness comes over them and they realise that their recently departed is ok and in a good place.

The whole time since Taine has been out of his body, he has noticed two things in the background, and just slightly out of focus. Firstly, in the distance he sees an incredibly bright, white light. This is the famous tunnel that many Near Death Out-of-body **(OBE's)** experiencers report seeing. The tunnel is literally a portal, or doorway between the Astral /Earth Plane and the Spirit Plane. The other thing he notices is a wispy, "human" shape or person hanging around. He does not fear this other person. In fact he is drawn to them. He feels a sense of comfort, peace and love coming from them. He feels secure knowing they are there, looking out for him.

Depending on the age and experience of the Soul, will depend on how long they stay on the Earth Plane. For now, think in broad terms as Souls being beginners, intermediate and advanced. As stated earlier, Taine would fall into the "Intermediate" group. So for him, as soon as he has comforted his loved ones, he is ready to move on. He feels an overwhelming urge to go to the Tunnel of Light. The person he feels nearby is his Spirit Guide. The Guide will try and stand back at this point, to allow Taine to make his way to the Light on his own. If Taine looks like steering off course, or gets distracted from his route, then the Guide will step in and make himself known, to try and correct the situation. But Taine's Soul has done this many times before, so he knows the way home without any help.

Jane Clovers on the other hand, is a Beginner Soul (4th Level Child Soul). Because she has not had much practice at dying, her Guide showed up to literally take her by the hand and show her the way home. Just a quick note on Guides – they will appear to the person in whatever way is most pleasing, or less alarming to that person. That is why some people see a little old lady, a young man or even Jesus! Rest assure, no matter what you see, it is a Guide, and as we will learn, your Guide is about the most benevolent being you will ever come into contact with.

## When Things Don't Go To Plan

Finally, poor old Kevin Stye. Kevin had amassed so much rage, greed and negative energy that his experience was totally different. Kevin is a typical 4th Level Young Soul. The human mind is the most powerful force in the universe, and unfortunately, it can be used for a negative cause as well as a positive cause. Kevin was so worried about other people getting to his rich stuff, that he inadvertently created a bond to it. He lived in a permanent, *Fear-based mentality*. He more or less anchored himself to the Earth Plane. So after the heart attack which killed him, everything went black. That is because he by-passed the normal death process and created his own version. Like hacking a computer program, Kevin created his own version of reality. However, because this reality was one based on pure negative thought, then that is what his reality reflected.

So, instead of waking up and seeing himself float above his body, or see a blinding white light, he found himself in an analogue of his earthly mansion. However, this version of his house was always in darkness. Cobwebs hung in every corner, dead leaves blew into the once beautiful foyer. It was empty, and without any positive energy what so ever. Here he would continually walk the halls, looking out for potential looters. He will become trapped in his house by his own mind. The longer he stays here, the more anchored he becomes. Kevin has become a Ghost!

Of course, on the Physical Plane the house still looked like a magnificent mansion, only it now has a very "dark" presence. Drug addicts, alcoholics and suicides are also at risk of creating alternative, negative realities. Because their physical world is so distorted, they carry that version of life over with them. But Kevin's Guides will never give up on him. They will continually surround his Soul with Love, until eventually, he is able to be bought home. This can take hundreds of earth years, but eventually he will "snap out of it" and realise it is all an illusion.

Once he sees through his self-created illusion, he will cry out for forgiveness. At this point, the Light will surround him and his soul will finally go back to the normal death process and the Light. He will spend even more time in a healing room where his battered and bruised soul can get some well needed rest.

Souls become Earthbound for many reasons. Sometimes, it is because they left something unfinished. I remember one story my mother told me about a good friend of my parents, Jim, that had unexpectedly died. A few days after his death, just before sunrise, both his adult son and wife would hear the back steps creaking as if someone was walking up them.

Both thought it was Jim, because he was a keen fisherman in life, and would often get up before dawn and go or come home from fishing and make the same sounds. Neither the son nor mother told the other what they were hearing. After about one week of this daily occurrence, the wife had a vivid dream that Jim was talking to her. He was repeating some numbers and asking her to remember them. Not really understanding what the numbers meant, she eventually told her son about the dream and the footsteps. He immediately said it sounds like an account number for something. The wife did some enquiries and uncovered a secret life insurance policy Jim had taken out years earlier, but did not tell her about. The policy was worth a lot of money and it meant Jim's wife and son would be looked after financially for the rest of their lives. The footsteps stopped after they had discovered the policy.

Other times they were killed and felt it was not their time. Sometimes for emotional love or hate. Like I said, there are many reasons, but ultimately the end result is the same – ghosts and hauntings. Kevin became the classic moan and groan, haunted house ghost. Others become the "lady in the upstairs window", or the Civil War soldier in the dry river bed. There are hundreds and hundreds of genuine, photographic evidence of ghosts from every country in the world. Disembodied Souls are actually more common than what most people realise. Luckily, these spirits rarely show themselves, or interact with humans in any way. That is because most of them do not even know they are dead.

## Noisy Ghosts

Poltergeists on the other hand are not Earthbound Soul's. The word poltergeist comes from the German words **poltern** (to make sound) and **Geist** (ghost), and the term itself roughly translates as "noisy ghost". This is because the Poltergeist will make noise – banging and rapping sounds, levitate objects like cutlery, open and close doors and cupboards. There have even been reports of physical attacks on human beings, such as pinching, biting, and hitting. Generally they scare the bejesus out of people for no good reason!

A Poltergeist is a result of extreme residual negative energy. For example, maybe there was a torture chamber somewhere that saw horrific scenes and absorbed tons of negative energy. Even after people leave, that left over energy stays there. Basically, because energy is on its own neutral, it can be programmed for Love, or conversely it can be programmed for Fear. So when it has been programmed for fear, it hangs around, but so does Love energy by the way!

For example, even if non-religious people walk into a church, they will often say they feel a solemn and respectful feeling. That is because they are picking up on the energy other people have left there. The same can be said when you walk into someone's house. Sometimes you feel nothing, other times you feel a warm loving energy, and other times you just feel creepy and want to get out of there!

If you like a really good ghost story, I recommend the **Rosenheim Poltergeist** incident. In it, the Physicists Dr.Karger and Dr. Zicha monitored experiments in the office and reached a chilling conclusion. "Karger and Zicha also felt that the telephone anomalies suggested that an intelligent force was at work, because it had 'chosen' to focus its attention on the speaking clock." (Brookesmith, 1988). Another famous incident occurred in 2010 in Sheffield, England. A poltergeist terrorised and attacked a family after the son brought home an antique grandfather clock for his mother (Project Reveal, 2012).

Some researchers now try and claim that Poltergeists are created by a person by means of **psychokinesis**[1]. This is simply not true. The spirits may be connected to a person, but it is not the person creating the disturbance.

---

[1] Psychokinesis is an umbrella term for any ability that involves using the mind to manipulate something, and some other, more specific, abilities may be acquired as a result. The word kinesis comes from movement and the other comes from the Greek meaning mind. (PsiWiki, 2014)

Poltergeists are very low form Spirit beings that exist only on the Astral Plane. Just like moths that are attracted to a light, these beings are attracted to negative energy. And like a drug, negative energy gets them high – and "hyper", so they start acting up. A Poltergeist is rarely a single entity. There are usually at least 3 beings acting as one.

A standard ghost (human Earthbound Soul) cannot, and will not hurt you in any way. A Poltergeist can, and will. Think of a Poltergeist as a spirit with psychoses. If you ever come into an area where a Poltergeist is active – leave. A human being, no matter how spiritually aware, or strong they are, cannot subdue a Poltergeist on their own. You are outnumbered and out muscled. Spirit will take care of them – don't feed their addiction with more fear! That said, real cases of Poltergeists are extremely rare, maybe 1 in 100 of hauntings, so don't start seeing a poltergeist around every corner!

I am always disturbed when I hear people say they have a "friendly" ghost in their house, or hotel, and they are "ok to be there" etc. In reality, it is not ok for a Soul to hang around on the Earth plane. They should be back in the Spirit Plane where they belong. That is why there are highly evolved Souls that will come all the way down to the Earth Plane to try and work with these Souls. Otherwise, these Souls will languish there forever. They achieve this by projecting Love energy into the ghost/spirit.

Just like surface cleaner on a greasy bench top, the Love energy neutralises the negative energy. But it does take a long time. The Advanced Souls cannot stay on these lower planes for very long. It is akin to you jumping into a filthy pool and trying and hold your breath while you clean a crystal glass. That is why there are many people on Earth that try and help them by "cleansing" houses or areas and sending the spirit into the Light. I did this work for many years with great success, with only the odd spirit getting the better of me!

Eventually, the Soul will snap out of it. They usually seem bewildered and discombobulated. Once they have their bearings, they begin to sob almost uncontrollably. It is at this point the Guides move in and take them to the Tunnel of Light. It can sometimes take as much as 600 earth years for an Earth bound Soul to find their way home.

## What About Old Soul's?

I didn't really go into Old Souls dying because there is not much to tell. Because they have done this hundreds, or even thousands of times, they usually go directly to the Light - do not pass go! They are so eager to get back home you won't see them for dust. They don't bother hanging around for funerals or wakes or final messages. They know the ropes and they know that those things are irrelevant in the big picture, so they would rather just get back home and start living their true life again. So into the **Tunnel of Light** we go!

## References:

Brookesmith, P. (1988). *Great hauntings*. 1st ed. London: Black Cat.

Brookesmith, P. (1988). *Rosenheim poltergeist*. [Image from book].

Gargett, R. (1999). *Middle Palaeolithic burial is not a dead issue: the view from Qafzeh, Saint-C\'esaire, Kebara, Amud, and Dederiyeh. Journal of Human Evolution*, 37(1), pp.27--90.

Lieberman, P. (1991). *Uniquely human*. 1st ed. Cambridge, Mass.: Harvard University Press.

Project Reveal, (2012). *Real Sheffield Ghost poltergeist Interview in Aston - Part 1.wmv*. [online] YouTube. Available at: https://www.youtube.com/watch?v=9S2ZTN7zd_s [Accessed 27 Jul. 2014].

PsiWiki, (2014). *Psychokinesis*. [online] PsiWiki. Available at: http://psi.wikia.com/wiki/Psychokinesis [Accessed 28 Jul. 2014].

Southport TV, (2012). *NEWS: Manchester Poltergeist Caught on CCTV - 1/11/2012*. [online] YouTube. Available at: http://youtu.be/IWV2PlojU0Q [Accessed 30 Nov. 2012].

Walker, J. (2012). *I Saw the Light: A True Story of Love, Death, and Fulfillment*. 1st ed. Seattle: CreateSpace Independent Publishing Platform.

# The Promise

I PROMISE IF YOU KEEP
SEARCHING FOR
EVERYTHING BEAUTIFUL
IN THIS WORLD,
YOU WILL EVENTUALLY
BECOME IT.

TYLER KENT WHITE

$$9$$

# GOOD VIBRATIONS - RETURN TO THE SPIRIT WORLD

*"I have come home at last! This is my real country!*
*I belong here. This is the land I have been looking for*
*all my life, though I never knew it till now...Come further up,*
*come further in!" (C.S. Lewis, The Last Battle)"*

### Death Process Stage 2 – Into the Light

*T*AINE HAS RESIGNED his Will and allows himself to float into the Tunnel of Light (Fig. 3). The light is so brilliant, yet he is amazed that it does not hurt his eyes. That is because Taine has still not realised he no longer has physical eyes! Although all souls travel through the tunnel, not everyone has the same experience. Indeed, some will hear music, others smell glorious fragrances and some even see choirs of angelic beings singing in some strange, but beautiful language. But the one thing that is in common for everyone, is the deep, overwhelming feeling of peace and love as you float along – drawn further and further into the tunnel.

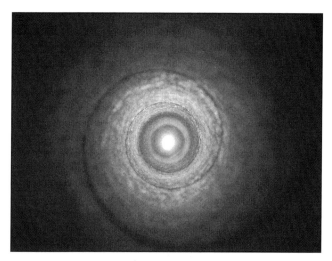

*Figure 3*

As the gateway to the Spirit World (Fig. 3) comes into view, Taine starts to see figures appear. This is Taine's "greeting party". All souls up to about 7th Level Mature will always be met by loved ones and Soul Mates that have passed over before them. Sometimes they will meet souls that did not appear in their life just completed, but who have incarnated with them many times before. They recognise everyone present immediately, so it is a highly, emotionally charged event. It is a literal home-coming that is so joyful it is hard to comprehend in the physical world. Again, these Spirits take on an appearance that is most recognisable, or pleasant for you, usually how you remembered them in the most previous life together.

However in reality, Spirits do not have gender per say and to see one in their native state you would only see a ball of light. They form into human shape just to make themselves recognisable for the younger souls. At the Old Soul level, they remain as Light, because Old Souls can feel, and sense their 'essence' and recognise them in this way. When Souls of any age embrace, it is not with arms. To embrace as Spirit to Spirit is akin to being enveloped in a blanket of Love, warmth and peace. Suddenly Taine spots his father who is smiling at him...

*        *        *

It is very common to be met by a Soul Mate. A Soul Mate should not be mistaken for a Twin Soul / Flame. They are very different and I will discuss them in Chapter 11. Another weird point is that some of the

Soul's that greet you may also be back on the Earth Plane in a new life. That is because a Soul leaves a part of its consciousness or 'being' in the Spirit Plane, while the rest of it is away. This is often referred to as your **Higher Self**. Again, we will look at this later.

The number of Spirits in the greeting party differs greatly. They start off with a lot, then the more experienced a Soul gets, the less turn up for the home-coming. So by the 7th Level Mature, there may only be 2 or 3 very key souls show up. In fact, with Old Souls, there is no one waiting for them at all, save their Spirit Guide. This may seem sad to you on the Earth Plane, but to the Old Soul this is a perfectly natural thing. They view it like when your parents finally think you are old enough to stay home by yourself without a babysitter.

It is at this point the Taine's consciousness fully awakens. He is now "all-knowing" as such, for his level anyway. Just like at school, each level has a certain understanding and knowledge. As you progress through the Soul Ages and Spirit Planes, your level of Universal Knowledge will increase. Universal Knowledge is all of the knowledge of how the universe works, what the Source is and your current relationship to it, as well as all past, present and future history of Earth, Galaxy, and Universe. You will also have limited knowledge of the different life forms that exists, particularly those that can accommodate a soul.

Souls are still fallible at this stage. That is, they still have Free Will, therefore they can still make decisions that may not be the best choice, although this is fairly limited, given how much extra knowledge they have access to. Taine will remember all of his past lives, that he is an eternal Soul, that this is home, and that he has a Spirit Guide patiently waiting for him, just off to the side of the greeting party. Eventually, each spirit in the greeting party returns to their own level. Once he is alone, his Spirit Guide will join him.

*          *          *

## Spirit Guides

Some people call them Guardian Angels, others call them Teachers, but most of all, we call them Spirit Guides! Spirit Guides are highly evolved beings that have been through the entire Maturation Cycle on earth just as you are doing now. So, they have been there, done that, and got the tee-shirt so to speak. They no longer need to incarnate any more, however, there are times when one or two of them may incarnate again for very specific reasons. These are not the "god men" like Buddha and Jesus. They are teachers, but as I said, for a very specific reason. Your Guides back in Spirit are your own support system or backup. They are there to guide you, not do it for you.

The younger the soul, the more Guides they have, however even older souls can have 2 or 3 at a time. Specialty Guides will come in at certain periods in a person's life, to help out with a particular issue or challenge. Specialty Guides also come in when a person begins to undertake a new profession, such as medicine or counselling, or when someone starts an alternative healing course or art classes. Any time you may need specialty assistance and guidance that falls outside the skill set of your main Guide, these loving Beings will be on call to assist you. It is also common for some of these specialty Guides to be non-human – in others words, of Alien origin! The most common are Pleiadians, Arcturians, and Sirians, but they are usually associated with Older Souls.

That said, humans have a need to anthropomorphises beings, particularly when they want to reach out to them in prayer or meditation, so usually Guides will appear as "human" looking. They know your fears, and they know what pleases you. So when a Guide makes itself appear to a person, they will always appear to the person as something that will not scare them or upset them. That is why many Christians who are on their death bed report seeing Jesus or a Saint. The fact is, it is their Guide coming for them.

Guides operate under a hierarchy, so the Guide for each person usually relates to the soul age of the person. Very Young Souls will have at least one Guide in training (assistant), as well as an intermediate and /or advanced Guides. Mature Souls usually have advanced guides, and Old Souls usually have an Advanced Guide and Master Guide, and sometimes several Speciality Guides. A **Master Guide** is the highest level Guides can reach. They appear as a deep, deep purple and have almost demi-god status in the Spirit World. They are so far up in vibration, that they do not spend a lot of time on the 6th level of the Spirit Plane, so there is a certain amount of mystique about them.

Guides are arranged so a Guide in Training and a Teacher Guide look after a Soul Group. Training Guides (Green) can begin training from as low as 3rd level Old Souls. Intermediate (Yellow and Green) and Advanced Guides (Blue-Mauve) will over-see 4-5 Soul Groups and a Master Guide will over-see the entire **Soul Cluster**, which can consist of 1000 plus souls. Each Guide (except the Master) is counselled and guided by the Guide over-seeing them.

So technically, every person has access to Guides all the way from Training right up to Master Guide!

Your Spirit Guide's main purpose is to guide you during your life, and be your adviser, councillor and teacher in Spirit. Before you came back to earth, you worked out a few lessons or experiences you wanted to achieve, and you asked your Guide to keep you on track to fulfil those lessons. It is very easy for humans to become distracted on the earth, so occasionally we all need a little poke in the right direction. Sometimes, we just need a good kick up the backside! As well as this, our Guides also comfort us in times of stress, as well as dispense moments of clarity, insight and inspiration.

Guides are graded on how well they affect positive change in their students, and each Guide will have their own unique style. Some can come across as stern disciplinarian, "head master" types, where others can be gushing with love and affection. However, the one thing they all have in common is their profound compassion.

It should be noted at this point that your Spirit Guide is not your Higher Self. I will talk about your Highest Self in the next section, but for now, just be aware that they are two different things.

Unfortunately, most people, when learning that they actually have a Spirit Guide, react in a subordinate way. They feel they are not worthy, and must bow down to their Spirit Guide. This is just silly. Your Guides will never ask you to be subordinate to them. You are in a team. You are on the field playing, and your Guide is like the coach on the sideline. They give you advice and strategy, a drink, and patch you up if you get hurt. But the player is no better than the coach, and the coach is no better than the player. They need each other to perfect their skills. So like a player on a field, it is ok to ask your coach for advice without feeling unworthy. Another point, is what I call "Guide Abuse". In my experience, I have seen many New Agers (7th Level Young Souls) use a pendulum or other devise to "ask their Guides something". The problem is, they will literally ask "what clothes should I wear today?"; "Should I buy the red car or the blue car" (when they are the same model). They ask silly, every day questions that they should be able to answer themselves. Unfortunately, they become too subservient to their Guides and they are not game to do anything without asking their Guides first. I can assure you that Guides do not answer silly questions or requests. They are there for the bigger challenges life throws at us. So please, have a little common sense when asking your Guides for anything.

As for "seeing" your Guides face to face, it is possible. However, it takes a lot of work by the person to achieve this. That is because you are asking your Guide to lower their vibration to such a dense vibration, that it is not possible for them to do it by themself. Imagine you had to go down 500 metres (1,640 ft.) under the ocean. Without a submersible specifically designed for this task, it is not possible. Even the toughest submersibles can only spend about 10 minutes at that depth, then hours to ascend back to the surface to avoid the occupants contracting the bends.

But what if you could raise the ocean bottom to 100 metres (330 ft.). That would make life a lot easier. The same can be said for your Guides. If you are able to raise your vibration to a higher level, then they do not have to descend to such great depths. To raise your vibration, takes discipline and time, and that is where most people decide it isn't worth it. In fact, they make a conscious decision that they would rather watch TV, than to speak with their Guide. That is ok, and that is their choice. I will cover ways to raise your vibration and communicate with your Guides in Book III, as that is more of a practical guide book, however, the most basic way to achieve this is to simply mediate, every day, for at least 20 minutes or longer.

Your Guides never judge you, and they never get mad or angry at you. They do display disappointment and frustration at times, but they also display great joy when they are happy.

As far as a Guide is concerned, we are their direct responsibility, not God's. That is because they are with us for many thousands of earth years, to assist before, during and after each life.

It is odd that in life, many people blame God for their problems or misfortunes, but in Spirit, Souls never blame God. Indeed, they nearly always take their frustrations out on their Guides! But our wonderful, beautiful Guides never react in kind, they just love us all unconditionally.

Younger Souls get constant help from their Guides, where Older Souls are left alone a lot to try and figure things out for themselves. It is very similar to school children. First year students may have several teachers to watch over them constantly, where a student in their last year of high school will be left alone for free study periods.

There is no correlation of gender of Guides to students. In other words, there seems to be an even number of male Guides with male students, to male Guides to female Guides, and vice versa. Maybe because Guides do not have gender by default. They have sufficiently raised their awareness beyond the male-female paradigm, so in essence, they are androgynous. As stated early, they all appear to the person in such a way that please the person. So if you want to see your Guide as a little old lady, and I want to see them as a young man, then that is how they will appear – even if we share the same guide!

I have a very strong respect for Guides, as they are powerful and compassionate beings that play an important role in our earthly and spiritual lives. However, I must admit that they can frustrate the daylights out of me at times! This is because they can be unpredictable, aloof and sometimes vague. I realise that is because it is part of my own soul's journey, and it is not for them to give me all the answers, but at the end of the day, I am human right now, just like everybody else, so I do get a little frustrated at times.

I know Guides only want what is best for us, so sometimes this means they must watch us from afar, and endure much pain in order to help us reach certain objectives. However, they do not come every time you call for them. Our Guides carefully evaluate each request based on its urgency and level of importance to our Spiritual growth. But Guides can only help us once we have made the conscious decision to change. They cannot, and will not force you to do anything against your will.

## How Do I Get Answers to My Issues?

People often express their own frustrations to me that they wished they knew more about many things. I simply say to them, "What is 25?" Every time is the same, they look at me blank. Some try and come up with an answer but to date, I have never had anyone answer that question correctly. So I will let you in on the secret. "What is 25?" 25 is 5x5. What does that have to do with anything you ask? Everything I say! Basically it is this – if you do not, or cannot formulate the correct question, what is the point of me, or your Guides giving you the answer? The answer on its own is meaningless, or even worse, you will try and make sense of it, usually with the wrong outcome. However, if you asked "What is 5x5?" and I or your Guide says "25", it makes perfect sense. Therefore, before you get frustrated with a lack of knowledge, try and formulate a very precise question. In my experience, exact questions will always be answered, but don't blame them if it is not the answer you were hoping for!

If you are asking a question out of pure fear or anger, they will not engage in your fear or anger. It is their purpose to guide you and to assist you on multiple levels, not just your conscious level.

## Should We Fear Our Guides?

Absolutely not! Sometimes we may be embarrassed to face them, and at times they don't always come when we call for them, but our Guides are our teachers, our confidants, and our best friends. They are the one constant throughout every life and death you will ever experience.

## Do My Guides or God Hear My Prayers?

Neither. When we pray, it is really being heard by your Higher Self. Therefore, your prayers will only be answered if the outcome is for your Higher good. When many people pray together for a common cause, this too is often answered. That is because they are creating an outcome through mass thought manifestation. What you think becomes manifest on the Astral Plane. It may disappear seconds after you think it, or it may stay there for years. It all depends on how much energy you give it. So, if many people are thinking the same thing, then it becomes longer lasting and more solidified. But no matter how much you pray, in a group or not, if it goes against the natural order of the Universe, the outcome will not change. The same can be said when you pray for another person. If that person's soul has chosen to experience that lesson, then nothing you or anyone else does will make a difference. That is why the best way is to make your request, then let it go – **Accept and Allow**. What will be, will be. Sometimes I find it helps if I end with, "and please allow me the strength, to accept the Universe's Will."

## Can My Guides Fix All of My Problems?

No. In times of trouble we often demand that our Guides help us at once, and set things right. But our Guides never "rescue" us or "save" us. What your Guides really do is step back, and illuminate alternative paths to your goals. It is best not to demand wholesale fixes, but rather, ask for help for just the next step, and prepare for unexpected possibilities!

Intent and appropriateness is very important. I knew a well meant woman who told me she would ask her Guides every day what colour outfit she should wear to work. She thought that by wearing a particular colour it would help raise her Auric energy for that particular colour (I will discuss Auras in Book III). I didn't have the heart to tell her that this was nuts! To put this into perspective, asking your Guides what to wear every day is like asking a PhD mathematician to help you count to 10. Don't waste your time asking your Guides silly questions that you can easily answer yourself.

## Can I ask my guides about my past lives?

Yes. They may or may not answer that question. It has to do with your intent of asking it and whether it is appropriate to discuss at that time. Your main focus is this life. If a level of understanding can be attained by discussing a past life, then they will discuss it. If they feel you will shift all of your attention on that life and not make movement on this one, they will not.

## Do Guides Work Together?

Yes. Guides work with each other to relay important messages to their students. For example, if I want to help a friend heal, I may ask my Guide, to ask their Guide, to pass on my healing energies. Guides are also the best "match-makers" in the Universe! They will work together to make sure 2 souls cross paths at the best time. Relationships are always arranged before you incarnate, and your Guides are well aware of these arrangements, as they helped to set them up. So when the time comes for you to meet your husband or wife, they will make sure the correct 'sign posts' are set up. That is not to say we always get it right.

In fact, many of us use our Will in choosing potential partners. From an Ego point of view, it may seem like a wise decision, but from a Soul perspective, it is usually disastrous. In those curcomstances, our Higher Selves will spend the next few months or years trying to get us out of disruptive or dysfunctional relationships.

But our old friend **FEAR** keeps us stuck, so we can stay in dud relationships for years and years. Then when you die and go back to Spirit, you remember you were supposed to marry so-and-so and would have had a beautiful life together. But you rejected them because they didn't have enough money, or they weren't physically attractive enough, or your family/friends didn't approve of them. This is just one example of how we can flounder on the same life lessons for lifetime after lifetime. Even still, our Guides work tirelessly dropping bread crumbs and setting up post signs. It is up to us to sit, breath, calm down and look around. The signs are always there for those that are ready to look.

*          *          *

Back in Spirit…Your Guide now takes you over vast fields of wild flowers or forest, or even through space to a **Healing Centre**. The Healing Centre is like a field hospital ready to take in battle weary Souls who have just arrived back from Earth. Almost every Soul that has been to Earth will be damaged in some way. Some will only have minor "dints" and scratches, while other Souls who have undergone several traumatic episodes in their life will have major deformations and deep running scars. These ailments need to be corrected before you can return to your final destination.

*          *          *

Taine is directed into an enclosed area similar to a cylindrical shower without walls. Although he is alone, the energy now appears like steam coming directly down like a column, and seems to be intelligently directed. It begins to circle and swirl around him until it finally touches and massages his very Soul, inside and out. The final process involves a Violet Flame being absorbed into the whole of his soul, healing and cleansing his Emotional and Mental Bodies. These are known as the **Subtle Bodies** which I will discuss in a later chapter, however for now, just be aware that after death, you carry your Emotional and Mental body back into Spirit with you.

*          *          *

Some souls that have had a particularly traumatic life on earth need extra treatments, and longer sessions in the healing chamber. That is why it is very important to deal with trauma on earth appropriately. There is nothing wrong with grieving, and in fact, it is an important process. However, when grief is held onto for extended periods, problems on a physical body and soul level can develop! Many people can become so addicted to their misery that they literally define their personality through it. On a distorted level, they find solace in their pain because they like the attention they get whenever they tell their sad story. They unconsciously use their hard luck story to solicit sympathy from others, which is really just a form of negative manipulation – a Fear-based mentality. Old Souls have learnt to process trauma, accept it, and then move on. They never use it to deliberately gain sympathy from others. Souls that do hang onto trauma can eventually develop holes in their Subtle Bodies. Although this can generally be repaired, the process can hold Souls back from their advancement. It is like being kept down a grade at school.

*          *          *

Good news for Taine, he is now free of emotional hurts, and his Subtle Bodies are now back in balance. It is time for a debrief and life review with the **Spiritual Council**. Once again, the surroundings will be unique for every soul, but for the younger souls, the process generally goes like this:

## Death Process Stage 3 – The Life Review

You will find yourself sitting in a room or place that had happy memories for you in your previous life. So in Taine's case, he finds himself in his childhood bedroom, complete with all his toys, wall paper and bed. This room was very meaningful for Taine because his father would come in every day when he got home from work and talk or play with Taine. But best of all he would tell the most amazing stories that always left Taine wanting more. Taine knew they were just fantasy, but they were better than any TV show he had ever watched. Taine's father died in an industrial accident when he was only 11 years old. So Taine treasured these moments with his father, in his room, above all else.

Jane Clovers on the other hand found herself in a beach hut in the Bahamas. This was where she spent her honeymoon, and it was the happiest memories of her life. Unfortunately for Kevin Stye, he never made it this far. He is still stuck on the Earth Plane moaning and groaning and rattling chains! Kevin is in a state of hard-core denial, so there is little anyone can do for him at the moment. His main Guide will remain in contact with him during his time in his self-imposed hell, and will constantly try and comfort and guide him back to the Light. Eventually all souls find their way out, but it can take a very long time in earth years.

In the room or location, there will be three figures. They sit on a slightly raised platform beside each other. They will appear as whatever is pleasing to you. Most people see them as older, professor types, or like court judges. They may be all males, or all females or even a mix. These 3 Beings are known as the Spiritual Council. These Beings were with you when you left for Earth, now they are here to welcome you home and discuss the events of your life just completed.

## The Spiritual Council

The Spiritual Council are made up from your own Over-Soul. The Over-Soul is not the Higher Self. The Over-Soul is the part of your Soul Group that has completed their incarnations and have merged back into one consciousness. Ok, I know this can be a little confusing, so let's take it slow, and from the beginning!

1. A SOUL COMES into existence with full Universal Knowledge – everything!

2. THIS SOUL IS HUGE, therefore, to learn even more stuff, it splits itself up in to many, many different, smaller souls.

3. EACH OF THESE smaller souls has independence, free Will and a unique perspective it can bring to the whole. Think of a large cut diamond, and each soul is a facet of the diamond. Depending on how you hold the diamond, will depend on which facets shines or sparkles light and which ones don't. Each facet has a unique shine or sparkle, just like each small soul.

4. AGAIN, JUST LIKE the diamond example, imagine if you slow the movement down, so only 100 facets have the light shone on them and you freeze. This becomes the first Soul Group to incarnate. Now we move the diamond again and the next group of 100 (or any number) is in the light – that is your next Soul Group.

5. BY THE TIME the second Soul Group is selected, the first group has already completed their incarnations, or have almost finished – as in, they have been through all of the Soul Ages or they are at Old Soul level and almost finished.

6. SO YOUR OVER-SOUL is made up of thousands of little souls that have either completed all of their earth lives, so they can contribute that experience to the whole, or, from the original fragments that still have Universal Knowledge. We call this your **Soul Cluster**.

7. YOUR ADVANCED SPIRIT Guides are from the group 2 or 3 times ago that incarnated and your Guides in Training are immediately before your Soul Group's incarnations. So, they are still in the incarnation phases, but are more advanced along the maturation cycle.

8. EVEN THOUGH THE Spiritual Council manifests as three individual beings of Light, the fact is, they are just a representation of hundreds of souls that belong to your Soul Cluster. I am sure you can imagine how impractical it would be, not to mention

overwhelming, to sit before 500 or 1000 souls! Spirit always likes to keep things simple – remember that!

Thus, I hope the reader can now understand, that the Spiritual Council are NOT there to judge you! On the contrary, they are there to counsel you on your life just completed. They will review the times when you were presented with your life lessons and see how you went. They look at how you interacted with people and how you conducted your life. They will say things like *"You may have made a different choice then – do you understand why?"* or *"Your treatment of your dying mother was commendable. Your level of compassion has risen since your last life so that is a great achievement"* and so on.

This review board knows everything about you, so don't think you can lie or cheat them! You have done this with them at the end of every life you have ever lived, and they helped you choose the life at the beginning of every new life. They know what your lessons were, what you set out to achieve, and what other Souls incarnated with you to help. They are in effect YOU! Or at least, a higher state of consciousness that you belong to. This is why it is so important to quieten your mind and mediate while on earth. Imagine the huge resources of knowledge and experience you can draw on – from your own Over-Soul! I am sure you would agree that you would be happy to help yourself if you asked.

The Old Souls by-pass the Spiritual Council all together. They go directly to their 'special place' and meet with the Spirit Guide(s) and Master Guide, who will take them through the exact sort of review and debrief but as a single entity one-on-one.

For all Souls, no matter what level they are at, there is one last process. At the end of this review you will experience every single emotion you have caused someone else. So if you are a happy, positive person that gave unselfishly to others, then you will feel a lot of joy and thankfulness. On the other hand, if you were a negative, nasty, fear-based person that took advantage of other people, then you will feel the pain and suffering you caused. This is not a punishment. This is not done to you by some other being or group. You are NOT punished by God. These are your own actions, and as per the Law of Karma, which we discussed in Chapter 1.

Remember, there is an equal and opposite reaction for every action you commit. Therefore, no one is punishing you, and furthermore, you are in complete control of how your review will go. Don't get hung up on this. The average person has almost balanced good behaviour/ bad behaviour in most cases. Even if you have done some not so nice things in this life, it is never too late to change. In fact, the more you change now that you are aware of it, the greater and more positive effect it has on your return to Spirit.

The purpose of this review is two-fold. Firstly, it resolves any outstanding Karma. Secondly, as a result of this it "sets" your "frequency" or Vibration.

## Good, good, good, - Good Vibrations...

Everything in the Universe, including the Universe Itself, vibrates at a particular rate or frequency. Science has finally caught up on this fact and they call it **String Theory**. Basically, the idea is that minuscule strands of energy vibrating in 11 dimensions create every particle and force in the universe. So everything in the Universe, right down to what atoms are made up of, are 1 of 2 types of vibrating strings. Type 1 looks like a wobbling rubber band, and Type 2 looks like the same rubber band, but it has been cut, so it can lie straight rather than be in a loop (Fig. 4). These strings attract to each other to form atoms, which in turn attract to other atoms to form molecules and molecules join to...well, you get the idea. Eventually it all forms **Matter**.

Even though that was the shortest and most simple explanation of String Theory in history, I think you get the idea. If you are interested to learn more, I strongly urge you to check out Physicist Brian Greene's TED Talk online (Greene, 2005).

Anyway, that is one science theory that is right on the money. What they haven't really figured out yet, is that those little strings vibrate at an exact frequency. So depending on the frequency, will determine

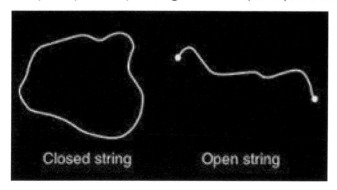

*Figure 4*

which strings are attracted to each other. For example, certain strings will attract to make each of the basic elements in the periodic table. So you know the old saying "Like attracts like" – well no words could be more true for every level of Creation. So much so that your very Soul vibrates by this Law of Physics.

So if you have a high (Love) vibration, your Soul will go to an area, or 'level' that is vibrating at the same frequency or rate. Alternatively, if your Soul is vibrating at a low (Fear) vibration, then you will go to a level that matches that vibration.

That is the reason why there are 49 levels in the Spirit World. Each soul may only have a slightly higher or lower vibration to another soul, so this way, there is a more suitable level for each soul to exist on. To put this into context, imagine you went on a holiday to any place in the world that you enjoyed the most. Once you arrive, it is stunning, and all the people there are just like you. They may look different, but their personality and nature is exactly like yours.

So, if you want to sit under a tree and quietly read a book, so do they. They would not start playing loud music or talking. Just as you might see someone reading, you would quietly walk by and not disturb them. Imagine living in a world where everyone behaved how you would behave.

So take your mind back to Chapter 1, where there was a diagram showing the 7 levels of the Spirit World, which were again divided into 7 sub-levels. It will be on one of these sub-levels that you will take up residency. Which sub-level you arrive at, will be determined by your vibrational frequency, and as we just learnt, your vibrational frequency is directly related to how you lived the life just completed.

## Moving Through the Planes

Souls who reside on level 3 and above can move to planes lower than the one they are on. They may do this for educational purposes, or to administer help to the souls existing on those planes. That said, they cannot spend a lot of time on the lower planes purely because their current frequency makes it difficult. So, with that in mind, imagine how difficult it is for Spirit Guides or other high Spiritual Beings to manifest or communicate with you on the Earth Plane.

Souls can also 'visit' higher planes, but only if they have a being from that plane to guide them and temporarily bump up their vibration to allow entry. Again, they cannot spend long periods in the higher realms. Spending time on the lower planes would eventually feel like an immense pressure, crushing you down. On the other hand, spending time on a higher plane would at first feel blissful. But eventually, you would start to vibrate so much, it would feel like your head and heart was going to explode. Thus, the easiest and most comfortable place to exist is on your Home Plane.

## Death Process Stage 4 – Your Home Plane

That is why this will be 'home' until you incarnate again. This is where you stay while you are back in Spirit. And as we have seen, your actions in your current life will determine which level you end up on. So again, I stress, this is not a punishment or judgement. You are wholly responsible for where you end up. But to be honest, the Souls that end up on the very low levels are not even aware that some better place exists. They are so entrapped by their own mind and negative vibration, that they become blind to all but their own misery and suffering.

Some very Young Souls even like residing on the lower levels, because they can still act like they did on earth. For example, they may be fixated on material things, so they will conjure up a red Ferrari. But then their spirit neighbour creates one, so they change it to a yellow Bugatti, and the neighbour follows…then they go for a game of golf, and every shot is a hole in one! They surround themselves with pretty girls (or boys), but so does everyone else. You see, eventually this will get very boring for this soul, especially the golf game right!

Eventually they may start to think that there is more to life than material things. At that very instance they make the conscious connection, they will snap out of it and realise where they are (which only comes with true sorrow and repent). They are automatically taken to the 3rd level of the Spirit realm. In the movie I mentioned earlier "*Astral City: A Spiritual Journey*" it is roughly the 2nd sub-plane of the 3rd Level that André is taken to. This is where the 'Astral City' is located. The majority of Child Souls and early to mid-Young Souls reside there. Levels 4 – 5.5 are Mature Souls and 5.5 – all of 6 are the Old Souls. The Over-Soul exists on the 7th Level of the 7th Sub-plane.

## What Happened to Heaven and Hell?

What is interesting, is that at some time in ancient, human history, someone had a sneak peek into these lower planes and came up with the concept of Hell. Maybe it was a Sharman, or a Priestess somewhere. No doubt at the same time, they saw these lower planes, they also got a glimpse of the 3rd or 4th plane and thought it was beautiful compared to earth, so they called it "Heaven". The idea took off and now it is entrenched in many cultures around the world.

Of course, the whole concept of the Devil and Hell was a completely made up concept that people used to explain evil in humans, as well as other negative events like natural disasters. Later the Devil was used to control the masses. Indeed, the history of the Devil is a fascinating topic, so I have included an article in **Annex 1.2.1.** Hopefully by reading the actual history of how the devil was created, and how it has evolved through history, will aid the reader to realise that these are manmade concepts that have no relevance in the Spirit Plane, or on Earth.

Hopefully by now, you understand why some humans do terrible things (as in younger souls) and why some people have horrific things happen to them (because of Karma or experience) and the rest of evil doings can be explained by science (eg: natural disasters). As for people born with disabilities, again, it was not God's fault, or God punishing the parents. It was that soul's choice – for whatever reason.

There are dark, demonic forces in the world, but they are not the Devil, and they do not come from Hell. They are part of Creation – you cannot have Light without Dark. However, the Dark Side is only interested in using and seducing those Souls that also vibrate at their frequency. Indeed, a demonic force coming into contact with a Spiritual person is akin to a bug zapper! They really don't like it, so they keep their distance. Book II will focus on the Dark Side as in what it is, who they control, and how to defend yourself from their influence.

However, the sooner you can move away from laying blame, whether on the Devil, God, the Dark Side or another person, and accept responsibility for your own actions, and your own life, then the closer you will get to the truly heavenly realms of the Spirit Plane. Furthermore, sitting around all day and praying for this and that is only going to hold you back. If you want change in your life, then you need to create the change you desire.

If you want God to punish someone for hurting you, then you are still stuck in Child or Young Soul level and you really need to work on that. If you only go to church because you think if you don't you will be punished, then you are still stuck in Child or Young Soul level and you really need to work on that. If you act the way you do for fear of retribution, then you are still stuck in Child or Young Soul level and you really need to work on that.

Part of being on a Spiritual Path means that you take responsibility for everything that happens or does not happen in your life. Stop blaming God, or the Devil or others. Stop kowtowing to a corrupt, religious industry, and communicate directly with God yourself. Don't think for a second you can buy your way into Heaven – remember the Spiritual Council? They don't take cash, credit cards or cheques – they deal in energy, or more specifically, VIBRATION!

I know how difficult it can be for people to turn away from their church or the religion they have followed for years. I am not saying you should. I am trying to say to stop using those institutions and icons as an emotional crutch. All the answers are within you, but there is so much clutter and noise, you cannot hear. Meditation is the key! I will explain meditation and include some practical exercises in Book III. If you can't wait that long, then there are thousands of excellent meditations online, on DVD's and in books. You can also visit my YouTube Chanel: Path to Ascension (https://www.youtube.com/user/PathToAscention) for free.

## Suicides Don't Last Long

Make no mistake, the Spirit realm is gorgeous, wonderful and it is home. But before you start thinking hmmmm, maybe I will just top myself and go back to bliss – beats this crappy life and miserable existence right? WRONG!!! If you suicide, you will be cutting your life off early. This means you will have to come back to earth and finish the lessons you missed, due to an early departure. Furthermore, you will have to be born again, and go through a childhood with similar circumstances to your original life. That is because you will require a life similar to this one, so the lessons can be tried again. As soon as you suicide, a completely different process is initiated, because you have violated the natural order of the Universe.

Your soul goes directly back to Spirit – no welcoming party, only a disappointed Spirit Guide waiting for you. You do go to the Healing Chamber, and then for a brief Spiritual Council review. Just on that, imagine having to face the Spirit Council just because you accidently took too many drugs, or alcohol, or killed yourself in a booze induced hissy fit because your boy/girlfriend left you? Just remember, there is nothing that is not fixable! Take out the high drama and view it from the **Wise Mind**.

The Wise Mind is a term I use to describe your Higher, perfect Self. If you had to counsel someone for their own good, what would you tell them? This is your Wise Mind. The Wise Mind does not know drama, angst, rage, bliss or any other emotion. It is like a professor that just deals in the facts, and does not get emotionally involved.

The Spiritual Council will now work very fast to try and find a new body with similar circumstances, to get the soul back onto earth. That is because the rest of the Soul Group are still progressing, and this soul has now fallen behind. Thus, the soul will spend very little time back in Spirit.

Usually Souls that suicide are kicking themselves, because they realise what a mistake they made and what a waste it was. This usually becomes apparent as soon as they get through the tunnel. However, all Souls will have at least one life where they will suicide – yet another experience they must have. But these Souls go to special healing hospitals, because they are particularly traumatised and need specialised healing.

After these 'planned' suicides, they will return to their home level as per the normal procedure. Planned suicides can happen at any Soul Age, but it is more likely to be in the early Mature Phase. That is because younger souls suicide because they lost all their money in a stock crash, or they are trying to save face in war instead of surrendering (false pride).

Planned suicide usually always involve intense, emotional states of separation. On a profound level, these souls become so separated from humanity, and from the Source, that they literally experience a *disconnect*.

A Spiritual Disconnect is about the most terrifying thing a soul can do, but luckily from their perspective, they are not even aware of it. Imagine for a minute you have a computer connected to the Internet. When you are connected to the Internet you can chat with friends, send messages, watch videos and look at pictures and many other things – you are 'connected' to the World Wide Web. Suddenly someone pulls the Internet plug and you are no longer connected to it. The computer still works (like your memories), but your connection to the outside world is gone.

Now you can't even check the weather forecast to see what's coming! For Souls that are always connected to each other and the Source for 99.99% of the time, this is a very destabilizing event. It is the first time the Soul will experience true being alone. They cannot even feel the Love of the Creator Source, nor see Its Light. They are in a very dark place, deep within their own minds. Thus, it can take the soul a long time to recover. These are the souls that often become trapped in their own insistent re-living of the event in their mind.

A very good example of this is in the movie *"What Dreams May Come"* starring Robin Williams, Cuba Gooding Jr., and Annabella Sciorra, (What Dreams May Come, 1998). The character played by

Annabella is Annie, and she kills herself and goes to "hell". There is no Hell remember, that is just a Hollywood euphemism for the experience I am talking about. Anyway, what happens to Annie is pretty much exactly what happens to many planned suicides. That is why many souls put it off for a long time, to when they have more experience, and also why the Spiritual Council and the Guides spend a lot of time preparing the soul for that particular life. By the way, unlike the movie, you don't have to send your soul mate to hell to try and "rescue" them. There is no rescuing in Spirit, just Unconditional Love, and a gradual realisation by the Soul that they can forgive themselves and reconnect with the Source whenever they are ready.

## Home Sweet Home

At some point, every soul that returns to the Spirit Plane will be ready to take their place in their natural home. I say home, because that is exactly what it is. Therefore, that is what we will look at in the next Chapter – **Home Life**!

---

### References:

Greene, B. (2005). *Making Sense of String Theory.* [online] Ted.com. Available at: *https://www.ted.com/talks/brian_greene_on_string_theory* [Accessed 28 Jul. 2014].

*What Dreams May Come.* (1998). [film] Hollywood: Director: Vincent Ward, Writers: Richard Matheson (novel), Ronald Bass (screenplay).

# 10

## WORK AND PLAY - YOUR LIFE IN SPIRIT

*"Every spirit builds itself a house; and beyond its
house, a world; and beyond its world a heaven. Know
then, that the world exists for you: build, therefore, your
own world." (Ralph Waldo Emerson)*

𝓘MAGINE FOR ONE moment what would be your perfect home. I
am confident that each person I ask this question to would have
a different description. So it is in the Spirit realm. You actually
design your home very early in your existence. Indeed, just as you
live in a home now, so will you do on the Spirit Plane. You may live
with other members of your Soul Group, or you may live with a single
Soul Mate or even alone. Others prefer the company of many and
will live in large open buildings and others again prefer a 'camping'
style abode.

You may think it is odd that you die, go back to the Spirit
world and live in a house. But the fact is, it is your earth life that is
imitating your Spirit World life! Remember this well, you are not a

human having a spiritual experience right now, you are a spirit having a human experience.

*Figure 5*

Just as your Soul evolves, so does your home base. Early on you may have designed a pre-historic round house (Fig. 5) as was popular in early Europe and Britain. When you move into your Child Soul phase you may replace the round house with a two story home, completed with shingled roofed and white picket fence. By Young Soul, your ambitions and experience have gone up considerably, so you may find yourself in a large condo or mansion by the sea, on a cliff or in a spirit city. Mature Souls opt for a small country retreat, away from other settlements, but still with regular contact for social gatherings. Finally at Old Soul level, you no longer need a house as such. They may spend time under a tree, then beside a lake, then high in the mountains and next floating among the stars. The Old Soul enjoys solitude and for them, everywhere and anywhere is home.

Younger Souls, including Mature Souls, like to have a house purely for psychological comfort. They still identify with living with others in family units or with friends, so what better place to hang around in then your own home. Old Souls, on the other hand, are no longer attached to such sentimental notions and are happy to just exist wherever they are. The fact is, anywhere can be your home, because you are no longer restricted by practicalities and limited building supplies. You are only limited by your own imagination!

On most of the 3rd Level of the Spirit Plane, there are many other buildings. They include learning facilities, as well as places of worship, what we may call churches. You see, as mentioned earlier, Souls are not all knowing when they return home. They understand their past lives and reincarnation, as well as their place in the Universe. But they do not yet fully understand the nature of the Source (God). They know about the Source, but they still feel it is necessary to pay homage and or worship. They do this in church type buildings. But you will not see religious icons or artefacts, like crucifixes or menorahs. However, what you will see, is the most stunning architecture, which is a combination of all world religions. For example, the high ceilings of Christian cathedrals, along with the breath taking Islamic arabesque carvings create beautiful buildings that all souls admire.

However, churches and religious type dedication is mainly seen on the lower levels 2-4. They do not exist on Levels 5-7. That is because the older souls on the higher levels have come to a realisation and understanding that actions and behaviour are the best form of worship.

## Learning

A common theme among all levels is learning. That's right, you don't get to sit around all day on a cloud, playing the harp! In fact, I have no idea where that stereotype came from, but it couldn't be further from the truth. Your spirit life is choke full of new experiences, profound retrospection and enlightenment. And lots, and lots of Love and fun!

## Soul Groups

Souls tend to hang out in their own Soul Groups. A typical Soul Group may start off with as many as 1000 souls, and by mature level it has dwindled down to about 100 or 200. That is because some of the Souls have finished their earthly reincarnations, and sadly because some have been left behind, because they failed to learn certain lessons. Most people are aware of the strong connection twins usually feel. Multiply this feeling x 1000 and that is how you feel about your soul group. They are your "family" as such. You sometimes incarnate with them, but more usually you go off on independent treks and come back and share your experiences with the group.

In these group sessions, it is common to see souls holding a large book type object. Well, that is what I thought when I first saw these nearly 20 years ago. Now I would describe it as an iPad ot PC Tablet! But rather than words in a book, it is like a screen. On the screen, souls can bring up any past life they have had for review, as well as potential new lives that may be considered for growth. With past life review, the whole group may contribute their thoughts, praise you for a good job, or help you understand where you could have made different choices. Overseeing all of this is your main Guides.

The Guides will also propose scenarios that will benefit the group in future. For example, let's say that this group is heading into the mature phase, so the Guide may say *"It is time to explore unconditional love. Create an experience where you think you can learn about unconditional love."* Each soul then looks in their life book. They will see full colour, moving pictures, complete with sounds, smell and feeling (as in temperature), as well as imagined emotional feelings. They can experience the scenario in the first person, as in you are in the scene actually experiencing it, or as a 3rd person, similar to a Guide's perspective and viewing the episode like a TV show. They may replay this scenario many times until the Guides feel that the souls have integrated this lesson sufficiently, that they then could potentially carry it out in their next life.

## Inspirations

As well as these group sessions covering more general topics, souls will also go through individual lessons just for them. They are similar to the group sessions, as in they will explore potential life experiences, but on a more personal level.

For example, a particular soul may have a passion for music or art. They have had many lives as a musician, but are not yet satisfied with where they have taken the skill. So, they will write or compose new music. The new music they create in spirit will often filter down into their next earth life as an "inspiration". In fact, all so-called inspirations or revelations in every field on earth, from art, to mathematics, to technology breakthroughs, to medical cures, ALL are worked out or invented in spirit, then are filtered down to earth for integration. But as you may be aware in your life right now, not all inspirations are acted upon.

You may feel your life doesn't have time, or your priorities have changed. It may be you did act on it, and invented a free energy device, but the powers that be took it from you or coveted it for themselves. The point is, it is not essential for you to act on every single inspiration in every single life. Think of them more as a potential treasure trove, should you decide to unlock it. At the more advance levels, every soul has the opportunity to go into Guide training. But the reality is, not every soul wants to be a Guide, and there is certainly no requirement to do it. It is the individual soul's choice. Indeed, many older souls opt to become "Creators".

## Creation

Just like art, literature, mathematics, technology, medicine, philosophy, and science are all created in spirit first, so too is all life. All older souls have the inherent ability to create new life. Just like anything, they start off small and work their way up. There is a whole section of the Spirit Plane dedicated to Life Creation. Think of it like one big university that is split up into different schools. For example, the School of Single Celled Life, The School of Birds; Dogs; Monkeys etc.

Have you ever noticed that all dogs, for example, share a common "theme" or template? We all automatically recognise a Chihuahua being a dog, as well as a Great Danes being dogs, even though there is an extreme in their size. It is similar to how we have a template for a car, but have thousands of interpretations of the basic car model. Now, before you get all hot and bothered thinking I am pushing an Intelligent Design theory, or trying to debunk evolution then stop and think again.

In a way, life is "intelligently designed", but not by God. Furthermore, there is evolution, but not caused by "random" genetic mutations spread out over millions of years. The mutations that occur are rapid, and planned.

## Let's break it down

**Step 1:** A very advance spirit being, usually Master Guides and above, come up with a new life form "model". They must factor in where it will fit into the Tree of Life, how it will behave, respond, and breed as well as which part of the earth it will live. Every single, little detail is worked out. It can literally take 1/2 million earth years to get this far, but in spirit there is no time, so it was completed very quickly in their terms. This becomes the prototype. In this example, we will pretend the model was the dog. It should be noted that the original template was the Wolf. They have now refined it into the domestic dogs that are better suited for human company. There will no doubt be failed experiments or abandoned trials, that can still be found in the fossil record today.

**Step 2:** The plans are filtered down to the lower levels ie. The School of Creation. Here the "teachers" will study the new form and learn about it inside and out. They will start to tinker with sizes, shape, colours etc., from a very broad perspective.

**Step 3:** This is where the fun starts! The students are basically given free reign (within reason) to "paint" and sculpture the new model. They do this via a form of biological programming. They literally write the DNA code required to bring about the changes they want to implement. Just like in the car example, one student may want a red "sports" car, with tinted windows and racing tyres. Another student may want a "family" wagon. The choices are endless! The same is with the dogs – some wanted big dogs, shaggy dogs, fast dogs, slow dogs, cuddly dogs, fighting dogs, hunting dogs and more.

It is important to note at this point, that cross breading and line breeding is not controlled by Spirit. These things are allowed to happen by their own accord. Genetic syndromes and disease are usually due to either poor programming, or a program that did not fit within the Universal Laws that govern all life.

Other genetic diseases can also be a result of inbreeding, or exposure to toxic environments. So, why were they allowed to be created? Free Will – never forget, your greatest gift from the Source is Free Will.

Once a new creation has taken root on the Earth Plane, they will be integrated with Soul beings. In other words, Soul consciousness will enter them. Thus, these forms of consciousness are like the test drivers, and may as a group, recommend upgrades or changes.

These upgrades are tabulated, and whichever requests get the most demand that is beneficial to the whole, then Creator Souls will make the necessary changes, and download the new 'evolved' species. On earth, these changes are recorded as evolution.

When you hear scientists talking about evolution, they will say things like, "That species developed a unique beak for finding food in that particular environment and that is evolution in play..." What they fail to answer is, HOW did that species decide as a WHOLE to change their beak? If 1 bird mutated with a different beak, it would die out within one or two generations. Furthermore, how does an animal think "If only I had a different shaped beak, then I could crack those nuts and eat more..."

The point is, they don't. It is the Soul Consciousness that has these ideas, and as a group, they take the ideas back to Spirit and implement them. Therefore, evolution can happen in one generation. There are also major environmental changes that can trigger a DNA change, which we will explore in Book III.

This method also explains the reason why some forms of life become extinct. It usually means that that particular experiment has run its course, so the model is scrapped, and something new is started. A good example of this was with the dinosaurs. They were an awesome way for Creator Souls to cut their teeth, so to speak on more advanced beings.

Think of it like programming a computer. Once they had mastered that experiment, they cleared the board to start again with an even more refined creators – mammals. It was later that humans came into the mix which I will discuss in Chapter 16.

This again, should demonstrate how precious life is, and how everything is connected. Furthermore, it also shows why some people in earth life have a certain affinity either with a species, or with all creatures in general.

Chances are, that person was doing Creation work back in Spirit before they incarnated to their present life. If you currently have a passion for animals now, there is a good chance you will be working with them on a much deeper level when you return to Spirit. In fact, that goes for any passion you may have on Earth. It generally means you have been working on it in Spirit before you came here.

## Lessons for All

There are lessons that come down from the higher levels for all groups. This happens a lot, when the earth is experiencing a massive shift in consciousness, like what is going on now. Say the general lesson may be "Tolerance", or "Unity". Each soul group is to incorporate these lessons into their current consciousness and next earth life. These lessons are usually delivered in person, so to speak by a very advance soul. You may see them as Krishna, or Buddha, or Jesus, or Mohamad. Again, they appear what is most pleasing to you as an individual.

## Healing

Another favourite pastime for some Souls is healing. This is a type of energy healing similar to the practice on earth called Reiki. Reiki is a spiritual healing practice developed in 1922 by Japanese Buddhist, Mikao Usui. It uses a technique commonly called, palm healing, or hands-on-healing as a way of transferring universal energy i.e., reiki

(Parkes and Parkes, 1996). On the 3rd and 4th levels, there are actual healing centres, similar to a hospital on earth.

Here, fresh souls from the lower levels that require intense healing come first, before they move to their Home Plane. It is also where new souls from earth come, especially if they have died in traumatic circumstances, like a war or natural disaster. As you can imagine, these places can get very busy during tumultuous times on Earth. That is why every soul will learn at least the basics of energy healing at some point of their training. During these high volume times, it is all hands on deck!

Healers on Earth are usually full time healers in Spirit. Spirit healers can be any soul from Level 3 right up to Level 7.

## Work, Rest and Play

Before you start to stress thinking it is all work and no play, have no fear. While you do lessons, you also have plenty of 'free' time in indulge in whatever you like. On the lower levels, they even have periods of rest, similar to going to sleep every night. But remember, you do not have a physical body, so you never get tired, sick, or hungry. Rest on the Spirit Plane is more akin to a deep, deep meditation, to help raise your vibration or calm your mind.

That is why it is good to get into interests on earth that you can carry back to Spirit. Things like collecting money, betting on the stock exchange, or playing competitive sport are not things you would do in Spirit. They are all Earth activities. Spirit activities always centre around creativity, thought, brain games type things etc. Did I mention that the Spirit Plane scenery is stunning, gorgeous and breath taking? If you are into beautiful nature, you will feel right at home.

As mentioned before, souls can get stuck in certain life cycles, and as such, get left behind by their soul group. This is about the worse thing a soul can experience, and everything is done to avoid it, however it is inevitable that some souls will get "kept down" a level at some point. Again, this is not a punishment. It is similar to a child at earth school, who is kept down a year because they failed to grasp the concepts or lack the necessary maturity. In effect, keeping the child down a level is being cruel to be kind. It all works out in the end, because everyone eventually "graduates". Most of the Souls that are kept down are incouraged to take up some form of creativity or healing so they can take those skills to Earth and perfect them. By channelling their energy into something other than their own negative thoughts is always a good start to passing lessons.

## Frequently Asked Questions:

### Do you eat in Spirit?

On the lower planes, yes. For some reason, soul's still like to eat together. But it is not for nourishment or health, because after all, you no longer have a physical body. It is more for social and psychological reasons. However, souls can only conjure up things they have experienced on the Earth Plane. For example, if they had never eaten an apple on Earth, then in spirit, they could only "guess" what an apple tasted like, or what its texture is like. Furthermore, they only eat things like fruit and soup – no animals. On the lower levels, they rarely eat. In fact, many of them experience starvation type scenarios. Even though they cannot die again from starvation, they still feel hunger pangs and believe they are starving. This is part of their illusion and self-entrapment. As soon as they realise they cannot die, they will stop feeling hungry, and stop feeling pain. Therefore, they will realise they are dead, thus, they will probably snap out of it!

### Do you sleep?

In the short term yes. When younger souls first get to the Spirit World they may experience a sleep like state during their healing process. Outside of this experience, souls do not sleep, nor do they require it. Not being in a physical body, you will never experience exhaustion or tiredness. You will however do many, deep meditations which will help you to raise your vibration for the next level.

### Do you get sick?

No, souls never get sick, however they can suffer from emotional turmoil. Damage to the Emotional Body can cause minor depression or melancholy, however these are quickly rectified by Spirit Guide Healers. In very Young Souls, they may convince themselves that they feel pain in their joints, arms and legs, or they can even feel thirst or hunger. These are all conditions created in the mind. It is only during separation, that is, the self-imposed hell on the very low levels, that a soul's mind can trick them into believing they are sick.

### Do you grow old?

No. Souls are ageless. As already stated, they may feel more comfortable projecting themselves to others as "old" or even a young child. However, most souls project themselves as a fit and healthy 20-30ish year old. Advanced souls approach as a vibrant colour of their grade, and just before they reach you, they will take on a physical form. After a little while, you will begin to recognise them just by their colour and energy vibration when you see them coming.

## Do you get married?

Yes, but not in the same sense as you would understand it on earth. Souls have a "union" ritual that is conducted between 2 souls on a very intimate and personal level. These souls are typically Twin Souls, but not Soul Mates. Twin Souls are two souls from the same Over-Soul. So in essence, they are the same soul split into male and female energies or essences. Soul Mates are souls that have arranged relationships on Earth in physical life. However, these souls are usually from two different Over-Souls. That is because they can learn more from each other, in particular when playing opposing roles. Twin Souls cannot and never will oppose each other on Earth or in Spirit. How could you? That is like being in a debate with yourself! Soul Mates are common, whereas Twin Souls are very rare.

Souls do not join in union for the same reason people get married. A soul's union is a joining of their consciousness. Although they experience deep and profound unconditional love, the union is more for growing in experience and knowledge. Even when souls are in union, they can still incarnate separate to one another, and they may still have human relationships with other souls. In Spirit, there is no such thing as jealousy, spite, and retaliation, as in the earth plane. So, a soul in union can incarnate and marry and have children, but their partner left behind feels nothing but love, support and happiness for them. In fact, the partner left behind will often work like a Spirit Guide and will encourage the human soul to marry or find love. It would upset the Soul in Spirit more to see their loved one alone and unhappy.

## Do you have sex?

No, not physical sex, but they do have a melding of energies which is better than sex! Think of two separated, coloured gasses – one is blue and 1 is green. When you put them in the same container, they can mix and swirl until they become one gas that is yellow! That is exactly how Souls experience sex. It is the ultimate in "being one". On the Earth Plane, it is possible to experience a physical oneness during sex.

This is when both parties have their Chakras open. Their Chakras join with each other and the Kundalini is awakened and raised. Kundalini is a divine, spiritual energy dormant in every human. Awakening, it results in deep enlightenment and bliss that is best described as Divine Union (Anand, Naslednikov and Hussey, 1990).

Part of the Separation from Source experiment reduced sex to an animalist act for the sole purpose of procreation or base pleasure. Sex was originally designed to be a spiritual experience and sacred contract between two Souls in human form. It is not possible to raise your Kundalini during homosexual sex. I am not homophobic, and I am not trying to marginalise anyone. However, it is just a basic fact of Universal Law. Think of the Divine Union being like two magnets with a North Pole and South Pole (male energy/female energy). Opposites attract, thus they form the union. Like poles repel each other. In order to raise your Kundalini, even on your own, you must have a perfect balance of male to female energy. That is why it is extremely difficult to do it on your own. Without the complimentary energy boosting and balancing your own, there is no way normal humans have enough gas in the tank so to speak to perform it on their own.

## Do you have children?

No, that is purely a physical experience. Remember, souls choose other souls to play the role as their parents or children, to help them learn the particular lesson they go to earth to learn. Therefore, having children in the spirit world would serve no purpose. Only the Ego would demand that, and the Ego is a part of the human brain, which dies and is left on Earth!

## Will I see my pets there?

Sometimes, briefly – they are on their own learning curve and journey, and generally your contract with that soul group is over for now. You may decide to incarnate with them at a later time, however for now, while you are in Spirit, you will not feel the same clinginess and need to have a pet. In fact, after your initial home coming, you may never see them again in Spirit, and this will sit very comfortable with you.

## What is the Source/God like?

I don't know! – hahaha! Every single Soul's relationship with the Source is unique. One thing I do know, is when you are in Spirit, God or the Source does not show up for chit chats or judgment. You become much more aware of the Source, but it does not manifest into any particular form. You have to remember that the Source is a massive, and vast state of consciousness, connected intimately with every level of Creation under Its guidance. Furthermore, the Source gave us Free Will. Therefore, It is not particularly interested in your daily comings and goings. Nor is it interested in the wars of men. It is only interested in knowing, and experiencing, as much as it can.

I realise this may seem like a cold and clinical explanation, but you need to look beyond your human understanding of things and see it from another angle. Does the Source love you? Absolutely. Does the Source feel pain when humans butcher each other? No, it examines the situation in order for it to understand it. Try and think of it like this. Imagine you are watching an ant colony. Suddenly a fly lands on it, and the ants attack it. They swarm all over it and begin to dismember it and carry it to the nest. Here it will be stored as food for the newly hatched larvae.

Using our Wise Mind, now pretend you are a biologist studying the behaviour of ants. Wouldn't you be more interested in how the ants caught the fly, and how they carried it away, and how it may sustain their young? I know there are probably some Mature Souls that want to jump in and save the fly! That is what I am talking about when I say you have Free Will. But if you save the fly, does that mean you think it is ok for the ant babies to die? You see, there is a reason for everything, and the Source knows these reasons. It knows that the fly made a choice before it incarnated to give up its body in order to sustain the ant colony. In human terms, the Source knows that the Old Soul, that incarnated into a 4 year old girl in Palestine, that was just horrifically killed in an Israeli missile strike, agreed to play this role before it incarnated. It was the desire of the Old Soul to try and teach humanity that bloodshed is not the way forward to reconciliation.

If no souls volunteered to do this, humans would never evolve. Furthermore, this particular scenario also allows souls learning about compassion, forgiveness, temperance, and unconditional love to have a reference point. You see, everything that happens in the Universe (not just on Earth!) happens for a reason. Right now, in this incarnation, you are trying to figure out what those reasons are.

You don't have to wait until you return to Spirit to have a relationship with the Source. All you need to do is sit quietly in nature – in a forest, on a beach, or in a desert. Sit there, and close your eyes. Now take three deeps breaths. Any moment, you will feel and maybe hear the Source. It was there all along. You just had the volume up too loud.

## Can you see the whole of the universe?

It is like looking at an earth globe or atlas. You can peruse it, then stop and focus in on an area that interests you. There are many planets and life-forms in the universe that can support complex souls like ours, so generally you are free to choose any life forms to experience. Souls mainly come to Earth, because it is the best training ground in the whole universe. Seeing the whole Universe in one look is something you can do on the 7th Plane. It takes a special kind of Spiritual awareness to do that.

## Can you see what everyone on Earth is doing?

No, not at the same time, but you can focus in on a single person. As you get more experienced you can focus on several people at once. It is not that normal for Souls to be particularly interested in seeing people on Earth. There is more than enough going on in the Spirit World to keep Souls occupied. That said, Younger Souls on Level 3 may still be interested in loved ones they left behind on Earth. This usually only lasts for a little while on returning to Spirit.

## Can I contact people on Earth?

Yes, however you would generally need to have a very good reason to. It is not like you just drop them a line or send an email just to say hello. The main issue with contacting the so-called "living" on Earth, is they probably won't hear your message. If they happened to go to a particularly good clairvoyant, then yes, the message should get through. Otherwise, the person may receive it as a vision, or inspiration. But as I said, if they are not inclined to meditate or sit quietly on a regular basis, then it may prove futile.

The fact is, that when souls return to Spirit, they really don't have a strong connection to the Earth Plane anymore. They are so busy with their new Spirit life. But don't forget, there is no concept of time in the Spirit World, so what may be an hour to you could be 20 years on Earth. So the person you want to contact may have moved on, or even died. If they are close to you, you will know before they do about which day and time they will die. That is so you can get ready to meet them at the Tunnel gate and greet them home!

This has been a very brief look at your life in the Spirit World. Just like Earth, there are so many places to visit, and so many things to do. Best of all, you typically experience the Spirit Plane with the innocence and awe of a child. Every moment there is filled with Love, Peace, Joy and overwhelming happiness. Look me up when you are back in town!

---

**References:**

Anand, M., Naslednikov, M. and Hussey, L. (1990). *The Art of Sexual Ecstasy: The Path of Sacred Sexuality for Western Lovers*. 1st ed. Haarlem: Jeremy P. Tarcher.

Parkes, C. and Parkes, P. (1996). *Reiki: The essential guide to the ancient healing art featuring the original Usui method*, 1st ed. London: Vermillion

# 11

## RETURN TO EARTH - REBORN AGAIN

---

*"The question shouldn't be is there life after death but is there life before death..." (Kate Miller)*

---

O YOU EVER find yourself reminiscing about the "good old days"? Maybe it was your first school camp, or when you and your friends got to stay out late in the warm, summer holidays. Most of us from time to time, like to sit around with old friends or family and relive some of the good times. The funny thing about this is, we hardly ever focus on the hard times we may have had. Don't get me wrong, that is a good thing! It's just that when you are back in Spirit it is exactly the same. After a while you will begin to reminisce about previous lives on earth. Your whole Soul Group will get in on the act.

You have been back in Spirit now for quite a while. You are learning new things and experimenting with new scenarios (via the Life Book). You start to get a little excited about how you may deal with that issue, or this issue, now you have your new found knowledge. Like anything you train for, you get to a point where you are bursting with excitement to do the real thing.

However, this is not something you will rush into. Leaving the blissful refuge of the Spirit World is not always easy. You are in  world of wisdom and pure love, without negativity and stress, and now you find yourself contemplating giving all that up, for another life on Earth. Your Guides will sense the push-pull within you and are more than ready to help you undertake the first steps.

## There are 3 main questions you will want to ask yourself:

1. Am I ready for another life on the Physical Plane?
2. What lessons/experience do I want to try?
3. What part of Earth and what gender will I need to achieve my goals?

Some souls are very reluctant to leave the Spirit World, while others can't wait to try out another Earth Life.  The enthusiasm, or lack thereof, is independent of Soul Age. Even though Old Souls incarnate far less than younger Souls, there are some that adore going to Earth and immersing themselves in the pleasure of physical life.  On the other hand, there are those that will go to Earth only out of a sense of obligation or duty. It should be remembered that Earth is not the only planet that the human soul group can incarnate into. There are literally thousands, on thousands, however Earth still offers by far the best learning experience in the Universe.  Particularly in the last 50 years, where soul from all levels of Creation have been lining up to get a place on Earth to be part of the "shift", which I will discuss in length in Book III.

Remember, it's all about direct experience. If a soul decides to stay in Spirit for too long,  they will fall behind their Soul Group. The Guides will gently nudge, prod, and poke you way before it ever gets to that point! They are also on hand, to make sure you do not bite off more than you can chew. Yes, we all do it, either from an overzealous attitude, that makes you want to take on the more difficult lessons in a misplace bravado, to: "holy crap!, I have some catching up to do!" There is only one thing for it – a trip to the Life Library.

## The Life Library

Remember back to when you were studying, and using your Life Book to try out different roles in different experiences.  This place is similar, but on steroids! I suppose the easiest way to grasp the enormity of the Life Library would be to compare watching a movie on your phone, and then watching the same movie in a movie theatre with surround sound, smell, and feel. The Life Library actually allows you to have a "dress rehearsal". Yes, you can actually get into a (simulated) body and feel what it will be like, from either "in body" or as an outside body observer. During these sessions, you are generally left alone to play as much as you want. So, just like clothes shopping, when you have found something you like, you will ask your friend (Guide) to come and have a look, but I doubt you would say *"does my bum look big in this?"* I may have mislead you by using the word "Library". This place is not a building as such, it appears as a huge, pink bubble of energy. Once inside, the walls turn into large screens where you can watch different lives, either one at a time, or several simultaneously. You float in the centre and can pause it, fast forward it and rewind it all by Will. I call this place a library because to me, that is what it is like. It has a massive catalogue of every possible scenario that one could experience in the Earth Plane.

## Location, location, location!

The first thing all souls look at first is the location. The country, the city, the village/suburb, right down to your potential house. The library will narrow down locations based on your Soul Age and requirements. As we have already seen, Infant Souls will choose rainforest and jungles for the most part, and Young Souls would prefer large cities and suburban sprawl. So to speed things up, only relevant information is displayed to each soul. The reason you look at location first, is because every society we live in, will imprint and condition you to a certain degree. A simple example is a sporting team. You may live in an area where everybody loves a particular sport and they all follow it with enthusiasm. Thus, it is natural if you have been brought up in that area, that you will also barrack for that team. The same can be said for religion, diet, health, etc.

Diet for example can have a huge influence. Suppose you incarnate into anyone of the current "first world" countries, that regularly enjoy a high fat and sugar diet. Now compare that to an Asian village in the mountains where 80% of their diet is fresh fruit and vegetables and meat is a rare treat for special occasions.

By living in a society that almost celebrates obesity, may lead you to become obese. This may be part of your plan, or it may not be. You may want to experience the many negative effects of being overweight, and that is great, as long as you deal with the lessons you want out of it. However, if that was not the goal of that life it will have a massive, negative outcome. It may cause you to become depressed, unhealthy and die early before you completed your goals. The depression will distract you from your primary task, whatever that may have been. Imagine if you decided to live a life as an elite athlete, that would one go on to be the inspiration to millions of children across the country. While you showed fantastic talent in pre-pubescent life, once you hit your teens, you start to live on a fast-food, junk diet and never end up realising your ambitions.

Cultural effects are just as strong, and often damaging, but they can also be incredibly subtle, to the point, that you may not even realise you were conditioned. On the other hand, some cultures can offer you a rich tapestry of experience over one that offers nothing but hardship. That is why it is so important in this life now, to regularly evaluate your goals, dreams and ambitions. There is a quote I like to remind myself and others of from time to time:

---

*"Love what you do and do what you love. Don't listen to anyone else who tells you not to do it. You do what you want, what you love. Imagination should be the centre of your life." (Ray Bradbury, an American fantasy, science fiction, horror and mystery fiction writer)*

---

I hope you can understand how critical this life selections can be. For that reason, many of the younger souls, including Mature Souls, will often return to countries or places they have lived before. But I also know many people, myself included, that have a special connection, or longing for a country, even if it may be on the other side of the world. A good friend of mine was raised in Australia like myself, but for some reason she developed a passion for Italy at about 10 years of age. She would study its culture, history, and eventually its language. She did not get to visit Italy until her mid-thirties, and the first thing she reported on her return was *"It felt like home"*. This is a perfect example of a soul that may have incarnated into lives in Italy for hundreds of lives, then for whatever reason, she selected a life on the other side of the world, yet she still felt the strong pull of her old country.

This very same scenario is also common for gender. Souls defiantly have a preference for gender. When a soul has had a series of disproportionate lives in for example, a female role, their Guides will encourage them to try a male role. Often, when they incarnate, and their security buttons get pushed, they revert back to their safety zone – of being feminine. This is the reason why some people have homosexual lives. But don't forget, that every soul will experience at least one or two lives as a homosexual or lesbian, purely because of the unique experience those lives offer. In the end, the Universe will always correct itself back into balance, so all soul end up with a 50/50 male to female lives. But for the most part, like I said, they have reverted back to familiar ground to make life a little easier, or at least to make sense! Of course, that is the crux of it all. You spend so much time in Spirit, working out every little detail about the life you are going to live. Then you get here, and you can't remember one, good reason why you chose it! That is why I often remind people when they ask *"Why would I choose this?"* and I reply: *"Yes, you have made the choice, and now you are trying to understand the question".* Maybe that is what life is all about – understanding why we made the choices we did before we got here.

No doubt, answering those questions with the Wise Mind, and not with the "Woe is Me" (victim) mentality will help tremendously. Just pause for one moment and try and think of something in your life you are not happy about, or what makes you feel sad, angry, frustrated etc. It could be your body, personality, friends, family members, your gender, your religion, your job – whatever.

Now, using the Wise Mind, try and think why your soul may have chosen that particular challenge. Once we can view the challenges in our life objectively, we can begin to address them in a positive way. Try and remember that your soul made these choices when it was still in a place of perfect knowledge, peace and harmony. So maybe now is not the time to second guess your soul's decisions, but instead, **accept and allow**. Lessons are taught to us in way of "challenges". How we deal with that challenge will determine whether or not we passed that particular lesson. Fail it now, and the Universe will, as per your instructions, deliver that lesson again, and again until you pass it. By the way, Souls are not influence by ethnicity or nationalism. These are human products of separation. Of course, the reason souls look at different lives is because each human body has a unique Ego.

## Ego – Is Not a Dirty Word!

The human part of your brain is the Ego or Self. It is the part of you responsible for survival. Therefore, depending on the situation, the Ego will respond according to its needs. For a Kalahari Bushmen, it is the Ego that tells the brain to RUN when it sees a lion coming. But it is the same Ego that treats women as little more than property. Soul Age has a lot to do with who controls the Ego – the Mind or the Soul. However, you still have to factor in the natural state of the Ego you incarnate into. It's like buying a car. If you are a new driver, it would not be wise to buy a Lamborghini super car! But Ego is not all bad. It can drive us to excel, and gives us the zeal to get up every day! The problem is that Egos come with their own set of filters. Yes, you have conditional filters that we spoke of before, but there are also non-conditioned filters people often view their world through. All filters are Fear based, no matter how trivial you may think they are.

So going back to the question from before, when I asked you to view a potential reason why you have a particular challenge in your life. If you can remove the [INSERT YOUR NAME HERE] filter, I can guarantee that it will not be a challenge for much longer. The main thing to remember about the Ego, is that it is not the real you! Indeed, at death, the Ego dies with the body. Only your everlasting Soul continues on its incredible journey of discovery.

## Money, money, money

Remember those filters and conditioning we spoke of earlier? Probably the single biggest one is money, or lack thereof. Money itself is not bad. It is like anything, it is your intent on how you use it. Imagine you wanted a life as a doctor, where you could help many people. It would make more sense to choose a life where you are born into a family, that has the means to support and encourage your dream to be a doctor. But wanting to be born into a rich family "just because", would be a complete waste of a life. Younger Souls often choose these lives thinking they will be easy. But as they discover, a rich person's life is just as limited, confusing, frustrating and unhappy as the next person. If you are not happy and balanced within yourself, no amount of money will ever fill that gap. So try not to see money as evil, and try not to see it as the be all and end all of your happiness. It is just a means to an end. The simple things come easy, when the best things in life are free. Wealth is a mindset. Remember, energy flows where attention goes. If you are always worrying about not having enough money, then the Universe will happily supply you with what your attention is focused on – no money.

On the other hand, be aware that we will always be given our needs, but rarely do we get our wants. A good way to make having little money a game, is to go to the market and see how many food items you can buy for $10. Each week, see if you can beat the previous total. Eventually, you will get a kick out of only having $10. You are never pre-destined to be poor. That is a limiting mindset your Ego imposes. If you don't think it is fair, then do something about it.

## Nothing is set in stone

While as souls we put a great deal of energy into planning every little detail of our lives, don't think for a minute that our lives are predestined and unchangeable. If that were the case, what would be the point? There would be no purpose or justice to our struggles.

What the whole purpose of incarnation is about is to practice Free Will. Challenges are really just opportunities for change. Granted, they often don't come at the best time, but we grow as a Soul depending on how we deal with those changes. If you want to go kicking and screaming, expect to come back life after life until you can accept change with Grace and Dignity.

We regularly get distracted from our Soul's plan. We may get back on track, or we may just make it up as we go. The plans we make before we are born, are made to give us the best opportunity possible to try and learn our lessons.

We are all born with amnesia. This is so our past lives don't influence the decisions we make in this life. That said, everyone has a complete set of blueprints for your current life stored in your subconscious mind, and the only way to get a peak in there is to meditate. More on that in Book III. If you have issues in your life right now, it is because you allow them.

## All Time is Now

I have mentioned many times that Time does not exist in the Spirit World. Now here is something that will really mess with your head. When you are selecting a new life, you have the benefit that past, present and future all exist now. Yes, you need to process that for a while. The reason is, you can incarnate into a different period in history that will be more conducive to your learning. For example, a life in colonial America would offer completely different experiences to a life in modern day America, even if it was in the same city or town. The same is for the future. Perhaps you want to help humanity with a technology that does not exists in our current timeline.

Imagine Louis Pasteur, the French chemist and microbiologists, remembered for his remarkable breakthroughs in the causes and preventions of diseases in the 1800's. His discoveries have saved countless lives ever since. What if he was born 200 years earlier? It is highly likely he would not have made his discoveries, because the required technology and know-how were not yet available. It's like the stories of the US government capturing alien spacecraft and not understanding even how to turn it on. We lack the technology to describe alien inventions that are years ahead of our own. The same can work in reverse – ancient technology that has been forgotten (hmmm, how did they build the pyramids?)

Therefore, it is important to incarnate in the correct time period. Just another point on the past, present future thing. The line we are all in now is just one example of this time line. Certain major events and inventions will happen on every time line, however certain events may not.

Adolf Hitler told a story about how In World War 1, he as a soldier on the Western front, got out of a trench after a battle. When he looked up it was just him, staring at a British soldier who was staring back. The British soldier was aiming his rifle directly at Hitler. Hitler accepted his fate and closed his eyes. But nothing happened. When he opened his eyes, the British soldier was walking away. Apparently he did not want to kill an unarmed man. Hitler says that it was at the moment, he realised he had been saved, because he was destined for greatness. People always ask, what would have happened if Hitler was killed in World War 1, maybe World War 2 would not have happened. I think it would have, or something like it, just with a different lunatic in charge. The point is, maybe in a different time line, Hitler was a nobody and Word War 2 never happened. Instead we became a space faring culture, and we all go to Mars for holidays now.

## Narrow it Down

By now, you should have come up with 3 or 4 potential locations, and bodies to incarnate into. You now find you are joined by your guides and the Spiritual Council. Remember those guys? They were the entities you spoke with on your return to Spirit. Well, turns out they are now here to help you choose the most suitable life.

It is also at this time you start to make "contracts" with other souls. These will eventually be your parents, siblings, lovers, best friends, bosses, work colleagues and "catalysts". The catalysts is a soul that will come into your life, often for only a brief time, to spur you into change and a new direction. These can be positive or negative changes (from your limited human point of view), but they were all set up before you got here. There are no accidents. People meet because they are destined to do so. Whether these encounters are short or long term does not limit their learning potential. My goodness, I can still hear some of you from here yelling "I chose my parents?? No way I did that!!!" Hahaha…yes, you did. So go back and ponder WHY you chose them.

By the way, you may have chosen a location, but the Spirit Council can only find you a suitable body in a town 200Kms (125 miles) away. This is common. Because our body choices are fairly specific, it is not always possible to find a body in the same place. It just means that in those contracts you made, may be one for your father to accept a job in the town you need to grow up in. Or maybe you don't need to go there, until you are an adult or at University. Again, these are part of all the little nuances that need to be worked out in advance.

Ultimately, you must factor in the Laws of Karma, that is, the cause and effects of all your choices will have on you, and on those around you. We do all strive to start a new life with Karma in balance. But ultimately, you ARE the architect of your own destiny. So if you have a complaint, go directly to the boss – you!

## Choosing Your New Body

Some souls will deliberately choose a body that is fit, healthy and robust. While others will more or less take what is on offer. The Spirit Council will come up with a group of potential bodies, and it is up to you, to choose the best one for your mission.

Souls that want deformed, crippled or brain damaged bodies usually request these specifically, well in advance. It may be they have a very unique lessons they want to learn, or they may be helping other souls to play the care role.

Children that die very young, under 2 or 3 years old, and even still births, nearly always come back in the very next child if it is possible. That was usually a lesson for the parents, not the soul in the child.

However, some cultures believe their ancestors reincarnate back into the same family or tribe. This is not the case as it would be counter-productive (effectively living the same experiences over and over).

You are generally given the best body they can find. So, it is more or less an even playing field when we are all born. However, it is the next 10 years, then teenage years, then young adult and finally adult, that will help mould and configure your present body. Some of the configuration is done by your culture, for example, an unrealistic expectation that all fashion models represent what all women are supposed to look like. This may lead to anorexia or bulimia. Then there is peer group pressure. You may choose to adorn it with body piercings and tattoos. You may abuse it by eating nothing but processed food, or you may treat it like a temple. Again, it is Free Will. However, the soul does not have absolute control over a body. Indeed, in extreme cases, like schizophrenia, conflicts will result in a dissociative reaction to reality. This is a sure sign that the soul is not always able to regulate and unify the human mind.

Admittedly you are reliant on your parents to give you a good, healthy start. But we know that is not always the case, so that is why now, as an adult, you must accept responsibility for your body. You cannot, and should not, use excuses your whole life. There is no excuse in the world for not changing right now. Only your mind needs to change, the rest will follow.

However, if we become obsessed by our physical body or get carried away with an emotional roller coaster in life, the soul can be undermined by its outer self. Like everything in life, it is all about balance. Souls search for self-expression, by developing different aspects of their character. Personality traits, such as extrovert or introvert, rationalistic or idealistic, emotional or annalistically dominated, are a by-product of the soul's 'spiritual energy'. This has nothing to do with soul age, but rather, the actual personality of the soul.

Ultimately, the Laws of Karma will prevail. If a soul chooses one extreme, somewhere down the line this will be counter-balanced by an opposite choice to even out development.

## All Disease is created in the Mind

Yes, you are not born with any diseases. God, the Universe, the Devil, your Guides, and ex-wife or husband – NONE of them are responsible for your health. When a soul 'plugs-in' to a body, it brings the Subtle Bodies I touched on earlier. They are the Mental body, and the Emotional body that join with the Physical body. Whenever you create an imbalance in any, or all of these bodies, the final manifestation is physical illness. You may argue that I have a genetic predisposition. Yes, but did you ever consider that you may have chosen to incarnate into that family specifically to show them that they do not have to live with that problem. Many people who are born with pre-dispositions, are told that their whole life until they believe it. If you believe it will happen, there is a good chance it will. However, most of us just get caught up in the Mind and Emotional dramas, so we get sick. Young people tend to burn the candle at both ends, so their physical body gets weak, which unbalances their Emotional, then Mental bodies. I would argue that there would be a huge drop in teenage angst stories if both parties were fit, healthy and got plenty of sleep! Pharmaceuticals and drugs are another big problem for the body to cope with. Just on this, how many times have you been sick with a flu? You feel terrible, then you finally drag yourself to the doctor. As soon as the doctor confirms that you do indeed have a virus, you automatically feel better. To the point you may even feel guilty that you were not that sick after all. The Mental Body has just got confirmation that something is really wrong, this triggers the Emotional Body to release feel good endorphins from the brain, and finally the Physical Body feels a little better, thanks to the endorphins. I will discuss the Subtle Bodies and their effect on health in more depth in Book III, however I mention it now because it does have a bearing on body selection.

## What Lessons Do I Want to Try This Time?

Your life lessons are your opportunity to share your wisdom, skills, creativity, talents, joy and love that you have gained in prior lifetimes, with others in order to be in service to Creation. We all have skills and knowledge we have learnt in prior lifetimes, even if we do not remember our past lives. Your soul has a record of all your past learning and experiences. The benefit to fulfilling your life purpose, is that it helps your soul advance. Indeed, the soul can only evolve through **Service-to-Others**. Souls that get stuck or flounder on a level, is because they get caught up in the **Service-to-Self** dilemma. Again, this is a by-product of the Fear mentality.

Some examples of a life In-Service-to–Others include a desire to help or heal others, to share any form of creativity, to bring joy, a wish to share your knowledge through teaching, writing, speaking or other means. The form these activities take is not important, it is your **intention** that counts. You do not need to be an expert in your field or licensed practitioner to teach or help. Informal teaching or helping is just fine. There are so many ways in which we can be of service. Even if you do not believe you are knowledgeable, there are always others who know less than you and can learn from you. In addition, through helping others, we learn what we are truly capable of. I find the best way to teach is to lead by example.

## Primary Soul Lessons

There are set of core lessons that every soul works through. These are your Primary Lessons. Think of them like a university degree, were you have set lessons that every student must master, then you have elective lessons that are unique to each student. You normally do not take on more than two Primary lessons in each life, purely because mastering one is hard enough, yet alone two! In fact, it is not unusual to see souls that choose just one, and then have to repeat that lesson over and over in many lives.

Primary lessons are the big issues, like communication (from the heart), unconditional love, trust, forgiveness, patience, generosity, acceptance, overcoming fear to name but a few. These are lesson that help you interact with all of humanity. Then there are the Personal Lessons, like learning self-love and discipline. Finally, there are Karmic Lessons that may just be something between you and another soul.

Your Primary soul lessons are what your soul incarnated on Earth to master. Your soul cannot evolve until it heals whatever is lacking in your understanding. You may recognise more than one lesson that you need to master, but there will be one primary one. You are sometimes challenged on a previous lesson you have learnt in a past life, just to keep you on your toes! Frustration, which I certainly succumb to, is created by the Ego – not a Lesson. In moments of frustration, try, try, try and breathe in, and say, "*I choose Love, I choose Love, I choose Love*".

To recognise your primary soul lesson, look back through your life and ask yourself, what have you learnt from your experiences and relationships? Do you see any repetitive patterns emerging, or the same issues coming up time and again?

Pay attention to when you blame others for the misfortunes and difficulties in your life. These are the lessons you came to learn and blaming others will not help you master your lesson, it will only prolong the inevitable. As you age, you may be able to recognise your primary lesson more quickly in new situations that arise. With this insight, you can now apply any learning from previous experiences to your current relationships. Almost universally, the main primary lesson that most souls have difficulty with, is Forgiveness. That is why I will often ask people to start with that one. Once you learn to forgive, the rest will come a lot easier. But don't try and kid yourself!

Often I hear people tell me that they have dealt with their anger or fear and believe they have mastered their soul lesson. Then in the next breath, they will complain about their domineering mother or partner. Even if they complain with a mild or even melancholy tone, there is still a deep, underlying anger that has not been dealt with. A simple way to test an undeniable truth, is ask tell yourself – "The sun is bright green!" You know this is not true, and you can laugh it off without any emotional charge. It is so absurd that it is not worth wasting any energy on, so you can shrug, have a giggle or smirk, then go about your business.

Now say, "I unconditionally love [insert person here – like mother, father, sister, brother, partner]". It is better if someone else asks you this question, because if you respond with an argument, or debate, or a pause, or anything other than the reaction you gave to "the sun is bright green" – then you still have a problem there!

Now ask, "[insert person here – like mother, father, sister, brother, partner] loves me unconditionally"

If this leaves a heaviness in your heart, or you don't really believe it, then that is ok. If that is how you honestly feel, then that is how you feel. So now you have confirmed there is an issue there, start planning how you could possible heal that relationship. It may just be that you have to accept, that they don't love you unconditionally. Once you realise, this is a limitation within themselves, then you can move on, and continue to send them Love. "The sun is bright green!"

Even if someone is abusive to you, you asked this person to play that exact role they are playing for your learning. From experiences of abuse, we learn to become strong, learn to say "no" and stand up for ourselves. If we did not experience abuse, we would not be motivated to learn these lessons. We all have relationships and experiences that we can learn from in our lives, so why not benefit from them and help your soul evolve.

If there is one thing you can be sure about, you will continue to meet your soul's primary lesson throughout your life, and if you do not master it completely, you will continue to face it through many future lifetimes until you master it. Most of the time, it is all about **SURRENDERING YOUR WILL.** If you can surrender your Will, then the battle is half over.

Whatever your primary lesson is, it will not change throughout your lifetime. You will discover that there will be many opportunities for you to master your lesson, as we do not become masters on our first attempt. Another thing you can do to increase your learning, is to ask what you can learn from every situation and person you meet. Remember, prior to incarnation, you made an agreement (contract) for these people to show up in your life, whether you remember this or not. You made this agreement with them, because these souls have the same lesson to learn as you do, but from an opposing perspective. Nothing happens by chance and there are no accidents, nor is there any co-incidences. By the way, a sure sign that you have mastered a primary lesson in a life will be that you are dead! I know those may come across as a bit harsh, however, there is no point continuing in a course if you have passed the final exam. Indeed, when someone dies suddenly, and unexpected, it usually indicates that they have finally mastered a lesson that they may have been struggling with for countless lives. Their soul would be so happy to have finally mastered the lesson that they would feel no ill will for dying so suddenly. For those left behind, we should feel at peace and happy for them, knowing that they have finally moved up and overcome a major stumbling block.

## The End is Near!

It does seem like a lot of hard work to plan a new life, find a body and decide on lessons, over and over again. However, I can assure you that the Spiritual Masters that oversee this stage in humanity's development are not indifferent to our cause. Indeed, they have been through the exact experience we are living now. It is not until the mass of souls, approximately 65% that we will stop the cycle of reincarnation as a whole. Once enough souls have graduated past the Old Soul level 7 stage and returned to their Over-Soul, then they will be able to 'pull' the rest of the souls up, and move to a higher level of existence. This is what the Ascension process is all about. For humans to naturally evolve to this level, may take about another 1,000,000 years. However, there are plans afoot that would see this process occur within 24 hours! I know you are getting sick of hearing this...but yep, I will be talking all about that in Book III.

## Do I know you?  Didn't we meet in the Spirit World?

You have made all of your arrangements, picked a body, time period, and location to incarnate into.    Now there is just one more, very important class to attend.   The Soul Mate recognition class!   You will attend a small class of about 10-20 souls, being conducted by a specialised Master Guide.   This Guide's speciality is Soul Mate Recognition.

There has been a myth created first in the New Age movement, which has now permeated the mainstream. That is, that Soul Mates are your perfect lover or partner. This is one potential role a Soul Mate can play, however it is not the only one. Each of the 10-20 souls present in the recognition class, are souls that will be incarnating at the same time as you.   Some of them are from your same soul group, but the majority are from other soul groups, and even other levels (higer or lower).   Each has chosen similar lessons to learn, either the same as yours, or from the opposite polarity of yours. For example, if you need to learn tolerance, then one of the other souls will incarnate with you to play the role of the antagonist. They will set up the situations that will allow you to learn tolerance.   Others could be your best friend (male or female), your business partner, teacher, major influence or husband/wife.

In order to know these people when you get to Earth, the Master Guide now gives you the clues to memorise. They may be a person's smile, their laugh, their hair, the way they talk, a pendant they wear. Smells and sounds are the easiest to remember.  There are hundreds of different types of clues.  Now it is up to you to remember then, so when you get to earth you will meet.  It is like cramming for a final exam.

## Do Souls Miss Clues On Earth?

All the time!  Yes, unfortunately souls get so distracted, and so caught up in the 'physical' world, that they do not trust their instinct.  A male friend of mine told me he was working in a shop as an assistant, and outside he saw a glimpse outside of a female, with burgundy/red hair.  He does not know why, but his pulse began to run, and he felt overwhelmed to meet this woman, and he had not even seen her face yet.    Luckily,  she  entered  the  store  and  he  immediately approached her.   When they looked into each other's eyes they locked.   Both knew there was a connection there, but could not explain it.   They went on to marry, have children and a wonderful life together. They have been married for 18 years.

Another not so nice story, is another young man I was once very close with.   He met a beautiful young lady on the Internet.   They conversed back and forth for over one year before they met.   This guy had been in a string of going nowhere relationships for years, so when he met X, he thought his "looking for the one" was over. She was the first woman he could talk to for hours and hours, about nothing in particular.   He was also part of an elite sporting team, so going to the gym and keeping fit were very important to him.   When they finally met, they hit it off famously.  He even introduced her to his family.   When she had to return home they were both teary and it was hard to let go.  I was very happy for him and said *"So I guess this is the one"*. He looked away and looking at the ground said, "No, I don't think so". I was shocked.   What had changed his mind?   Basically, X was very beautiful (especially her personality), but she carried a few extra pounds, mainly around the hips and buttocks.  In his world ruled by "beautiful people" i.e. Sports stars and fashion models, this was not acceptable.   Many people in his family and friends begged him to reconsider.   He did not.   The short story is he broke it off (she was devastated) and he consumed his guilt with alcohol and drugs.   He then went on a sexual binge for years, having casual sex with less than reputable women.  He retired from sport, because he could no longer keep up.  He developed a big beer belly, and now has no one, which further exacerbates his drug and alcohol problems.   This is classic example of a soul who turned his back on a Soul Mate.  But this same guy has other Soul Mates he did connect with.  His business partner, who has supported him through highs and lows.  His best friend from his sport team, that stuck by him all these years.  It seems he had no problem with male Soul Mates.

The secret to finding love, is to first love yourself. Then stop looking, because it will find you.

Believe it or not, that story is not particularly unusual.  Younger souls always have difficulty reconciling their heart (soul) and their mind (ego).  Their mind will nearly always call the shots.  This goes on until the Mature Soul phase.

## Time for Departure

Once the class is finished you will probably have a little going away party with your soul group. After this, with just your Guide, you will make your way to the Area of Departures, like the departure lounge at an airport. Your Guide will give you some last minute advice, and you begin to gather your thoughts. This is your last chance to experience unconditional love, peace and knowledge...it is time.

You feel yourself begin to move away. Down, sliding down, down you speed, getting faster and faster. Your Guide is no longer holding your hand, but you can feel their presence just behind you. Faster, faster, down, down you travel, through thick white clouds and silky shining light...then, nothing. Stop. Dark, cold...now warmth. You are in your mother's womb.

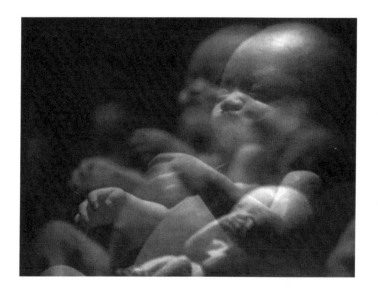

# 12

## PLUGGING IN THE SOUL

*"So we grew together like to a double cherry,
seeming parted, but yet an union in partition,
two lovely berries moulded on one stem." (William
Shakespeare, A Midsummer Night's Dream*

**Y**OU JUST WENT through a dark tunnel, but it was not your mother's birth canal. It was the gateway between Earth and the Spirit World. It is much quicker coming from Spirit to Earth than it is to leave. That is only because when you leave Earth, you are dazed and confused, so they need to take it slower so you have a chance to figure out what is going on.

Now it is time to integrate your Soul with your new body. This can be a slow and complex task, depending on your Soul age. For younger souls (under Mature level), the task can be a little daunting, so they will have their Guides on hand. But for Older Souls, it is like riding a bike. They have literally done this thousands of times, so they get pretty efficient at it. In fact, I have heard of some cheeky Old

Souls that jump into the body as it is coming out of the mother! Now that is some slick timing, and amazing skill. But for the normal souls, the process goes like this:

## Plugging in the Soul

First of all, the soul must enter the body. It does this via the **Pineal Gland**, situated in the middle of the brain. Once in, it has to send out thousands of little feelers, like vines, growing out to every direction, millimetre, by millimeter of the brain and nervous system. The soul must map the brain and nervous system in exact detail. It is creating a spiritual analogue, or exact copy. For less experienced souls, this process can take up to 6 months. However, once it has mapped about 25%, it can start to probe the mind of the child.

Remember back when we spoke about each body has a different Ego? This is when it counts that you picked one that you can deal with. If an Ego is too strong or aggressive, the Soul will not be able to join with it. The Ego will block, and push away the Soul trying to enter. But this is not an alien take over. There is a part of the human brain that is empty, ready to accept a soul. Indeed, the Soul brings a great deal of positive attributes to the Mind and body.

Some human babies will resist the probing purely from fear, so a Guide may have to come in and assist. They calm the child's mind, and take it very, very slowly. It is an extremely gentle process, and there is no stress to the child what so ever. The more advanced a soul is, the easier it is to make the connection with the human mind. The average soul completes Soul/Mind conection at about 30 weeks into pregnancy.

Once the Soul/Mind union is completed, the Soul will go back to mapping the rest of the brain and nervous system. Once the mapping is complete, the spiritual "vines" now sprout little connectors that enter the nerves and neurons in the brain. Once the Soul is completely connected to the nervous system, it downloads and installs the Subtle Bodies – Mental and Emotional from its Higher Self. The Soul must now use the child's own internal body energy to boot up, or turn on the Subtle Bodies.

The Soul must map the body systems accurately so as it can gain control over the human body. Indeed, there are times when the Ego is controlling the body, as in arms, legs and talking, and other times when the Soul is running things. Older Souls get to control the body almost all of the time, where younger, less experienced souls, get religated to the back seat. So the mapping process is a means to wire the Soul in, so it can drive the body, so to speak!

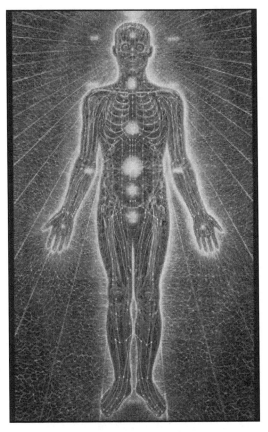

*Figure 6*

## The Chakra System

There are 7 energy centres positioned throughout the human body, that spin when activated. Each is attuned to a different frequency and help to regulate different areas of health and well-being. In Figure 6, you can see the 7 Chakras and the Soul map of the brain and nervous system. The Chakras protrude from the front and back by about 30-60cm (11-23 inches), and are coloured from the bottom and moving up as: Base (Red); Sacral (Orange); Solar Plexus (Yellow); Heart (Green); Throat (Blue); Third-Eye (Indigo); and Crown (Violet). At this stage in the unborn child, the Chakra System is on, but not fully charged. The fact is, the nervous system, including the brain, is made up of billions of interlinked neurons. This vast interconnected

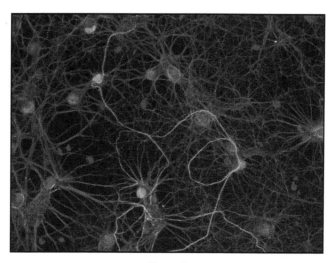

*Figure 7*

web is responsible for all human thinking, feeling, and behaviour (Fig. 7). If the Chakras were switched on at this point, it could literally fry the nervous system. The child's brain and nervous system is not strong enough yet to handle the full Chakra system load, nor does it have the required energy/power anyway. You see, the Charkas are powered directly from the brain and nervous system. Later in life, when you can successfully meditate, you can power them via connecting to Spirit Energy (prana). Imagine this is like adding solar panels to your house. It won't work when it's cloudy. In Book III, we will discus how you can turn your Pineal Gland into a WiFi connector, and download information and prana wirelessly!

But as I was saying, the Soul does not fire up the Chakras to full capacity until the body is around 6 years old (Fig. 8). There are two other Chakras – one above the head (about 60cm / 23 inches) which serves as an antenna back to spirit, and one below the feet (about 1 meter / 40 inches), which acts as an anchor to the Earth. There are also minor Chakras in the palms of the hands, feet and over major organs.   No other creature in the Third Dimension (3D) Creation has a Chakra system so advanced. This is something unique to humans.   Animals have basic auras, the energy field created by all living things, however, they do not have a Chakra system as such.   That is because the consciousness in animals does not have the experience or know how yet to wire up a full chakra system. It is a bit like an apprentice electrician. They do not have the skills yet to wire a whole building on their own, particularly if there were billions of cables to run and connect.

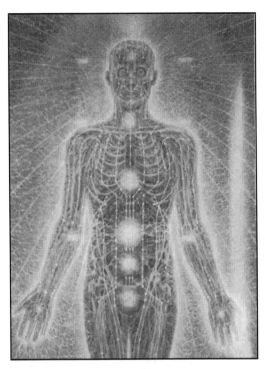

That is why Spirit gave humanity Reiki – hands on healing, so we could heal animals and children under 6 who do not have functioning Chakra systems.

Acupuncture also works on the energy lines that the Soul has laid down over the nervous system. That is why they can unblock energy and get it flowing again.

In the early days, humans walked around with a fully visible Aura, and just visible Chakras. When they got excited or happy they would glow more. When they were sad, or ill, they

*Figure 8*

would almost disappear. Eventually, due to the Separation Experiment which we will discuss in Chapter 14, the ability to naturally show your Aura was lost. However, not before the last section around the head disappeared. That is why "holy" people were always painted with halos around their heads. I will discuss Chakras and Auras in full details in Book III.

Getting back to the soul coming into the new body. Even though the soul is busy with integrating with the body, it still has time to spare. Most souls will leave the body and go and seek out their friends (from their Soul Group) who have also incarnated. They get together to play or just chat. Older Souls use the time to explore parts of the Earth, or observe the family it is about to become a member of. If something happens to the child, the soul is zapped straight back in a heartbeat. That is because now, the soul is tethered to the body. Whenever they travel outside of the body, they are connected by a thin, silver chord. Again, it is connected via the Pineal Gland. When souls duck out for 5, they are still on the Earth Plane. In other words, they are not going back to Spirit or even the Astral Plane.

By the time the child is born, the soul is fully integrated. The shock that comes to the child from the birthing process is the trigger to wipe the memory of both the Soul, and the child. Full memory loss is not always achieved at this point. Particularly in Old Souls that will deliberately try and fight the amnesia. Not because they want to know what will happen in the new life, but because they do not want to forget the Spiritual knowledge they hope to impart to humanity. Regardless, at some point full amnesia kicks in.

I am sure you have heard stories about a child who has an "invisible" friend. Or the baby that starts to giggle when it is in a room by itself. These are interactions with their Spirit Guides. Babies and children can still see Spirit because they are not long out of Spirit. However, as the amnesia sets in, or the child is berated for "making up lies" about invisible friends, or they are constantly told by adults that "there is no such thing", they will eventually lose the ability to see their Guides.

Hopefully now, you can see that during the whole 9 months, and the birthing procedure, everything was taken care of for you. So, why now do you doubt that everything else is not been taking care of for you?

---

*"Wisdom is nothing more than the marriage of intelligence and compassion. And, as with all good unions, it takes much experience and time to reach its widest potential."* (Vera Nazarian)

---

### References:

Fig. 7: Source: Photo courtesy of GE Healthcare,
   http://www.flickr.com/photos/gehealthcare/4253587827/

# PART
# 2

## BACK ON EARTH

---

*"A well-ordered life is like climbing a tower;
the view halfway up is better than the view from
the base, and it steadily becomes finer as
the horizon expands". (William Lyon Phelps).*

---

### Congratulations!

If you have made it this far, then you now have a firm understanding of what Soul's and the Spirit World are all about. Part 2 has got to do with the physical side of things, and where humans came from, and how we fit into the Universe.

It is no accident you are reading this material. Your Soul wants to learn and grow, so thank you for listening, now, let's give it what it wants!

# KARMA

## HOW PEOPLE TREAT
## YOU IS THIER KARMA
## HOW YOU REACT IS
## YOUR KARMA

WAYNE DYER

# 13

## LET THERE BE THOUGHT

*"The Creator, at a certain point in its evolution, said:
I want to explore everything; I want to learn;
I want to grow; I want to understand everything."
(The Master Vywamus via by Janet McClure, 1996)*

SCIENCE, RELIGION AND folklore have all at one time or another strived to explain the Creation and evolution of the Universe. Each has based its assertions on man-made laws and dogma, but none have to this time managed to give a definitive explanation to this query. In fact, it seems these schools of thought have resigned to putting forward a vague, at best, general assumption of what they believe to be the nearest they can get to the truth. Therefore, this chapter will endeavour to explain the true meaning and depths of our Creation as told by Spirit. For some this may be old news, for indeed this knowledge has been widely available throughout the esoteric schools for millennia. However it should be remembered that this Higher Spiritual Knowledge has not been available to the general populous and thus, given this crucial time in our evolution, it is time to change the balance.

## All That Is

Creation refers to the construction and implementation of all that is. It includes the planets, solar systems, galaxies, universes, all dimensions, all life and all physical matter – down to the smallest atom and to our very Souls. So far, humans have come up with two main explanations to account for the creation of all that is. Science argues that all matter is the result of a 'Big Bang' which led to 'Evolution' and religion claims that 'God' created the Universe in six days branding this school of thought 'Creationism'.

So began the great debate between Evolutionists and Creationists. To fully understand the shortcomings of both these theories we must first examine each in a little more detail. Oddly enough, both of these ideas once shared a common root.

## Cosmology

The word Cosmology comes from the Greek κόσμος, kosmos meaning 'universe' and -λογία, -logia meaning 'study of'. It is the study of the Universe and all that is and humanity's place in it. The word cosmology is relatively recent, being first used in 1730 by Christian Wolff in *Cosmologia Generalis*. However the study of the Universe has a long history involving science, philosophy, esotericism and religion. The first recognised cosmological theory is *Brahmanda* from the Hindu *Rigveda* (1500-1200 B.C.). Rigveda is part of the ancient sacred texts of Hinduism known as the Vedas. Brahmanda states that the Universe is cyclical or oscillating and infinite in time. They believe that the universe is a cosmic egg that cycles between expansion and total collapse. It expanded from a concentrated form — a point called Bindu. The universe, as a living entity, is bound to the perpetual cycle of birth, death and rebirth.

Cosmology predates modern physics, however, in recent times physics and astrophysics have come to play a central role in shaping the understanding of the universe through scientific observation and experiment; or what is known as physical cosmology shaped through both mathematics and observation in the analysis of the whole universe. In other words, in this discipline, Cosmologists propose that the history of the Universe has been governed entirely by physical laws (Singh, 2005).

## Young Earth Creationists

Young Earth Creationism (YEC) is the religious belief that the Universe, Earth and all life on Earth was created by the Abrahamic God of the Bible and Jewish Torah during a very short period, sometime around 6000 years ago. Its primary adherents are those Christians and Jews who believe that God created the Earth in six 24-hour days, using a literal interpretation of the Genesis creation narrative as a basis.

YEC is described by themselves as *"an endeavour that holds that the events associated with supernatural creation can be evidenced and modelled through an interpretation of the scientific method"*, however, the consensus among scientists, is that creation science is unscientific, in both conception and methodology.

Since 1982, between 40% and 50% of adults in the United States say they hold the creationist view that *"God created humans in their present form at one time within the last 10,000 years"*, when Gallup asked for their views on the origin and development of human beings. As of 2012, the percentage of believers decreases as the level of higher education increases. Only 25% of respondents with postgraduate degrees believed compared with 52% of those with a high school education or less. A 2011 Gallup survey reports that 30% of U.S. adults interpret the Bible literally.

YEC's latest attempt to legitimise the Young Earth theory was something called *"Intelligent Design"*. That is, the Universe was 'obviously' intelligently designed, so the designer must have been God. Suffice it to say, it had just as many shortcomings as the young Earth Theory.

For a very funny, but factual look at YECs I highly recommend going on YouTube and looking up Phil Mason's (AKA Thunderf00t) *"Why Do People Laugh at Creationists"* series.

## Unification

The Creation Process that Spirit speaks of, goes beyond the heavy physical matter we associate with. Indeed, Creation can be broken down into three main areas: Mental, Physical and Spiritual. The initial stage is Thought. This is the stage of planning. The second stage is the manifestation of thought into solid matter - Physical. Finally, the third stage is concerned with what is termed 'Life-force'. Life-force is the 'spark' that gives life to otherwise inanimate objects. When Life-force is mixed with created matter it allows a once inanimate object to come 'alive', and through interaction, evolve, thus contributing to the creative process.

As stated, all Creation is a direct result of pure thought. That is, only through the application of pure thought-energy can anything come into Creation. Without the initial thought form, nothing could or would exist. You can view this concept in your own life. For example: if you were to build a new garden in your backyard, you would first need to conceptualise the garden in your mind (Thought). Next you would manifest this concept into physical matter in the way of a plan, or drawing (Physical). Finally, you would plant your garden and nurture it to bloom, completing the cycle of Creation (Spirit). And so it is with everything in the Universe – first we must conceptualise – then we must plan - and finally we can create. In its purest form, Thought is a force or power that precedes all creative manifestation no matter what level it is on. Thus, it follows that the organization of this Thought force in our Universe is that which we call our Prime Creator – also known as God. God is in fact the Source of All That Is - the original Thought Force. Thus from this point on it would be more appropriate to refer to the Prime Creator as The Source.

The Source came into existence within the Void, which is incomprehensible to us. We as humans, with human thinking, find it difficult to conceptualise the nature of the Source whilst we are trapped in our 3rd Dimensional logic. Furthermore, our dense physical brains lack the psychological and physiological means to contemplate such a concept.

For example, in the 3rd Dimension we know everything to have a definite starting point, and finishing point. We know we are born as babies and grow old, eventually dying, completing that cycle. This concept is easy for us to understand as we can relate it to many things in our everyday life.

However, when we try and contemplate a much higher dimensional truth we cannot. For instance, try to imagine a colour that does not exist. It is impossible to do so in a 3rd Dimensional mindset. Automatically you try and visualise something you can compare to something you already know. This is how the 3rd Dimensional mind works – we can only understand something by comparing it to something we are already familiar with. Higher thinking though tells us that the Source is not a 3rd Dimensional being and thus it is not bound by the laws and physics of this plane. So in view of this higher thinking, we can start to understand that the Source has no beginning or end – it just IS. Of course, the moral of this story is to not allow ourselves to be trapped in the boundaries of the 3rd Dimension. True knowledge comes by traversing all levels of Creation – not just the level you are manifest in.

To extrapolate the Source even further, it is very likely that the Source we attribute with Creation in our Universe is in fact part of a larger surrounding Cosmos or Cosmic Entity. As we will investigate, ours is not the only Universe in existence.

## The Creation Process

In the beginning of Creation the Source projected its Thought-force out into the Great Void. This Thought-Force in turn created a vast expanding matrix with which the Source surrounds itself.

By stepping-down the frequency of the original Thought-force, the Source then energised these matrices with Light. This Light-force energy could then be further lowered in frequency for the Creation of more solid matter, which became the network of expanding Worlds of Matter (dimensions).

Finally, into these newly created worlds of matter, the Source projected elements of Its own being. These elements were in the form of Consciousness, which would themselves grow and evolve outside of the Source, adding a Spiritual ("alive") aspect to the worlds of Created Matter. Through the individual Spirits, multiple interactions and experiences of life in the Worlds of Matter, they would greatly grow in knowledge and awareness. The Spirits' or Souls' evolving consciousness and experience could then be added to that of the Source's own continuously evolving consciousness, allowing the Source to expand into yet an even greater Entity.

## Stage 1 – Thought (Mental)

Before the Source could begin the first stage of Creation , it had to first establish what is known in esoteric teachings as the *Ring-Pass-Not*. The Ring-Pass-Not can be viewed as an encircling barrier of limitation (Fig. 9). Without the barrier of limitation, the Thought force projected by the Source would have dissipated and been lost in the surrounding Void. Indeed, if the Thought-Force energy would have been lost in

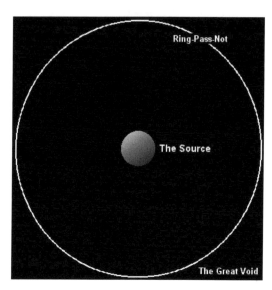

*Figure 9*

the vastness, then no effective Creation would have been possible. It is the constant outward projection of the Source's Thought energy against the Ring-Pass-Not that creates a continuing cycle of outgoing and returning Thought energy.

This flow manifests as a wave of rapidly alternating energy with a positive-negative vibratory frequency. To illustrate this concept, imagine you are standing in a perfectly circular swimming pool. As you move your arms, waves are sent outward to the edge of the pool. If these waves are strong enough they will hit the pool's edge and then bounce back to you. If you were to continue this motion, eventually the water would appear to bob up and down where the outward and returning waves intercept. In fact, you wouldn't really see the water moving outward any more, you would just see the waves bobbing up and down on the spot.

This is the driving force behind our known Creation. ALL life and matter within all levels of our Creation vibrates to a particular frequency or responds to a specific vibration rate. Generally speaking, the denser the matter, the lower the vibrational rate, and the lighter the matter, the higher the frequency. This is why beings that vibrate at a frequency, higher than our own, appear translucent, ghost like or are invisible all together. The Positive and Negative polarities which exist in every faction of Creation are a direct result of the outgoing and returning energy of the Creator's Thought-Force. These positive and negative energies are the very basis of all matter. The Positive and Negative polarities are the basic components of all Creation, thus everything within Creation manifests within this duality of energy. We can view these two energies as opposing forces; however, in reality, the Negative force acts as a 'friction block' against which the Positive force can become manifest as Matter.

## Stage 2 – Matter (Physical)

The second stage of Creation is concerned with the manifestation of Thought into Matter. This is achieved by the interaction of the outgoing and incoming vibrating Thought waves. By now, these energies have slowed down by their to-and-fro movement to the point that they are now vibrating at the frequency of light. It is at this point where these two opposing forces meet each other, that Matter is made manifest. As the two forces cross over, friction is generated. This friction leads to a 'locking up' of energy at this point. The movement of these energy waves is effectively neutralised at this time. This 'locked-up' force then allows, through a combination of attraction and repulsion, the build-up of material (matter) known to us as atoms.

It is the nature of atoms to attract other atoms. The atoms establish 'lock-up' orbits of magnetic attraction and repulsion. This in turn attracts more atoms, causing the matter to increase in size and density and the process continues to build upon itself. It is this basic 'building block' process of atoms which is responsible for all the solid material worlds around us.

As this process continues there is an ever-increasing density and complexity of matter, resulting in the matter moving further and further from the Source. The distance from the Source determines the vibratory rate and density of matter. Moreover, as the energy extends further and further from the Source, the vibration rates become slower and denser.

In order to understand the nature of these vibration rates, imagine 3 concentric circles between the Source Centre and the Ring-Pass-Not (Fig. 10). These 3 circles represent the 3 major vibration or density levels of Creation. The first is referred to as the Spiritual Plane, which is located nearest to the centre or Source. The next is known as the Etheric Plane and finally the farthest and densest is the Physical Plane. It is on the Physical Plane – the plane furthest from the Source, and thus the densest - that matter builds up to an incredibly tight ball or

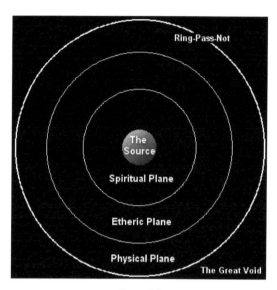

*Figure 10*

"egg" of matter. This "Cosmic Egg" becomes so dense and so hot it explodes! Science calls this the "Big Bang".

## When Something Went BANG!

The origins of the theory came from a Belgian priest named Georges Lemaître. He first suggested the big bang theory in the 1920s when he theorised that the universe began from a single primordial atom. He first called it a "Cosmic Egg", but later changed it to the Big Bang. He observed that other galaxies were moving away from our own at great speed, in all directions, as if they had all been propelled by an ancient explosive force.

Before the Big Bang, scientists believe, the entire vastness of the observable universe, including all of its matter and radiation, was compressed into a hot, dense mass just a few millimetres across. This nearly incomprehensible state is theorised to have existed for just a fraction of the first second of time. The theory contends that it probably happened about 13.73 billion years ago, because that's how old the oldest stars are and they think that stars began to form almost immediately after the Big Bang.

When the Big Bang happened, it let loose a huge amount of energy in an instant. The energy expanded at the speed of light, from its pin-head size origin to astronomical scope. Expansion has apparently continued, but much more slowly, over the ensuing billions of years.

Inside the Universe, the energy (in the form of photons (light) and bosons) went zipping around like crazy all over the place. But at some point, the first hydrogen atoms were formed. Once there were clouds of these hydrogen atoms floating around together, they formed nebulas, which were the birthing grounds for the first stars (Singh, 2005).

The Big Bang theory leaves several major questions unanswered. One is the original cause of the Big Bang itself. I remember asking that question the first time I heard about the Big Bang in about Year 10 science class. Several answers have been proposed to address this fundamental question, but none has been proven. Another issue that has plagued Astronomers from day one is known as the "Horizon Problem". The Horizon Problem states that the Universe has basically the same temperature, density and other properties in every direction you look. Technically, there has not been enough time for areas far away from each other to become the same. However, an explanation for this problem came about in the early 1980s.

Alan Guth argued that inflation was the answer. Inflation says the universe underwent a brief period of rapid accelerated expansion very early in its history. Inflation accounts for the observed likeness of regions within the universe, as well as the flat geometry of the universe (a separate issue). Although the Inflation Theory is not without its own set of problems, it continues to be, overwhelmingly, the best scientific explanation for the beginning of the universe (Greene, 2010).

## Spirit Answers

Alan Guth was close, but no cigar! Prior to the Big Bang, everything in the primordial mass was 'raw' and unconditioned by the Laws of Physics. Therefore, at the time of the explosion, light could travel faster than the speed of light. (Science says nothing can travel faster than the speed of light – thus the Horizon Problem).

A trillion-trillionth of a second after the Big Bang, some matter went flying off faster than light to the far flung reaches of the Universe. As the explosion died down, so did the speed of the matter. The matter that went speeding off was super-heated by the time it stopped due to friction. That meant that it started to cool at around the same time as the matter that was closer to the centre. Therefore, everything cooled at almost the same time. The 3rd Dimension is long and thin. That is why the Universe became finished with a flat geometry.

Imagine exploding something in a pipe. The explosion will shoot out the ends, but the top and bottom are flat.

Another anomaly of the Big Bang is Dark Matter. Visible matter is all the things we can see - stars, galaxies, planets etc. It is thought to comprise only 4% of the Universe's energy. Approximately 23% is dark matter and the remaining 73% is thought to be Dark Matter's even more enigmatic cousin, Dark Energy (Greene, 2010).

It is important to understand just how much Dark Matter and Energy makes up the known Universe. Dark Matter is the raw, unconditioned matter. As Dark Matter began to leave the centre of the explosion, it was the heat and light generated by Big Bang that Dark Matter reacted with. When a certain amount of heat and a certain amount of light hit a piece of Dark Matter, it caused a reaction. The Dark Matter was transformed into one of the elements on the periodic table. So matter that travelled very quickly away from the centre became element 'Y' and matter that left last and was closest to the centre became element 'Z' and so on and so on. However the majority of the Dark Matter was not transformed at all. Imagine a ball of rice. All the rice grains on the outside will be affected by a flame, but the grains in the middle of the ball remain unaffected.

Dark Energy is the 'glue' of the Universe. It is what holds everything together. However, if you could tear a hole in Dark Energy then you would create a worm-hole. A worm-hole in space allows you to travel vast distances within the blink of an eye. Imagine you had a piece of paper and drew a small circle on one edge (Point of origin) and another circle on the opposite edge (Destination). Now fold the paper to so the two circles line up and touch. This is how a worm-hole works. But instead of folding paper, it folds Space!

Scientist have currently discovered or synthesized 118 elements. There are many more that cannot be discovered yet, due to inadequate technology. However, it is possible to create any element you desire. If you experiment and calculate the heat/light ratio required to produce gold for example, then all you need is some Dark Matter. It really is that simple. It comes down to a calculation. If I expose this bit of Dark Matter to 'X' light and 'Y' heat I can produce 'Z'. Unfortunately, science does not have the technology at the moment to harness Dark Matter. But ancient Alchemist did. We have all heard about how they changed base metals to gold.

A few seconds after the Big Bang every Law of Physics and every element was created and set in stone right? No. This is a human thinking constraint. Just like the rules of a computer some can be bent and some can be broken. Even now, the Speed of Light is not the speed limit science thinks it is. Remember, Thought is the fastest and most powerful energy in the Universe. Light is a step down in frequency. So if Thought is faster than Light, that should give you some idea about how ETs power their craft.

This process has been explained to you, so as you can realise that Creation is not some 'magical' event nor is it the result of some clumsy and random 'big bang'. It is a process based on simple principles that can be incorporated into your own life to 'create' and bring about change.

## Planes of Creation

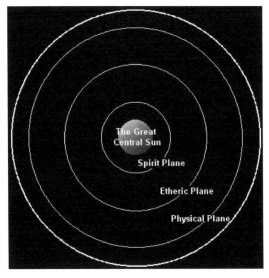

*Figure 11*

## The Spiritual Plane

The Spiritual Plane is the first level of the Creator's Thought-Force (Fig. 11). It is at this plane that the original Thought-Force is lowered into a denser vibratory rate and it becomes the energy known as Pure Light. Even though this level is vibrating at a slower frequency than that of Thought, it is still at a very high spiritual level and thus is expressed as a golden-white luminance. This luminance can be viewed emanating directly from the Thought Centre (which is the Source). It is the only object visible on all dimensions/levels. We refer to the Source's incandescence as the Great Central Sun of our known

Cosmos. This is the Plane that all Souls transcend to at the moment of death - this is home! This is the area we spoke about in Chapter 1.

## The Etheric Plane

Spiralling further down in vibration and complexity is the Etheric Plane. The Etheric Plane contains those levels referred to as the Astral Planes. Etheric energies are able to inter mingle, inter act, observe and interpret our own physical matter. We can view the Etheric Plane as the halfway point between the Spirit Plane and the dense Physical Plane. It is through the Etheric Plane that we are able to communicate and interact with Spirit. Occult scientists refer to the energy of this plane as the Ether. Ether has at times been made manifest in a physical form called *Ectoplasm*.

The lower levels of the Etheric Plane are an exact mirror image of the Physical Plane. It was from this mirror image that the original template for the Physical Plane came into existence. Once it was created on Etheric Plane, it was lowered in vibration further to what we now know as the Physical Plane.

## The Physical Plane

The 3rd Dimension is our perception of the lowest density plane called the Physical Plane. The Physical Plane contains the most solid matter of the planes of Creation we have discussed up to now. This apparent solid state of matter allows the best 'training ground' available throughout Creation. It is on this plane that souls are able to experience the very depths of the Creation process, thus enabling these souls to learn at a more advanced rate than is achievable on any other plane of existence. Planet Earth is the best known of these 'training-grounds' through which one may experience the necessary lessons to accelerate Spiritual Evolution, however it is not the only 3rd dimensional planet that is inhabited. This is the lowest plane consciousness has been birthed into and therefore, it is unlikely that any form of life/consciousness exists on the plane below the physical.

The Creation of Matter exists due to the cycles of Pure Thought moving back and forth at varying rates of vibration and density. The further these waves move from the Source, the denser they become and then manifest into matter, creating the different levels of Creation we have discussed. This simple process of outward Thought cycles moving back and forth is repeated many, many times over.

## Beyond the Physical Plane

The discussion so far has focused on the Planes of Creation involved in the descent of Thought through to the Physical Plane. There is however a Plane that goes beyond the physical. In all honesty I have not been given very much insight into this Plane, as it is not particularly pertinent to Humans at this time. All I can say is that this is the lowest plane the Source Created in Its original scheme. This Plane is what is referred to as the 2nd Dimension. Contrary to popular belief, Black Holes are not vortices to other Universes, but rather, they are doorways to the 2nd Dimension. Since a Black hole is capable of bending and distorting light, it would seem unlikely that any form of life or consciousness could exist on this Plane.

## The Great Central Sun

*Figure 12*

The Great Central Sun (Fig. 12) is the central focus of all Creation in this Cosmos. It is from the Great Central Sun that all Pure-Thought emanates. It does this by radiating an intense Light force throughout the Cosmos. There are at least 12 Universes that orbit the Great Central Sun. Each of these Universes in turn has its own Central Sun, around which orbit further systems of galaxies. Again, each galaxy contains its own Central Sun around which solar systems and planets orbit. Be it Cosmos, Universe, Galaxy or Solar System, each of these is governed by the same simple system of varying planes of density. These Central Suns become the central focal points of intersecting Thought energy. This allows different levels to offer different degrees of learning and experience, as each Central Sun amplifies the Thought of that particular system.

If you take your mind back to Chapter 1 (*"Eventually the Super Soul is assimilated back into the Source (God) and all of the information that has been accumulated over the eons is downloaded and shared."*) The information is shared via the Great Central Sun. We can see this process in our own recent history. In the late 19th century there was a great spiritual revolution. Indeed, during this period many people rose to prominence including Madam Blavatsky and Rudolf Steiner. Séances, ouija boards and Mediums were everywhere. In fact, at its height it was considered 'trendy' to hold a séance at dinner parties (as entertainment). Once it was taken up by the mainstream like this and reduced to parlour games, it declined. But those true pioneers eventually died and returned to Spirit. All of their combined knowledge and experience was assimilated, downloaded and shared via the Great Central Sun. Thus, the end of the 1960's and early 1970's, there was a new spiritual revival. The same process repeated. So it was, by the 1980's we began to see 'New Age' shops, crystal shops and esoteric book shops pop up everywhere.

Mediation circles became all the rage as did 'Spiritualist' churches. Into the 1990's it had gone mainstream and re-branded 'Mind-Body-Spirit'. There are now Mind-Body-Spirit fairs and expos lasting 3-5 days at a time, held regularly on the social calendar. What is interesting is that in the 1970's the average (God fearing) person would not even consider going for a Tarot reading. This type of occult practice was deemed the work of the devil! Now I walk down the street and see signs out the front of coffee shops advertising Tarot reading available! It is not uncommon to see business men and house-wives lining up for a reading – my how times have changed.

That is because of all the Souls that lived through the 1800's, 1960's and 1980's spiritual revivals. They learnt new insights before dying and returning to Spirit. They shared the information, thus, those still on Earth were showered by the new energy from the Sun (via the Great Central Suns) and consciousness in humans on Earth changed. There are literally hundreds of examples through history where humanity has undergone massive consciousness shifts via this method. The Renaissance, the emancipation of slaves and the Industrial Revolution to name but a few. It is literally a snowball effect. Each wave of incarnations brings/receives the knowledge of previous souls. The time frame between each resurgence is less and less, and the knowledge and awareness is increased exponentially.

Using our own Solar system to illustrate, our Sun is the Central focal point for our Solar System with an individual and unique consciousness, as do all of the planetary bodies surrounding it. Whilst we are governed by the Great Central Sun of our Universe to "do no harm" (a Universal Law), locally our Sun attempts to influence all life on Earth to care for our planet. This is a (local) Solar System Law that has no real relevance to life in distant star systems. The Great Central Sun radiates one particular Thought for all that resides in this Universe and dimension and our Sun is concerned with the local inhabitants of this Solar system. On a human level, we can compare it with our own earthly governmental systems. For example, a federal government is responsible for the wellbeing of the 'whole' nation. A state government will then set out laws and regulations best suited for that state's environment. Finally, a local council will regulate its population via unique rules that pertain to that local area. The main and obvious reason for this system is that some laws pertain to all, whereas some laws only have meaning to a particular audience.

## Stage 3 – Spiritual

The last stage of Creation involves the birthing of spiritual life forms that are able to create, interact, experience and grow, thus contributing to the Creative Process. It is at this final stage that the Creator initiated Its great Divine Plan. This plan involves the Source, introducing elements of Its own being into the Worlds of Matter. These elements are in fact Spiritual elements (part of the Source's own Spiritual Consciousness), which are projected outside of Itself. Therefore, the Source has birthed parts of Its own Consciousness to evolve independently & autonomously from Itself. The Source did this in an effort to learn more about Itself. Many people ask why the Source would need or indeed want to learn more about Itself. Moreover, why would the Source need to learn anything? After all, the Source is 'all-knowing 'right?

Firstly, the Source is all-knowing about that which It has created, however as explained earlier, the Source did not create Itself, It simply came into existence. Therefore, the Source has a profound yearning to learn more about Itself - much in the same way we as humans/Spirit seek to learn about ourselves (after all, we are 'of' the Source, so no doubt we share many traits). A simple example would be as follows: Imagine that you have never seen yourself in a mirror, a photograph, painting or drawing. So since the day you were born, you had never seen your own image nor had you been in contact with anyone else. How would you know what you looked like? How would you know what colour your eyes were? How would you know what the back of your head looked like? You see, the only way you learn these things is to separate yourself from your 'inner' world and view yourself as others do – from the outside. Indeed, even the way your voice sounds to you is different to how other people hear you (try recording your voice and play it back – you will be surprised!).

Hence, the Source spawned parts of Itself to be Its mirror, to be Its self-recording, to be Its outward view of Itself. Moreover, the Source sent forth these newly birthed parts of Its own Consciousness into the Cosmos, to every part of the great Creation, to learn all manner of experiences and lessons, allowing It to further grow and develop. All the while allowing these Spiritual Extensions to become fully developed, separately aware beings with Free, Independent Will. We know these Spiritual Extensions as Souls.

The first Souls were sent forth into the yet undeveloped Worlds of Matter. Even though the Source had created the 3 major planes, these were in effect 'empty-houses'. It was the task of these Souls to 'furnish' the planes of Creation.

They started in the first plane, the plane of Pure Light. These Souls became known as Elohim meaning 'Shining Ones' or 'Light Beings'. The Elohim began to 'co-create' the lower vibratory material worlds of solid matter. These original beings were extremely good at co-Creation. At a point that the Source felt they had developed enough knowledge and experience, It encouraged them to birth a part of their own Consciousness, as the Source had done for them. This created the Spiritual hierarchy of Souls, which in turn began the great cycle of Spiritual Evolution.

After a long period of experimentation, learning and co-creating, the Elohim moved downward from the Planes of Light and into the realms of the Etheric Plane. Here they created all the worlds and Kingdoms that would one day solidify into the realms of the Physical Plane. Even though the Etheric Planes were a Spiritual and 'easy' place to exist (compared with the physical realms), these Souls yearned to delve further into the matrix of Creation. Therefore, they birthed even more Souls, who in turn lowered their vibration and entered the Worlds of the Physical Plane.

Here these Souls set about creating the very fundamentals of our dense physical world. But it was not just Earth they were creating. Indeed, there are many other inhabited worlds within the Physical Plane just as there are within the Higher Planes. In time, through much trial and error, the Physical Plane was complete. These Souls became known in future eras as the Gods and Goddesses of old. They had created worlds so complex and diverse, that the Source inspired them to birth the final Souls that would inhabit these worlds. These Souls would be given complete freedom to explore, learn and grow. This then sparked the very cycle of rebirth, as discussed in Chapter 1.

As it was, the Source pre-empted this achievement and accordingly birthed a special group of beings that became the Order of the Angelic Realm. These 'Angels' were created to evolve on a completely separate evolutional path to the other Souls. In fact, the Angelic realm does not have the gift of Free Will. They were created with the sole purpose of serving Creation, which would see them acting as Heavenly Messengers to ensure the maintenance, nurturing and growth of all forms of created matter in the various Universes. The Angelic Realms exist in all Planes of Creation. Here on Earth, we know them as Deva or Nature Spirits. They include all manner of Nature Spirits, Elemental Spirits and Faerie, as well as those Spirit Messengers that some people refer to as Angels. These beings ensure the well-being, growth and maintenance of the Mineral, Plant and Animal Kingdoms as well as assisting humanity. They are also the literal eyes and ears for the Source, with a direct link to it.

The most important and often overlooked Consciousness that independently volunteered to assist and nurture the burgeoning new Souls was **Gaia**. Gaia is the Consciousness that inhabits planet Earth. Without Her, life as we know it could not exist. Gaia is the patron of humanity, the Deva and Nature Spirits.

This concludes our basic overview of Creation. To be sure, the Universe is in a constant state of flux, ever evolving and changing as the Source expands and grows in Its quest for knowledge.

Hopefully you will now understand that both the Creationist and Evolutionist were partially right in a roundabout way. The Earth and indeed the Universe was "created" as was the mechanism for generating a Big Bang. As we will learn in the next chapter, the process of creation and evolution continues. But for now, know that each and every one of us is playing a key role in growth and learning. For in reality, you are of the Source and the Source is of you. We really are Divine Beings – but we have just forgotten that at the moment. So go forth into this world knowing that you are contributing to the greatest Plan that was ever conceived – the **Divine Plan of Creation**.

## In the words of The Master ZEN TAO:

*"This Earth is a very special place. You have been given the supreme gifts of the God-Head: divinity, creativity, and free choice. You are, in essence, Gods in the making and this Earth is a school for Gods. You are highly privileged to incarnate on Her, to be a part of the school of Earth and to advance your spiritual consciousness through the exercise of those Cosmic talents. There are many Beings on other planets who are not permitted to achieve consciousness in this way. You may now see why Earth is looked upon with envy by the other planets in the Solar System, for they do not all possess that potential. You have, in fact, the potential and the destiny to outstrip every other plane of consciousness within this Solar Body if only you could but harness your being and direct it with wisdom and love." (The Master ZEN TAO, 1996)*

## References:

Greene, B. (2010). *The Elegant Universe: Superstrings, Hidden Dimensions, and the Quest for the Ultimate Theory.* 2nd ed. New York: W. W. Norton & Company.

Singh, S. (2005). Big bang. 1st ed. New York: *Harper Perennial.*

*The Master ZEN TAO,* (1996). Glastonbury: Ramala Centre

> # WHAT WOULD LIFE
> # BE IF WE HAD NO
> # COURAGE TO RISK
> # ANYTHING?
> *Vincent van Gogh*

# 14

## THE SOUL'S JOURNEY THROUGH TIME

*"We are your ancient Family. We have been with you from the beginning, and now we are here to assist you in returning home." (Pleiadians)*

### Our Celestial Ancestors

GOING BACK MANY millions of years, a group of beings where birthed by the Elohim. These beings became known as the Lyrian Race. The Lyrians are in fact the 'root' of all humanoid type beings in existence. The original Lyrian race is referred to as the 'Giant Race', as they average between 5.5m and 6.5m (18ft – 20ft) in height. As part of their original learning, they birthed four sub-groups: The Red Headed Race; The Black Headed Race; The Bird Race and the Feline Race. The original Lyrians have pure white/silver haired, fair skinned and bright blue, violet or mauve eyes. Even though they are ancient, they always appear to be in the mid-20's to early 30's. Most have moved to very high dimension, or have moved out of this Universe all together. There are still a few who have remained as Watchers and Teachers. They built civilisations throughout the Milky Way galaxy, many of which were re-settled by their sub-races. Theirs is one of the highest technologies that has ever been achieved in all Creation and this made them the envy of many of the non-humanoid races. All of these beings share their DNA, as we are all related. There are many, many other alien families/races, however these are not related to the Lyrians so they will not be discussed here. I will be looking at other alien races in Book II.

## The Sub-Races:

### PLEIADIANS

Pleiadians are very tall, standing about 2.5m – 3.5m (8ft-12ft), very slim, with straight, long hair, high cheek bones and almond shaped eyes. Their eye colour ranges between violet, electric blue and golden. Their skin is smooth and chalk white, however they often appear to glow a light blue haze around themselves. Males and females usually wear a long robe in pastel colours. Their personalities are very spiritual, loving and like teachers/parents.

### RED HEADED RACE

The Red Head Race are about 2m – 3m (7ft - 10ft), very muscular, hair bright red/orange, varies from shaggy to frizzy and sometimes a dreadlocks look. Males usually have beards and they are sometimes plated. They often appear in armour with weapons. Their skin is smooth and a ruddy complexion. They resemble the Norse Gods of old. Their personalities are aggressive and war-like.

## BLACK HEADED RACE

The Black Headed Race are average to humans in size (1.80m/6ft.) with dark skin hair and eyes. The main group of the Black Headed Race is known as P'taah. They are stunning in their beauty, not unlike the Nubians of ancient earth history. Their personalities are very calm, loving, caring and helpful.

## BIRD RACE

The Bird Race, or "Bird People", are slightly taller than humans, about 2m – 2.5m (6.6ft-7ft). They have bird like faces, with a beak, but with human eyes. They have feathers in place of hair, but have a human like body. They have wings and can use them for flight and they also have human type arms, but with 3 long fingers per hand. Very intelligent. They wear tight fitting pants, shirts and boots. The colour of their feathers varies as much as human hair colour, however their eyes are always a light amber/gold colour. Their personalities are very analytical and science like.

## FELINE RACE

Also known as "Cat People". About the same height as the Bird People, they have fur like a cat and faces like a cat. They resemble lions, with human bodies. Their bodies are very muscular and they have paws with elongated fingers, similar to human hands. They wear pants and tunics with black boots. They have normal cat eyes or varying colours. Their personalities are very diplomatic.

Below is a basic family tree showing the main Lyrian race and their direct descendants. We all belong to the same family!

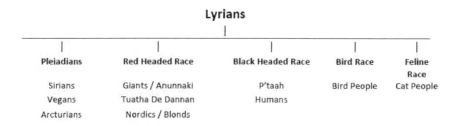

**Lyrians**

| Pleiadians | Red Headed Race | Black Headed Race | Bird Race | Feline Race |
|---|---|---|---|---|
| Sirians | Giants / Anunnaki | P'taah | Bird People | Cat People |
| Vegans | Tuatha De Dannan | Humans | | |
| Arcturians | Nordics / Blonds | | | |

Many hundreds of thousands of years ago the P'taah existed on the 11th dimension. Their civilisation reached a high, technological level and they began to travel throughout the galaxy. They were free-will beings and thus had control of their destiny. At a certain point in time they felt restless and yearned to learn more about the Source and Creation. Therefore, they decided to conduct an experiment that is still going on today.

In basic terms, they wanted to separate themselves from the Source and all creation and see if they could still find and love the Source without prior knowledge of it.

The P'taah were not under any illusions - they knew exactly what they were getting themselves into and this is why they jumped at the opportunity. In effect, the P'taah would have to lower their consciousness so far down the vibrational scale that they would forget who they were and where they came from. Moreover, they knew the experiment would result in Separation.

Separation refers to a soul separating itself from the Source. This is not the same as a Disconnect, as we discussed with Suicides. All beings throughout Creation are connected and consciously aware of the Source and their relationship to It. What the P'taah wanted to do was deliberately forget about who they were, who the Source is and where their place in Creation is. To say this was a risky undertaking is an understatement! But they had good reason. The ultimate Spiritual lesson and advancement would be to see if they could find their way home again. Without conscious knowledge of the Source and still finding their way back to the It, would be one of the greatest achievements ever undertaken. Imagine it something like this:

Imagine you were born in a fine house on a hill. You had everything you could ever desire and there was never any pain or suffering.

One day, your father comes to you and says that in order for you to inherit all his wealth and glory, you must first prove yourself worthy by travelling to a far distant land and live with the inhabitants there for 5 years.

You decide to accept this challenge; after all, it is only 5 years. Along the way you encounter many hardships, make many friends and learn many new things. Whenever it gets hard, you tell yourself – it's only for 5 years. Eventually you get to your destination. A tribe of very primitive but kind beings takes you in. Here, you live and work with this tribe of people, side by side. The work and living conditions are very hard compared to where you have come from, but you put up with it because you know it is only for 5 years.

At the prescribed time you go back home to the house on the hill. Here your father is waiting for you. He welcomes you home and asks what you have learnt. You tell him you have learnt many things, you tell him of the hardships you endured and you tell him how much you missed being home in the house on the hill. Your father asks: why didn't you help the old woman in the village when she was unable to fend for herself anymore? Your reply: She had family to do that, I was only a visitor and it was not my place. Father asks: Why didn't you marry and learn of love? Your reply: I couldn't get married or fall in love; I was only going to be there for 5 years. Father asks: When the village people needed your help to finish their new temple, which you convinced them to build, why didn't you stay? Your reply: it was time for me to return home for my 5 years had finished. Father says: I am sorry child, but you have learnt nothing that would allow you to inherit my wealth.

Now we look at this story in a different scenario. In this story, your father takes you from birth and places you in the care of the tribe's people. They adopt you as their own and you grow up as a member of the tribe, with no memory of your father or the grand house. Throughout your life in the tribe you occasionally have dreams of a beautiful house on a hill, but you are not sure what this means. You marry and learn love. Holding your partner you remember another time when you felt warm and secure, but you can't remember and shrug it off. You have children and their laughter reminds you of another time that was filled with laughter and happiness.

After your children have grown, you start to feel an overwhelming urge to travel. Your dreams of the house become more and more frequent. One day you decide to listen to your heart and go in search of the house on the hill. After many years of travel and hardship, you are old and almost dying. You sit down and reflect on the life you have lived. It was a good life, filled with love and happy memories. As you struggle to your feet for one last time you are greeted by an angelic glowing figure. They pick you up and take you over the mountains, till at last they set you down – in front of you is a beautiful house on a hill – your father runs down the stairs, smiling broadly with his arms out stretched - you are home – you suddenly remember everything. In that instant, you are young and fit again. You are home!

*          *          *

Hopefully that story reiterates the reasons for the P'taah to separate themselves from the Source. If you know your destiny, then you will subconsciously avoid learning the lessons that will help you advance. If you have no knowledge of your destiny, you are more likely to follow your heart – which is the way home. By successfully returning to full consciousness after separation you will automatically transcend into a much higher Spiritual vibration then you ever experienced on the 11th dimension.

## When the Earth was Young

The Earth was chosen to be the 'playground' for the P'taah to experiment on. It was the P'taah's loving cousins, the Pleiadians, that found the young earth. At this time the consciousness known as Gaia had already assimilated with the planet and it was in the cooling down period, preparing for new life to start. A planet cannot support life without a highly evolved being merged with it. This also includes stars and habitual moons like Jupiter's Europa. You never know, your own consciousness may one day be the host of a planet or star, but we will talk more about that later.

## The Spark of Life

For a planet to start life, there is another group of highly evolved Spirits that initiate the process. When all souls finish their incarnations and merge back into an Over-Soul, they have the opportunity to perform many tasks in service of Creation. One of those tasks is to start life on new planets. If you were in the 3rd dimension and you were to witness this event, it would look like a massive rainbow coloured gas covering the planet. The rainbow effect ripples. On the surface of the planet, it is hot and steamy and pouring rain. But it is not normal rain. It is a special liquid, like water, but it contains the life creating elements that are the building blocks for all life. At the same time, the gas, or more correctly, "life energy" is also "charging" the rain. The two combine to create the "spark" that creates life. The first form of life that starts to grow is a plant. This plant is like a vine, but with massive tendrils. Each leaf would cover a hectare (2ac), and the vine is about 20metres (65ft) in diameter.

This will eventually grow all over most of the surface of the planet. When the rain stops and the gas dissipates, the plant breaks down. This is what creates the top layer of fertile, top soil. In this, all manner of bacteria, nematodes, and algae start. This process is what scientists would call "Terraforming". The templates i.e. prototypes for animals and insects are created in the Spirit World and then sent down to the planet to breed and evolve, as discussed in Chapter 10. The gas is the actual physical manifestation of the Over-Soul. Each Over-Soul has a singular name, but still maintains group consciousness. In other words, it is like 20 people in a bus all talking to each other. The bus is the vehicle they get around in, that is the Over-Soul.

The Over-Soul that performed the Life Creation Process was called **Ti-Amat**. You will see this name again in Chapter 18, but I won't give it away just yet. I will say however, that the name Ti-Amat was later used by the ancient Sumerian people to mean "Mother of Life".

Before the P'taah could start their experiment of Separation, they needed to create a "home base" to run their operation from. They would also use this area for R&R (rest and recreation). As we have already discussed in the previous chapter, the Source created all levels and dimensions and then tasked the Elohim to "furnish" those levels. To furnish a level simply means to build areas within it. Imagine someone gave you a house and garden, but with no furniture or plants in the garden. Your job would be to furnish the inside of the house and plant out the garden. By doing so, you transform the house into a functional and beautiful place. Dimensions work in the same way. The Elohim at this point were the P'taah and the "house" they furnished for their home base was what we now call the Spirit World – all 7 levels, within 7 levels! They created the Spirit World while Ti-Amat was sparking life on Earth.

## RAW – The Four Elements

At this stage, the Earth had no life as we know it. There were no forests or grasses. No animals or insects. There was only the four elements – Earth, Air, Fire and Water. Therefore, the P'taah merged their consciousness with these elements. They needed to do this in order to form a symbiotic relationship with Gaia. It also anchored them to the planet and in effect, held them in the 3rd dimension. It also served to teach them some of the fundamentals of living in the 3rd dimension, which would later help them create more complex and dense beings to inhabit and experience at a later time.

At this early period, the P'taah were still experiencing a group consciousness. That is, they were aware of each other on a consciousness level and could communicate with each other simply by thought. They could also feel what others were feeling. Once they had mastered and understood the Elements they undertook their first step in gradual separation. They incarnated into the Mineral Kingdom.

## Mineral Kingdom

## Stage I

The mineral Kingdom is made up of all rocks and crystals – not earth or soil. Earth, sand and soil are the remains of 'dead' rocks whose consciousness has returned to Spirit. When I talk about consciousness at this level, do not think of it like your own. Consciousness at this level is barley understandable from the human perspective. These 'Souls' are not even close to the same level of sophistication that your own consciousness is. Indeed, imagine you have just gone from a very bright lit room into a tiny box that is in complete darkness. Your ears and nose are plugged, so the only sense you have working is touch, but you are in a thick body suit, so only very heavy touch is registered. Even this example still does not come close to understanding consciousness in the Mineral Kingdom because there are no senses at all – only a very low level of perception. There is no concept of time at this level nor is there any concept of self. You are still part of the collective.

Consciousness starts in the oldest rocks of all - felsic rock. Felsic rocks include igneous rocks, the most common being granite. Next is Igneous volcanic rocks. These are very early lessons in birth and rebirth. Then come the Metamorphic rocks. They are in a transition learning new attributes. Finally, Sedimentary rocks are starting to break down and die. But like all life on earth, everything returns to the Earth for recycling and renewal. This is Stage One of the Mineral Kingdom.

## Stage II

When a Soul Group feels it has learnt all it can at the rudimentary level of Stage 1 of experience, It moves up the vibrational ladder to semi-precious and precious metals. The highest vibration of metal is gold. The ancients understood this and that is why they treasured gold as a metal of the 'gods'. They saw no intrinsic wealth in gold, it was a metal to honour the gods. But not so in modern humans. Modern humans see gold as wealth, which is part of the experiment of separation. They hoard it and use it to display their power and you can't get more separated than that!

## Stage III

The final stage of the Mineral Kingdom is crystals. Crystals have a very high energetic and spiritual vibration compared to other minerals. They literally work like a battery, storing High Divine Energy. Many are used for healing humans, animals and plants. This is their service to creation which helps them learn about becoming human on an energetic level. Some of the more common and useful crystals are Amethyst, Clear Quartz, Rose Quartz, Lapis Lazuli to name but a few. There are literally hundreds of different crystals that are beneficial to life.

Once again, modern man uses crystals to power weapons like lasers and defence systems like sonar in submarines. Furthermore, they also crush up certain crystals for basic construction work. Again, these uses and abuses are part of the big experiment of separation. On the one hand, they help the consciousness that inhabits the crystal to serve humanity, which helps them to move higher up the vibrational ladder and on the other hand, they have contributed to the separation of man from the Source. Once consciousness has traversed all of the levels of the Mineral Kingdom they return back to Spirit to assimilate all of the experiences back into one consciousness. Once the information and vibration is assimilated, the Soul Group splits apart again and prepares for the next incarnation into the Plant Kingdom.

## Plant Kingdom

## Stage I

The Plant Kingdom includes all manner of algae, grasses, weeds, shrubs, bushes and trees. Consciousness now moves from the crystalline structure it experienced in the Mineral Kingdom to its first experience in cellular structures. Again, this is part of moving closer to human form (i.e. cellular form).

Ocean plants consist of a very large and diverse group of simple, typically autotrophic organisms, ranging from unicellular to multicellular forms, such as the giant kelps that can grow to 65 meters in length off the coast of Californian and other places. Most are photosynthetic and "simple" because they lack the many distinct cell and organ types found in land plants, so this is where the Soul Group incarnates first. Here they perform many duties of service to Creation. They willingly give up parts of themselves to feed many other life forms. They also create most of the Earth's oxygen. This self-sacrifice to feed others is the highest vibrational achievement in this level. Furthermore, others contain medicinal qualities, many of which have not yet been discovered by humans. They provide shelter for sea life, as well nurseries and mating locations. Humans also harvest seaweed and kelp as well as many freshwater plants like the superfood spirulina.

## Stage II

Land plants are more complex and sophisticated compared to water plants. Many have sexual organs for mating and bear fruits and other edible treats for animals and humans. They provide shade and building materials. Certain tree saps are used for incense like frankincense while others are used to heal wounds. There are literally hundreds of uses for plant materials. Just look at the cloths you have on now. Are they made of cotton, hemp or silk? How many wood objects do you see in your home? Wood, grasses and reeds have been used for thousands of years for human transport. From simple dugout canoes, to large ocean going vessels. They provide material for chariots, wagons and wheels. Early aircraft were built from wood and all manner of furniture, sculpture and kitchen/eating utensils, not to mention houses and buildings.

## Stage III

As with the Mineral Kingdom, and indeed all of the Kingdoms, the consciousness in plants strives to serve Creation. You can probably see yourself that they have increased their value to both humans and animals as compared to the Mineral Kingdom. This is because they have taken the valuable lesson they learnt in the Mineral Kingdom and applied them to the Plant Kingdom. You may have also work out that each Kingdom has a symbiotic relationship with each other. Plants need minerals to grow. Plants help minerals to break up and be dispersed. Both minerals and plants combine to provide early and modern man with solid structures to live in.

Many, many land plants have medicinal value. Modern science has not even begun to discover most of these yet. Unfortunately, it is cheaper and easier to artificially concoct a drug in a lab, then it is to send a scientist out into the field to find natural plant remedies. Medicinal plants have a very high vibration, along with those plants we use to feed, clothe and shelter ourselves. Medicinal plants vibrate in harmony with animals and humans and lab drugs do not. That is why lab drugs often come with many side effects. Plants also supply fragrance and oils. Bach Flower Essences are about as high a vibration as you can get in the Plant Kingdom. They are akin to the high vibrating crystals.

Majestic trees like Oak, Norfolk Pine, Redwoods and others are in their last experience in the Plant kingdom. Before the wholesale deforesting of these magnificent trees, this was their reward for hundreds and hundreds of lives as food and shelter. They take this opportunity to spend a long time in the Earth's vibration, known as the Schuman's Resonance which I will discuss in depth in Book III. They need this time to attune to the Schuman's Resonance because this is a prerequisite to move into the next kingdom – the Animal Kingdom.

## Animal Kingdom

The Animal Kingdom includes single cell amoeba, all insects, fish, reptiles, mammals and birds. Just like in the previous kingdoms, consciousness starts off small and simple, then gradually goes up into more complex creatures. While insects do not have a brain as such, they do have nerve clusters which are a type of proto-brain. This is the first time in the Spiritual Evolution that consciousness can integrate with an organic "operating system" or brain. This is essential to move into human form. The soul must learn the very tricky and complex task of integrating itself with the brain and later the Chakra System. Thus, they start with more simple creatures and work their way up.

Like before, insects that serve humanity are usually in their last lives as insects. For example silk worms. In the previous kingdoms the soul consciousness served Creation in a more general sense, but now in animal form, they move to contribute or "serve" humanity in numerous ways. That is because the consciousness is striving to move into human form, so by being close to humans or serving humans as a source of food, they learn more even quicker. Early humans did not eat meat, however it became the norm to help speed up the development of the human body and also create a lower and denser vibration in humans to complete the separation experiment. As the Separation Experiment draws closer to its completion, humans will once again be non-meat eaters simply because their vibration will be too high to digest and process it. They will lose their appetite for meat and will not even like its taste anymore.

**Stage I**

The simple creatures that Consciousness went into were Insects, worms and simple celled creatures. They learnt a great deal about being in a 3D body that is effected by temperature and hunger. Worms are simultaneous hermaphrodites, meaning worms have both male and female reproductive organs. During sexual intercourse among earthworms, both sets of sex organs are used by both worms. If all goes well, the eggs of both of the mates become fertilized. You can imagine this is a highly efficient way of ensuring the survival of the species. This allowed P'taah to split their male and female energy. This was good practice for when they would be in male or female bodies.

## Stage II

Next they evolve into crustaceans, fish and birds. Laying eggs was their first attempt of live breeding. This went passed even the dinosaur period. It took the Creation programmers a long, long time to come up with live, placental births, which eventually came next.

**Stage III**

Enter the world of mammals! Mammals are also unique in having hair, although it may be scant and mammary glands. They are warm-blooded and air-breathing, and all but the whales and sirenians(sea cows), have four limbs. All mammals except the platypus and the echidna from Australia, which lay eggs, give birth to live young. Mammals care for their young for longer periods than other animals do. Mammals have a more highly developed brain than other animals, with correspondingly higher intelligence. By studying other mammals, P'taah gained insight into human behaviour which they knew would be their next big incarnation challenge. (Burnie, 2002)

Mammals appeared more than 200,000,000 years ago; they evolved from reptile-like animals called *therapsids*. The earliest known mammals, called *triconodonts*, resembled shrews, but laid eggs. Marsupials (mammals with external pouches in which young are nourished) and placentals (mammals with wombs in which unborn young are nourished) appeared about 100 million years ago. About 65 million years ago (the beginning of the Cenozoic Era, or Age of Mammals), mammals increased in number, diversity and size. To give you an idea how creative and amazing the team in Spirit are, the largest mammal and the largest animal that has ever lived, is the blue whale. It measures up to 30 meters (100 feet) long when fully grown. The smallest mammal is the Kitti's hog-nosed bat of Thailand. It is about the size of a bumble bee and weighs no more than a penny! (Hayward, 2011)

## Stage IV

The final stage before human incarnation is domestic animals and pets. Souls evolve through the previous Kingdoms to get closer to humans. Thus, the closest you can get to being human, is to be a pet of a human. Many people say how "human" like their pet cat or dogs are. We have all heard stories of dogs that save humans from fire and other dangers. Indeed, we call dogs, "man's best friend" and I would have to agree. Here is an animal so imbued with Unconditional Love, they could teach many humans a thing or two. And that is exactly the point. The beautiful, docile, loyal and loving pet dog is in its last life before it incarnates into a human body. By now, the Soul has evolved and learnt everything it can about the 3rd dimension, so the only thing left is to experience life with a sense of self, isolation and deep thought and reasoning.

## The End Game

It should be noted at this point that the goal of each Consciousness is to eventually evolve into Human Consciousness. To do so, they must first learn a little bit at a time about humans. Therefore, in each of the first 3 Kingdoms there are several types of mineral, plant or animal that works closely with humans. There is a twofold advantage to this. Firstly, some consciousness allows themselves to serve humanity in the way of benefiting mankind such as in iron ore – a mineral essential for modern living. In the case of plants and animals, they serve humanity by either providing shelter, suppling fruits and berries or allowing themselves to be used as food and clothing for humanity.

It would be remiss to think that these consciousness have the same feelings or views that human have. Many Mature Souls in particular, like to humanise animals and sometimes even plants. By doing this they assume that the animal thinks and feels the same way they do. So when they learn that some species of animals freely give up their life in order to sustain humans, they find it difficult to accept. Animals in particular do this, as it helps them rapidly climb the Spiritual Evolution ladder. They make the ultimate sacrifice for their brethren who have already incarnated into human bodies. Other animals serve humanity as beasts of burden or as pests.

Again, humanity would not have advanced to where it is today without certain species doing most of the grunt work. The service of horses, Oxen and Donkeys should never be underestimated. The work of pet dogs, cats and any other "pet" creature has also been incredibly important.

However, in the bigger picture, this has allowed humanity to progress technologically so there is no longer the requirement for animals to do all the hard labour. Eventually this will also led to humans not eating animals. But for now we must accept the way it is and honour those that make such heroic efforts. That is also why we should never abuse or mistreat any living creature, be it mineral, vegetable or animal. They are all primitive versions of our own consciousness striving to reach the same goals we have already achieved. And yes, you have been through all of these states already, so you should know from experience to be kind to all life.

## Human Kingdom

Life began on Earth about 3.8 billion years ago and the P'taah have been here from the beginning. In case you haven't worked it out yet, YOU are part of the P'taah! Almost every human on Earth is. I say almost, because there are other alien species, some good, some not so good, that also reside on the plant. Some have for almost the entire history of humans. The modern human (homo sapiens sapiens) has only been around for about 30,000 years, but the P'taah souls have been in some form of humanoid body on Earth for several million years. Just like the plants and animals, the souls had to gradually incarnate into humans. They started off with smaller and more simple brains and gradually over time evolved more sophisticated brains and bodies. Humans are now at their peak for this dimension. There will be no more major genetic upgrades, except for those that require advanced, spiritual awakening. From the very beginning of souls incarnating in human form, things have not always been as they are now. Indeed, since the great Atlantean catastrophe, we are now living in the Fifth Age. But going back to the start, humans were very different.

In early days, humans were still part of the collective conscious, similar to herd animals. It was not that they could read each other's mind, but they could sense danger through each other, they could find food, water and shelter. They had a "tribe" mind. At this point there was still no sense of Time, so day and night blurred. They were still very close to the Spirit realm, so they could see Elementals (Faeries, Devas, nature spirits etc.)

Gradually, over time, their connection to Spirit waned and the separation began to take root. For about the first 2-3 million years, humans did not eat meat, and they were more or less friends with animals. Animals did not run from humans and they all got along just fine. However, with each generation, the Separation crept in more and more. Animals began to see humans as food, so they would attack and eat them. Humans then began to hunt the killer animals and out of superstition, they began to eat certain parts of the animal. Eventually during hard natural times when food was scant, they would eat all of the animal. Then they would use the hides for clothing and shelter. That is when animals would run and hide from humans. Humans began to make tools and covert them. People started to identify with "That is my spear"; "Those are my beads" etc. Prior to this time there was no sense of ownership. Eventually it grew into "This is my/our hunting grounds/land" and fights over territory turned into wars. This was all part of the experiment.

It was the evolving human Ego that created ownership and aggression. Ego was programmed to feel separated from everyone and everything, including God. This was deliberately programmed into the human body. The P'taah required a mechanism to generate separation and individual personality as opposed to the "tribe" mentality. They did maintain enough connection to the Spirit World to record certain information that would be beneficial and some of that knowledge has remained to this day. Eventually the "Priest" class grew and used this knowledge as power over the masses. This grew to a head just before the Atlantean catastrophe. This was a really big deal! Some major, major things happened then that have dictated human history ever since.

- The Spiritual clock was set to Zero
- Time, as in the concept, came into being
- Humans, for the first time felt isolation. They were no longer connected to anything. This is why the clock was set to 0 and Time began. Because from that point, the Experiment of Separation would officially begin (up til now was preparation)
- The old doorways/vortexes to the Spirit World were shut for good
- It was also at this point that some Souls remained in Spirit for extended rest, while others forged ahead to build the new world. That is what created the stagger of Souls, thus forming the different Soul Ages

All this seemed bad enough compared to how humans originally lived. However, as we will find out in the next Chapter, events unfolded which the P'taah did not foresee. These unforseen events certainly did allow things to speed up, but on the other hand they have imprisoned humanity to this day.

Immediately following the Atlantean catastrophe was the Fourth Age, known as the Graeco-Latin period. This was a time when thought, ideas, feelings and the general 'earth-will' was governed by the Greek and Latin peoples. The Third Age was Chaldaic-Babylonian-Assyrian-Egyptian period, the Second Age was Old Persian and the First Age was ancient India. Prior, in antiquity to the ancient Indian period, we will find the pre-catastrophe Atlantis which was the Sumerian-Atlantis-Trojan period.

As stated, we are now in the 5th Age and this is the Age that the experiment is meant to end. But we are not there yet! It is the Age of Aquarius that will herald the New Age and the completion of the Experiment. There is still about 120 years before we will be right in the middle of Aquarius and the New Age of Enlightenment. All this will be discussed in length in Book III. In the next chapter, we will look at some of the major events that you were never taught in school. These events have had a profound influence on all humanity's history to this day, not to mention how they nearly screwed everything up! So get your crash helmet ready, because next, we look at the Cosmic Collision!

## References:

Burnie, D. (2002). *Animal*. 1st ed. Madrid: Pearson Education.

Hayward, K. (2011). *Ultimate book of mammal*. 1st ed. London: DK Pub.

# 15

## COSMIC COLLISIONS

*"Far beyond the solar system's nine known planets,
a body as massive as Mars may once have been part
of our planetary system -- and it might still be there;"
(Science News of April 7, 2001)*

THROUGHOUT HISTORY, HUMANS have tried to explain many things, not least of all how the Universe and Solar System were formed. Modern science attributes the creation of the Universe to the 'Big Bang' theory and the Solar System was formed due to "Accretion". However there is another theory based on ancient texts, that shines a whole new light on this topic. Whilst science has done an excellent job of trying to unravel these mysteries there still remains some missing pieces to the puzzle. Therefore, it is my intention to fill in those pieces and hopefully reveal the whole picture.

## Planetary Accretion Theory

Modern science teaches that a long time ago, our sun exploded into existence. Around the sun, was left over material and gases that began to revolve around it. Small chunks would bump into bigger chunks and they would stick together forming an even bigger chunk. Eventually, after billions of years, these chunks grew into planet size bodies. However, accretion only explains the inner rocky planets and does not explain the outer gas giants like Jupiter and Saturn at all. Furthermore, Cosmologists are not sure how the asteroid belt between Mars and Jupiter got there either. There is too much material to be a broken up asteroid, but too little material for it to be a destroyed planet.

## Sumerian Cosmology

Many years ago now, I came across a book called *"The 12th Planet"*, which is part of a series called **The Earth Chronicles** by Zecharia Sitchin (Fig. 13). Although not everything Sitchin puts forward gels with what I have been taught by Spirit, it comes pretty close to the mark and

*Figure 13*

therefore warrants close examination. In fact, the reason for dealing with this subject at this time, is that the past will revisit us in the future and will have a monumental impact on all who dwell on this planet.

Zecharia Sitchin (July 11, 1920 – October 9, 2010) was born in Russia and raised in Palestine, where he acquired a profound knowledge of modern and ancient Hebrew, other Semitic and European languages, the Old Testament and the history and archaeology of the Near East. He is one of the few scholars who is able to read and understand

Sumerian. Sitchin attended and graduated from the University of London, majoring in economic history. A leading journalist and editor in Israel for many years, he moved to New York until his death at age 90. Sitchin's books have sold millions of copies worldwide and have been translated into more than 26 languages, converted to Braille for the blind and featured on radio and television.

The Earth Chronicles series is based on the premise that mythology is not imaginary, but rather a storehouse of ancient memories; that the Bible ought to be read as a historic/scientific document; and that ancient civilizations, older and greater than assumed, were the product of knowledge brought to Earth by the Anunnaki, "Those Who from Heaven to Earth Came."

The Sumerian civilization, thought to be the oldest on the planet, has left us an enduring portrait of their society, philosophy, religion, courts, art, economy and daily life in the countless records they left behind.

*Figure 14*

The Sumerians created an alphabet called cuneiform that was a series of wedge shapes in different combinations. When they wanted to write something down, they used a stylus to press the wedge-shaped marks into a slab of clay (Fig. 14). When the clay was fired in a kiln, the result was a very durable document, of which thousands have survived to this day, some 5000 years later!

The Sumerian language is well understood and for many years archaeologists have studied the so-called myths as told about the Sumerian gods in stories such as the **Epic of Gilgamesh** (Gilgamesh and Sandars, 1972).

In 1976, Sitchin revolutionised understanding of these Sumerian "myths" through his book, The 12th Planet. According to Sitchin (The 12th Planet, 1976), the "Story of Creation" in the book of Genesis, is in fact an edited and condensed version of a much older story – the Sumerian Epic of Creation - the **Enuma Elish** (also called the Babylonian Epic of Creation). Moreover, Sitchin argues that this story has passed through many generations throughout many cultures, usually in oral tradition. He has managed to trace the story from the Sumerian, Akkadian, Babylonian, Assyrian, Hittite, Egyptian, Canaanite and Hebrew peoples. Thus, it is no doubt then that the original story was 'cut down' and edited, considering it had been told orally over hundreds of years. When the early Jewish scribes did finally record this edited version whilst in exile in Babylon, they named it the Book of Genesis. Different cultures and traditions tended to 'localise' the events and characters, giving more meaning to their own peoples. I am sure you are familiar with the game called Chinese Whispers. This is when you have around 10-20 people in a line or in a circle. The first person is told a message to pass on. Each person then passes it on to the next. By the time the message comes back to the original person, the message is usually so different they can hardly recognise it! Imagine this game played over thousands of years, with hundreds of people.

The first major breakthrough Sitchin made was the realisation that the apparent Sumerian 'gods' where in fact the celestial bodies of our solar system. Indeed, an ancient Sumerian cylinder seal dating from the third millennium Before Common Era (BCE) clearly depicts our solar system, with all of the planets in their correct positions around the Sun (see Fig. 13). However, instead of the usual 9 planets we are familiar with in modern times, the ancient Sumerians mapped the solar system with 12 planets. The Sumerians included the Sun and Moon as the tenth and eleventh bodies, with the final shown as a planet considerably larger than Earth, yet smaller than Jupiter or Saturn. This final body is what Sitchin refers to as the 12th Planet.

The Sumerians called this planet **Nibiru** and stated in a very detailed narrative (recorded in clay tablets using ancient cuneiform) that it was the home planet of the Anunnaki. The Anunnaki, Sitchin states, are none other than part of the Nefilim, an enigmatic group mentioned in the Old Testament. Translated, Nefilim means "those who from heaven came down" or more appropriate – The Fallen (Angels).

According to the Sumerians, "in the beginning", (approximately 4.6 billion years ago) only three celestial bodies existed - Apsu (the Sun), Mummu (Mercury) and an unfamiliar planet they called Tiamat (larger than Earth and covered entirely with water).

Next, the planets of Lahmu (Mars - no moons yet) and Lahamu (Venus) were formed, followed quickly by Anshar (Saturn - no rings yet) and Kishar (Jupiter). Some time then passed and a third pair was brought forth. First came Anu (Uranus), followed by its twin Nudimmud (Neptune).

There was yet another planet to be accounted for among these outer planets, the one we call Pluto. The Enuma Elish tells us that Gaga (Pluto) was actually a moon of Saturn. This is interesting, since in 2006 scientist demoted Pluto to a Dwarf Planet as it was not deemed big enough to be a planet. If only they had read the Sumerian story they would have known from the start that Pluto was never a planet!

As Stage I of the Sumerian creation story came to an end, there was a solar system made up of the Sun and nine planets:

| MODERN NAME | | SUMER NAME | SUMER NAME MEANING |
|---|---|---|---|
| SUN | .... | Apsu | One who existed from the beginning |
| MERCURY | ... | Mummu | Counsellor and emissary of Apsu |
| VENUS | ... | Lahamu | Lady of Battles |
| MARS | ... | Lahmu | The Muddy One |
| ?? | ... | Tiamat | Mother of Life |
| JUPITER | ... | Kishar | Foremost of Firm Lands |
| SATURN | ... | Anshar | Sky Pivot |
| PLUTO | ... | Gaga | The Announcer |
| URANUS | ... | An | He of Two Faces |
| NEPTUNE | .... | Antu | The Twin of An |

So where were the Earth and the Moon? They were yet to be created, products of the forthcoming cosmic collision. With the end of the majestic drama of the birth of the planets, the authors of the creation epic now raise the curtain on Stage II, on a drama of celestial turmoil.

The newly created family of planets was far from being stable. The planets were gravitating toward each other; they were 'converging' on Tiamat, disturbing and endangering the primordial waters. The epic then explains how the unstable planets surged back and forth toward each other, till finally Neptune "cast a spell over Apsu (Sun)" putting it to sleep and thus ending the gravitational turmoil of the planets. This also meant that any new planets could only come from outside the solar system, as Apsu could no longer create new planets.

## A Cosmic Collision

*Figure 15*

In Stage III (approximately 4 billion years ago), a new celestial 'god'—a new planet—now joins the cast (Fig. 15). He was formed in the deep, far out in space, in a zone where orbital motion had been granted to him. Nibiru originally form around a Dark Star called Nemesis. Nemesis is locked into orbit by our own sun, making our solar system a Binary System. Nemesis is located about 50 AU away and because it is a Dark Star, it is not easily visible. It is detectable with infra-red telescopes, as well has the gravitational effect it has on our outer planets (The Daily Telegraph, 2002). NASA has been looking for this Dark Star for many years. They know it is there, but they just aren't telling us. In 1991, Dr. Robert S. Harrington, the chief astronomer of the U.S. Naval Observatory, did an investigation into the existence of Nibiru and Nemesis. After he discovered what has been described as spectacular and possibly the great scientific find in history, he suddenly died under mysterious circumstance. Indeed, Harrington dispatched an appropriate telescope to Black Birch, New Zealand to get a visual confirmation, based on the data leading to the expectation that it would be below the ecliptic in the southern skies at this point in its orbit. On Harrington's early death the scope was immediately called back and as one observer noted, "almost before he was cold". (DiNardo and Manning, 2008)

## From the Deep

Nibiru was attracted to the solar system by the gravitational pull of the outer planets. As it appeared from outer space, the new planet was still belching fire and radiation. As Nibiru entered the solar system, many things changed forever.

The epic's narrative now takes us along Nibiru's steady path toward the Sun. *"He first passes Neptune, the planet that pulled him in. As he passes, the gravitational pull causes Nibiru to bulge, as though he had a second head".* No part of Nibiru was torn off at this point, but as he reached the vicinity of Uranus, chunks of matter began to tear away, resulting in the formation of the four satellites (moons) of Nibiru.

*Figure 16*

Judging by the description, Nibiru was entering the system in a retrograde direction or counter clockwise (Fig. 16), the opposite of the systems orbital direction. It soon entered the mighty clutches of Saturn's pull, then Jupiter's, causing its path to venture further inwards—into the centre of the solar system—into the path of Tiamat. In fact as Nibiru passed the giant Saturn, its gravitational pull managed to dislodge Saturn's largest moon Gaga (Pluto), there setting Pluto into its own orbit where it still remains to this day.

Keeping in mind that Nibiru is a much larger planet than present day Earth, as Nibiru approached Tiamat and the inner planets (Mars,

Venus, Mercury), the gravitational battles greatly affected these heavenly bodies. The pull of the large approaching Nibiru soon began to tear away parts of Tiamat. From her midst emerged eleven satellites that "marched at the side of Tiamat". Of particular importance to the epic, and to Mesopotamian cosmogony was Tiamat's chief satellite, which they named Kingu. Subjected to conflicting gravitational pulls, Kingu began to shift toward Nibiru, however it did not suffer the same fate as Gaga/Pluto.

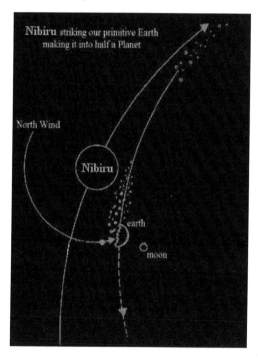

*Figure 17*

After much drama, Nibiru left the system, only to return 3600 years later to create even more havoc. On the planets return trip, it upset Uranus's tilt, forcing it onto its side. Modern day astronomers did not realise this fact until 1977 when the first colour images were beamed back to Earth via NASA's Voyager 2 space probe, yet the Sumerians described it as such 5000 years ago! As Nibiru approached Tiamat, one of Nibiru's moons, *Northwind*, split away and impacted directly into Tiamat, causing the giant water planet to crack (Fig. 17). Almost half of Tiamat is obliterated and thrown into the orbit that is now the asteroid belt between Mars and Jupiter. The second half (approximately 62%) of Tiamat was forced onto a new path—a path that no other planet was using. We now know that the remaining half of Tiamat as Earth! Nibiru continues on its massive elliptical orbit, encircling Apsu/Sun before returning on its path. It will return to the inner solar system every 3,600 – 3, 700 years.

## Modern Science Agrees!

The most favoured mainstream theory for how the Earth's moon was created is called the *Giant Impact Hypothesis* (Wikipedia, 2014). It basically says that the Moon was formed out of the debris left over from a collision between the Earth and a planet the size of Mars, approximately 4.5 billion years ago (Fig. 18). Wow, so I wonder if Northwind was roughly the same size as Mars? Interestingly is that the mainstream theories have a lot of holes in them that scientists can't really explain. However, if they followed the Sumerian version of creation then all of their questions would be explained!

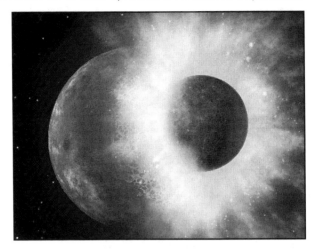

*Figure 18*

In the 1970's a massive geological survey was conducted over the entire ocean floors of the world. What they found shocked them. If you drained all the water away from the earth, the land mass that would be left would only be about half a planet! To give you an idea, they also measured and mapped the *Mariana Trench*. The Mariana Trench is the deepest part of any ocean in the world. It is located east of the Mariana Islands in the western Pacific Ocean. The trench is about 2,550 kilometres (1,580 mi) long with an average width of 69 kilometres (43 mi). It reaches a maximum-known depth of 10.911 km or 6.831 mi. Some more recent measurements put the depth at 11.03 kilometres (6.85 mi). That is one mighty big hole! So how else would it get there unless half the planet was smashed away? (Drain the Ocean, 2009)

## Science Meets Planet X

*"There is new evidence that a sudden barrage of deadly debris crashed against the Earth and the Moon 3.9 billion years ago... What*

*triggered this onslaught?    Something in the structure of the Solar System must have changed."* (Semeniuk, 2001)

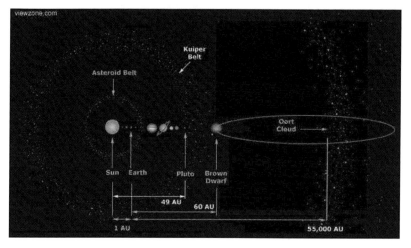

*Figure 19*

As we have discussed, Tiamat was a large water covered planet. After the collision with Nibiru, almost half of Tiamats solid mass was obliterated. As is the nature of planets, the remains of Tiamat reformed and became spherical again. The result was a much smaller planet with landmasses now visible, as most of the water was gone. Indeed, it is my own theory that the water ended up in what we call today the *Oort cloud* (Fig. 19). The Oort cloud or Öpik–Oort cloud, was named after the Dutch astronomer Jan Oort who discovered it in around 1950. It is a spherical cloud of mainly icy asteroids, some almost as big as Pluto! The Oort cloud is thought to occupy a vast space from somewhere between 2,000 and 5,000 AU to as far as 50,000 AU from the Sun. This would explain where all the water for the Oort cloud came from – from Tiamat!

Back on Earth, the main rift where the shattering took place is located in the vicinity of the Pacific Ocean. As stated earlier, the impact forced the remains of Tiamat into a new orbit around the Sun. This new orbit is the very reason that the reformed planet Earth would one day be able to support life. If ended up in what astrophysicists call the "Goldilocks Zone" of space i.e. not too far from the sun, not too close to the sun, but just right to support liquid water and life.

Tiamat eventually recaptured Kingu in its gravitational pull. Kingu was securely positioned on the opposite side of the planet when Tiamat and Nibiru collided. After the remains of Tiamat reformed into Earth, Kingu remained by her side. We now know Kingu as the Moon! According to the Sumerians, the moon was once destined to be a small planet, however whilst it was still forming, the collision of Tiamat and Nibiru occurred. Therefore, Kingu was never able to finish 'growing' and thus it died, becoming the stark, desolate moon we know today. Indeed, most modern astronomers would agree that our moon is too large for this size planet. Of course, the moon was once the satellite of a much larger planet, Tiamat.

According to Sitchin, geologists in recent times have successfully mapped a topographical image of the entire Earth. From this, he argues, the Sumerian version of events can be verified. Indeed, if one were to drain all of the oceans of Earth away, one would only be left with a solid mass that resembles approximately 2/3rds of a planet(Drain the Ocean, 2009). In fact, parts of the Pacific Ocean are hundreds of kilometres deep, so one can begin to understand that the Sumerian creation story is not that far off the mark. This lopsided planet theory would also explain the tilt of the Earth and its 'wobble'. Indeed, only an off-balanced sphere (i.e. one that is not completely spherical) would wobble.

Another interesting point the Sumerians make concerns the debris of Tiamat after the collision. The Sumerians tell us that the debris ended up between Mars and Jupiter. This is exactly where the Asteroid Belt (Sumerians called it the **Hammered Bracelet**) is located, with which modern day astronomers are so familiar. One contemporary theory argues that the asteroid belt is the remains of primordial matter that failed to coalesce into planets. Another theory is that the asteroid belt is the remains of a planet that did form there, but somehow broke up. The inability to explain how or why it broke up has been largely responsible as to why scientists have not embraced this idea.

New revelations in science have once again vindicated the Sumerians version of events. Actually, NASA launched a probe several years ago (February 17, 1996) for the purpose of learning more about asteroids. The main focus was on the asteroid named Eros (one of the largest in the Asteroid Belt). This mission was successfully completed on St. Valentine's Day, February 14, 2000.

NASA chief project scientist Dr. Andrew Cheng reported *"Eros has an ancient, heavily cratered surface."* He added, *"There are also tantalizing hints that it has a layered structure, as if it were made up of layers, like plywood."* Such stratified features, Dr. Cheng explained, could occur if the asteroid was melted while it was part of a planet. (Lawrence Journal-World - Google News Archive Search, 2000)

Returning to the Sumerian Epic of Creation, all of the planets had by now settled into stable orbits around the Sun including Nibiru. However, Nibiru's orbit being a massive retrograde elongated ellipse, only returns to loop close to the Sun once every 3,600 earth years. Indeed, to live on Nibiru would offer one a moving observatory since it must pass relatively close to each planet in our system before it loops and goes back the other way. Is this why the Sumerians always depicted and described the solar system from the outside in – i.e. coming from Pluto and heading toward the Sun?

According to the Sumerians, a group who call themselves Anunnaki inhabit Nibiru. It was the Anunnaki that dictated the Epic of Creation to the Sumerians. How else would the Sumerians be able to explain in such great detail the outer planets of our solar system? After all, let us not forget that the Sumerians did not have telescopes. Modern astronomers did not discover Pluto until the 1930's! So how is it that these ancient people could describe these planets – down to their size and colour and in reverse order?

Zacharia Sitchin was able to give such graphic detail about the outer planets from his translations of Sumerian texts, that he was able to describe to NASA their appearance well before NASA had sent any probes out that far. Much to his delight, when the NASA probes finally did send back pictures of the outer planets for the first time, they matched the Sumerians description exactly!

In recent years, much debate and controversy has surrounded what some astronomers are calling 'Planet X'. Science News of April 7, 2001 headlined: **A Comet's Odd Orbit Hints At Hidden Planet** reports the conclusions of an international team of astronomers who have studied an unusual 'super' comet discovered last year (2000), designated 2000 CR/105. It follows a vast elliptical orbit around our Sun – an orbit that takes it way out to some 4.5 billion kilometres from the Sun and brings it back at its closest to the Sun to the vicinity of Neptune. According to Sky & Telescope News of April 5, 2001, this 'super' comet's orbit *"takes roughly 3,300 years"* to go once around the Sun.

In fact, the journal Science (April 6, 2001), in its Discovery News section was headlined: "**Comet's Course Hints at Mystery Planet.**" The special report, written by the Dutch astronomer Govert Schilling, summed up the findings in the following lead paragraph:

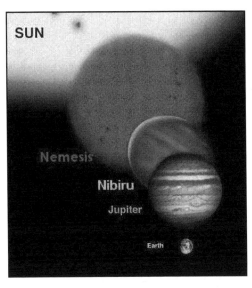

*Figure 20*

"A Supercomet following an unexpectedly far-flung path around the sun suggests that an unidentified planet once lurked in the outermost reaches of the solar system, an international team of astronomers report. What's more, the mysterious object may still be there."

R. Cowen in Science News (April 7, 2001), also stated, "Such an oblong orbit is usually a sign that an object has come under the gravitational influence of a massive body..." (Fig. 20)

Was this the gravitational pull of Neptune? In a study to be published in the Journal Icarus, the team of astronomers (led by Brett Gladman of the Observatoire de la Côte d'Azur in Nice, France), analysed all the possibilities, and concluded that this is not the case. Indeed, they offer an alternative solution. They argue that, "the comet's orbit could be the handiwork of an as-yet unseen planet...as massive as Mars...that would have to lie some 200 AU from the Sun," in the Kuiper Belt of cometary and other planetary debris. This would also explain "why many members of the Belt have orbits that angle away from the plane in which the nine known planets orbit the Sun."

Sitchin was so elated by this news that he wrote to them to ask that if they do discover this planet, could they please call it by its original Sumerian name of Nibiru!

## The Return of Nibiru

It is now up to us to overhaul our own understanding of who we are as a species so that we can, as Sitchin says, "be more prepared when the Anunnaki arrive." For although we may not agree on the return date of Nibiru, one point is for certain from both sides: Nibiru will return in our lifetime! On the record, Sitchin has stated that his calculations show the return of Nibiru to be at the end of 2063. However, several other people have calculated the date to be between 3750-60AD.

So doesn't look like we will see in our lifetime! Don't be disappointed, if it did come, chances are we would not survive the massive earth changes and upheavals it would cause.

On the 20th April 2013, an interview appeared on YouTube called **Wormwood passes Earth in Aug. 2013** (Wormwood is what some people call Planet X/Nibiru) between George Noory of Coast to Coast radio and Gordon James Gianninoto. Gianninoto claims to be an 'alien contactee' who told him that they have informed President Obama to release the information about Planet X to the public. The aliens, he says, foretold a time a great volcanic activity and massive social change just prior to the announcement. Not long after the world announcement, Planet X will be visible in the sky. Only time will tell on that one! But as I detail in Book II, don't expect any government to come clean on anything that may 'disrupt' the economy.

We have seen how an ancient culture has recorded events in universal history that are far more detailed and encompassing then our own 'modern day' theories. Did the ancients record these events as a warning to future generations? This is a topic I will detail in length in Book II & III and we will also look at strategies to avoid any impending disasters.

In the next chapter we will learn more about the mysterious Anunnaki and how they came to relate this amazing sequence of events to the Sumerians in the first place. So prepare yourself for the most enlightening revelation of them all – the origins of Homo Sapiens!

---

## A Mystery Revolves Around the Sun, MSNBC, October 7, 1999

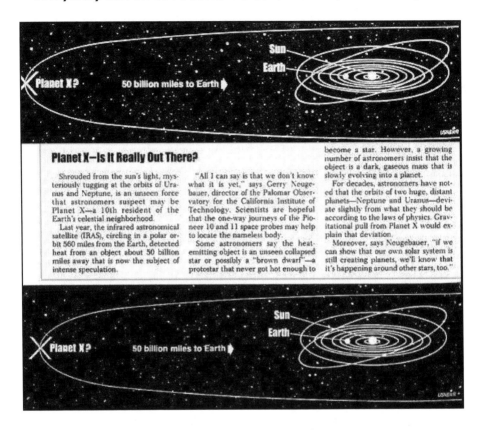

### Planet X—Is It Really Out There?

Shrouded from the sun's light, mysteriously tugging at the orbits of Uranus and Neptune, is an unseen force that astronomers suspect may be Planet X—a 10th resident of the Earth's celestial neighborhood. Last year, the infrared astronomical satellite (IRAS), circling in a polar orbit 560 miles from the Earth, detected heat from an object about 50 billion miles away that is now the subject of intense speculation.

"All I can say is that we don't know what it is yet," says Gerry Neugebauer, director of the Palomar Observatory for the California Institute of Technology. Scientists are hopeful that the one-way journeys of the Pioneer 10 and 11 space probes may help to locate the nameless body.

Some astronomers say the heat-emitting object is an unseen collapsed star or possibly a "brown dwarf"—a protostar that never got hot enough to become a star. However, a growing number of astronomers insist that the object is a dark, gaseous mass that is slowly evolving into a planet.

For decades, astronomers have noted that the orbits of two huge, distant planets—Neptune and Uranus—deviate slightly from what they should be according to the laws of physics. Gravitational pull from Planet X would explain that deviation.

Moreover, says Neugebauer, "if we can show that our own solar system is still creating planets, we'll know that it's happening around other stars, too."

*"Two teams of researchers have proposed the existence of an unseen planet or a failed star circling the sun at a distance of more than 2 trillion miles, far beyond the orbits of the nine known planets... Planetary scientist at Britain's Open University, speculates that the object could be a planet larger than Jupiter."*

# References:

Cowan, R. (2001). *A comet's odd orbit hints at hidden planet | Science News.* [online] Sciencenews.org. Available at: https://www.sciencenews.org/article/comets-odd-orbit-hints-hidden-planet?mode=magazine&context=293 [Accessed 10 Jan. 2010].

Cowing, K. (2001). Is There a Large Planet Orbiting Beyond Neptune?. [online] Spaceref.com. Available at: http://www.spaceref.com/news/viewnews.html?id=309 [Accessed 9 Sep. 2010].

DiNardo, J. and Manning, J. (2008). Planet X and the Mysterious Death of Dr. Robert Harrington. [online] Yowusa.com. Available at: http://yowusa.com/planetx/2008/planetx-2008-05b/1.shtml [Accessed 30 Jul. 2014].

*Drain the Ocean.* (2009). [film] http://channel.nationalgeographic.com/channel/episodes/drain-the-ocean/: National Geographic Channel Writers: Steve Nicholls, Victoria Coules.

Gilgamesh., and Sandars, N. (1972). *The epic of Gilgamesh.* 1st ed. Harmondsworth, Middlesex: Penguin Books.

Gladman, B., Holman, M., Grav, T., Kavelaars, J., Nicholson, P., Aksnes, K. and Petit, J. (2000). *Evidence for an Extended Scattered Disk?.* [online] Www-n.oca.eu. Available at: https://www-n.oca.eu/gladman/cr105.html [Accessed 17 Oct. 2010].

King, L. (1999). *The seven tablets of creation.* 1st ed. Escondido, Calif.: Book Tree.

Lawrence Journal-World - Google News Archive Search, (2000). *Asteroid heavily cratered.* [online] Available at: http://news.google.com/ newspapers?nid=2199& rs?nid=2199&dat=20000218&id=8ZgyAAAAIBAJ&sjid=IugFAAAAIBAJ&pg=5167, 3703370 [Accessed 25 Jul. 2014].

Nelson, T. (2011). The King James Study Bible. 1st ed. Thomas Nelson; Lea edition.

Semeniuk, I. (2001). Neptune attacks! - 07 April 2001 - New Scientist. [online] Newscientist.com. Available at: http://www.newscientist.com/article/mg17022854.600-neptune-attacks.html [Accessed 8 Jan. 2010].

Sitchin, Z. (1991). *The 12th planet.* 1st ed. Santa Fe, N.M.: Bear & Co.

Sitchin, Z. (n.d.). *The King Who Refused to Die: The Anunnaki and the Search for Immortality.* 1st ed. Bear & Company.

The Daily Telegraph, (2002). *Does the Sun have a doomsday twin?.* [online] Bibliotecapleyades.net. Available at: http://www.bibliotecapleyades.net/hercolobus/esp_hercolobus_1_03.htm#does_the_sun [Accessed 30 Jul. 2014].

Wikipedia, (2014). *Giant impact hypothesis.* [online] Wikipedia. Available at: http://en.wikipedia.org/wiki/Giant_impact_hypothesis [Accessed 28 Jul. 2014].

YouTube, (2013). *Wormwood passes Earth in Aug 2013.* [online] Available at: http://youtu.be/2XhWEWaOh7Y [Accessed 25 Jul. 2013].

# 16

# ADAM & ET - THE CREATION OF HUMANS

*Anunnaki – "Those who from heaven to Earth came."*

SCIENCE AND ARCHAEOLOGY have toiled for many years trying to identify that missing link that would vindicate Darwin's theory of evolution. This line of thinking argues that humans shared a common ancestor with the great apes. This apelike ancestor, which probably lived 5 to 11 million years ago in Africa, gave rise to two distinct lineages. One resulting in hominids, i.e. humanlike species, and the other resulting in the great ape species living today.

One of the earliest defining human traits is bipedalism, which is the ability to walk on two legs. They believe this trait evolved over 4 million years ago. Other important human characteristics such as a large and complex brain, the ability to make and use tools and the capacity for language developed more recently. Many advanced traits including complex symbolic expression, art and elaborate cultural diversity emerged mainly during the past 100,000 years

(Parker, 1992). On the other hand, Young Earth creationist, religious fundamentalists, have dismissed evolution out of hand, and claim that the Bible tells them that God created man and the earth in 7 days – precisely in 4003 BC making the Earth about 6000 years old! (Creation Today, 2014)

So collectively, on one side we have the 'evolutionists' and opposing them, are the 'creationists'. However, after many years of debate, neither group has been able to substantiate their claims. As we will discover, there is no missing link and furthermore, the biblical verses dealing with the fashioning of The Adam are actually condensed renderings of the much earlier and more detailed Sumerian and Akkadian texts.

Just on a cynical note on Science and Evolutionist – when the Christians say "God made it", scientists scoff, but when scientists say "Nature made it", they all nod and agree. But wouldn't this in effect make "nature", science's god? Seems a little hypocritical to me!

Approximately 4 billion years ago, the solar system and the Earth were very different from what we see today. As previously discussed, the Earth had once been part of a much larger planet, Tiamat. After the cosmic collision between Nibiru and Tiamat, the ensuing aftermath

*Figure 21*

found Tiamat smashed in two and the remainder being thrust into a new orbit around the Sun. This became planet Earth, and with her new orbit around the Sun, temperatures became more conducive for supporting life. Thus, over many millions of years, Earth was able to create an atmosphere, which in turn led her waters to become suitable for sustaining basic life forms. At this same time period, the planet Nibiru was also developing and changing, but at a much more accelerated rate.

Jumping forward to about **450,000 BCE**, we find Nibiru is inhabited by a race of giant hominoids, standing on average 2.8m - 3m (9ft-12ft) (Fig. 21)) and far heavier and more muscular than humans. They look very similar to humans or rather, humans look like them. Because of Nibiru's vast elliptical orbit, 1 year on Nibiru is equivalent to 3,600 years on earth. Therefore, they have extremely long lives. In fact, the ancient Sumerians thought they were immortal because the 'gods' would be on earth for many, many generations of humans. They are known to the Sumerians as **Anunnaki** *"those who from heaven to earth came"*. In the Bible it says: **Genesis [6:4]** *There were giants on the earth in those days; and also after that...* (Figs. 22 & 23)

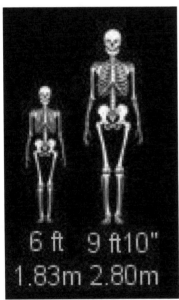

Figure 22                                    Figure 23

For further evidence for giants on Earth check this reference: (twelphsoul human agenda), 2012.

By all accounts, the Anunnaki were already a very technologically advanced race by our standards and according to Sitchin, the Anunnaki had already mastered space travel within the solar system. Being a military dictatorship, they had developed very advanced weapons, as well as medical procedures and a sophisticated society. That said, they still displayed basic forms of behaviour in the way of constant in-bickering, family feuds, wars, greed, cheating, lying and extra-marital affairs.

It was at this time that the Anunnaki realised that their planet had some major problems with its atmosphere, similar to our own ozone dilemma now, but far worse. Their atmosphere was leaching out into space. After several failed attempts using different methods, they had come to the conclusion that the only way of fixing this problem which threatened to destroy them, was to suspend a layer of gold dust high up in the Nibiru atmosphere. This, they hypothesised, would reflect the harmful radiation of the Sun and help to keep their atmosphere intact. This is a theory that NASA scientists have realised in our time. Indeed, NASA use to coat the windows of the space shuttle with a thin film of gold particles designed to reflect harmful radiation, which is an unavoidable hazard of space travel.

*Figure 24*

They would have to crush and grind the gold up into a powder known as **monoatomic gold**[2], (Fig. 24) thus, they would require substantial amounts. Assuming they could fix their atmosphere with gold was one thing, finding enough gold to complete the task was something else. Gold was an extremely rare metal on Nibiru, so they would need a new, abundant source. So far, they had only detected gold in 2 places within our solar system. One was in the asteroid belt, the other was a small planet they called Ki.

## The Main Players

At this time, the leader of the Anunnaki was Anu. Anu had two sons, **Enki**, their Chief Science Officer and eldest son, and **Enlil**, who was Enki's half-brother, having a different mother. He was mainly involved with administration and logistics. They also had a sister called **Ninmah**

---

[2] They later found out that monoatomic gold also has miraculous healing properties, promotes longevity, youthfulness and much more. Will talk about it in Book III.

(later called Ninhursag) who was the Chief Medical Officer. There are many other sons, daughters, cousins, uncles, mothers etc. Anu had 80 children to several different concubines. But these are the main characters that will change planet Earth forever.

Anu had literally just won the throne through single combat. The previous king, Alalu, failed to fix the Nibiru atmosphere as promised, so Anu called him out on it. After Alalu was defeated, he was very humiliated and facing death, so he stole a space ship and headed to Ki to follow a hunch he had – that the 3rd planet from the sun may have gold on it in abundance. On the way to Ki, Alalu actually had to nuke some asteroids in the asteroid belt between Jupiter and Mars that blocked his path. He hoped that if he found gold the people of Nibiru would praise him as a saviour and reinstate him as king, if not, he could hold them to ransom. He did find the gold and straight away he contacted the new King, Anu from Earth.

*"If you want the gold, restore my rule; recognize me as King of Nibiru and of Ki"*, he demanded, *"Otherwise I have missiles locked onto Nibiru and I will blow you all away!"*

Don't panic! Enki volunteered to go immediately to try and resolve the issue as he was related to Alalu by marriage. Much to the absolute disgust of Enlil, Anu sent Enki with Alalu's grandson, pilot Anzu (an expert pilot and navigator) and 50 men to Ki. Enki had pre-empted the job half-brother Enlil coveted. Enlil seethed while Enki and Anzu rocketed for Ki.

Ki was at this time a primordial swamp. The temperatures were hot and humid, volcanoes and earthquakes where a regular event, and life, though plentiful by now, was still very primitive. Even so, Ki had available vast amounts of gold, which the Anunnaki would eventually exploit.

When Enki landed, he declared, *"Here on Ki I am the commander! On a life or death mission we have come. Nibiru's fate is in our hands"*. Much to Enki's relief, Alalu did not object or challenge his authority. Being alone for so long on Ki had soften Alalu and for now he was just happy to see regular faces from home.

They had splashed down in the area we now know as the **Persian Gulf**. Back then, the area was lush and wet, not the desert we see today. In the next 7 days, Enki and his crew set up a base camp. It was the first time they had witnessed a sunset, and at first they thought something bad was going to happen. They were also amazed at how short the days and nights were.

*"On the seventh day Enki gathered the heroes (Igigi) around and spoke: We've undertaken a hazardous journey, overcoming much as we traversed from Nibiru to the seventh planet. We successfully arrived on Ki, which we now have renamed Earth[3], established an encampment and completed much good. Let this, the seventh day be a day of rest. And hereafter the seventh day always to be a resting day. Henceforth let this place be called Eridu, meaning Home in the Faraway. "* (Sitchin, 2004).

(**Genesis [2:2]** *And on the seventh day God finished the work that he had done, and he rested on the seventh day from all the work that he had done.*)

The Anunnaki had a band of professional soldiers/astronauts they call Igigi (pronounced Eye-jee-jee) - the Bible calls them Nefilim – **The Fallen**, but we will have to wait until Chapter 20 to find out why! The Igigi were the only working class inhabitants that went on the Earth mission, whilst the rest of Anunnaki were considered the royalty or aristocracy.

As a boy, Sitchin was extremely curious about a reference made in the Old Testament concerning the Nefilim. This is what eventually gave him the impetus to learn cuneiform, which in turn enabled him to translate the term 'Nefilim' to its literal meaning of "those who came down". This same line of reasoning led him to believe that the Elohim in Genesis, were the Anunnaki – "Those who from heaven to Earth came". Although I only offer a cursory overview of Sitchin's conclusions here, I would encourage the reader to follow up these arguments for themselves, as I am confident you will fully appreciate the veracity of Sitchin's work.

Around **445,000 BCE**, Enki led a landing party that establish **Eridu** – Earth Station 1, for purpose of extracting gold from the waters of the present day Persian Gulf. In modern times, the site of Eridu is now called **Tell Abu Shahrain**, in Dhi Qar Governorate, Iraq. Given the climatic and geographic state of the Earth, the work proved

---

[3] Enki was originally called "Ea", but was later named Lord of Earth "En-Ki", and Earth was named after "Ea" – his original name!

very trying, however they persisted, as their end task was a matter of survival for their home planet. Enki was an extremely talented scientist. During this period he managed to document many varieties of wild plants and animals including wheat, barley and rice along with goats, oxen and other beasts. He hoped to get samples back to his lab to see their DNA and try and domesticate them. In fact, most modern day botanists are perplexed as to how wild varieties of rice, wheat and corn became domesticated. There appears to be major changes in the DNA structure of wild and domesticated varieties of these plants.

Figure 25 shows wild corn on the left and the fully domesticated variety on the right. However, as we know, Enki was responsible for this amazing feat of science. Indeed, Enki created an environment so hospitable compared to the rest of the world that his 'garden' became the seed of legends. The Sumerians called this area **É.DIN**. This is what the ancient Jews called "Eden".

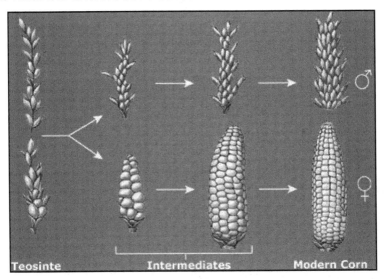

*Figure 25*

By 430,000 BCE, the earth's climate had mellowed somewhat and Enki was joined on earth by his half-sister, Ninmah, who was Chief Medical Officer and his son Ningiszidda (pron: Nigi-shee-dah). It should be noted at this point that one must remember that 1 year on Nibiru is equivalent to 3,600 years on earth. Therefore, the typical life of the Anunnaki spanned many hundreds of thousands, sometimes millions of earth years.

Many of the Igigi workers had toiled in the harsh conditions of Earth for many, many years mining gold. The point had come when they had had enough. For a start, they were soldiers and pilots, not labours. On top of that, the working conditions were hellish. What ensued was a mass riot – they refused to mine anymore gold. Gold production stopped and many Anunnaki on both sides were slain. A compromise needed to be found and in a hurry. The unrest had forced Anu himself, accompanied by his other son Enlil, to come to Earth and personally try and negotiate a settlement.

Anu felt the rebellion was caused through Enki's inability to manage the workforce. Moreover, he felt Enki was too 'soft'. Anu acknowledge and respected Enki's scientific achievements, however he felt that Enlil could better manage the Earth colony on a day to day basis. Enki was always away, exploring and cataloguing new species. Otherwise he was in his lab working away. He didn't have the time or the impetus to run a mining operation, still, it hurt him deeply that he would have to hand over everything he had built to his ungrateful and spiteful brother Enlil. But it was done, Enlil was now the new Commander of Earth Station 1 and everyone, including Enki had to take orders from him.

After Anu spoke with the aggrieved workers, he realised very quickly that an alternative workforce must be found and quickly. There was a sense of urgency as Nibiru was moving out of the solar system again and the problem with the atmosphere had still not been rectified.

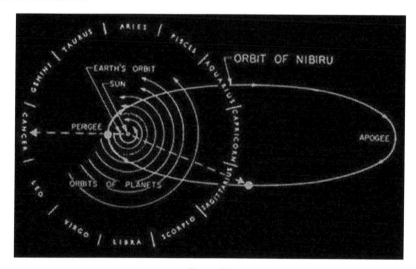

*Figure 26*

The best time to travel from Nibiru to Earth is when Nibiru neared the Sun, at perigee (Fig. 26). Therefore, they only had a span of 13 to 18 Earth months to ship stuff back and forth. They also used specialised shuttle craft to transport gold mined on Earth to and from a base on Mars. From Mars it was on-shipped to Nibiru. (Sitchin, 1991)

Anu ordered Enki and Ninmah to find an alternative worker to replace the rebelling Igigi. As it turned out, Ninmah had already been assisting Ningiszidda, who was a top level geneticist. He had been experimenting with the life forms of Earth, using advanced genetic splicing techniques. Enki saw the amazing and odd creatures they had created. Many of the creatures we associate with mythology such as Griffins (Fig. 27), Minotaur (Fig. 28), Centaurs and Unicorns were but a few. This gave Enki an idea. Perhaps they could create a "beast of burden", capable of carry out the mining work. It would have to be a creature that could understand and follow basic orders, but be docile enough not to rise up and mutiny like the Igigi did.

Over much time and many experiments, they still had not created a being capable of carrying out the work required. Anu was about to shut the whole operation down because Nibiru was moving out of the system. It was then, at the 11th hour that Ninmah saved the day!

But before we get into that, we need a little lesson in **Human Evolution** and the Family Tree!

*Figure 27*

Griffin

*Figure 28*

Minotaur

## References:

Creation Today, (2014). *Creation Today | Impacting our world with the creation message.* [online] Creationtoday.org. Available at: http://creationtoday.org/ [Accessed 29 Jul. 2014].

Parker, S. (1992). *The Dawn of Man.* 1st ed. New York: Crescent Books.

Sitchin, Z. (1991). *Genesis revisited.* 1st ed. Santa Fe, N.M.: Bear & Co.

(1991). *The 12th planet.* 1st ed. Santa Fe, N.M.: Bear & Co.

(2004). *The Lost Book of Enki: Memoirs and Prophecies of an Extraterrestrial God.* 1st ed. Santa Fe, N.M: Bear & Company, pp.67 -78.

(2010). There were giants upon the earth. 1st ed. Rochester, Vt.: Bear & Co.

Tellinger, M. (2012). *Slave species of the gods.* 1st ed. Rochester, Vt.: Bear & Co.

twelphsoul (human agenda), (2012). *Giant Skeletons 7 to 12 feet tall.* [online] YouTube. Available at: http://youtu.be/tQlxFF_gAi8 [Accessed 31 Jul. 2014].

# 17

# HUMAN EVOLUTION - THE FAMILY TREE

---

*"Human evolution, at first, seems extraordinary.*
*How could the process that gave rise to slugs*
*and oak trees and fish produce a creature that*
*can fly to the moon and invent the Internet and*
*cross the ocean in boats?" Steven Pinker*

---

*H*UMANS ARE MEMBERS of the genus **Homo**. Modern people are **Homo sapiens sapiens**. However, we are not the only species of humans to who have ever lived. There were earlier species of our genus that are now extinct. In the past, it was incorrectly assumed that human evolution was a relatively straight forward sequence of one species evolving into another. We now understand that there were times when several species of humans and even other hominines were alive living in the same regions at the same time.

This complex pattern of evolution emerging from the fossil record has been aptly described as a luxuriantly branching bush on which all but one twig has died off. Modern humans are that last living twig. The

*Figure 29*

striking similarities in appearance between the human genus Homo and our distant ancestors, the genus **Australopithecus** (pron: Austral-o-pith-ikus) (Fig. 29), is sufficient reason to place us both into the same biological tribe (Hominini). Both genera are bipedal (walk on 2 legs) and normally have an upright in posture.

Like australopithecines, early humans were light in frame and relatively short. They were only about 100-135 cm (3 ft. 4 in. to 4 ft. 5 in.) tall and weighed around 32 kg (70 pounds) – similar to a modern 6-7 year old child. The evolution of larger bodies occurred later in human evolution.

The differences between australopithecines and early humans are most noticeable in the head. Humans developed significantly larger brains and relatively smaller faces with progressively smaller teeth and jaws. In addition, humans became ever more proficient in developing tools to aid in their survival, while the australopithecines did not.

The immediate ancestors of early humans were most likely late australopithecines. At present, the leading contender for that ancestral species is Australopithecus garhi or possibly Australopithecus africanus.

There may have been one or possibly two species of the first humans living in East Africa--**Homo rudolfensis** and **Homo habilis** (literally "handy or skilled human"). The few rudolfensis fossils that have been found are somewhat earlier, dating about 2.4-1.6 million years ago, while the more common habilis remains are around 1.9-1.4 million years old. Rudolfensis apparently was a bit taller and relatively larger brained on average. However, many paleoanthropologists consider the differences to be too slight to warrant a separate species designation. Some have suggested that rudolfensis were males and habilis were females. As a result, they classify them both as a single species--Homo habilis. That is the approach taken in this book.

The evolution of the genus Homo beginning around 2.5 million years ago coincides with the beginning of a period of prolonged climate instability in Africa. The overall trend was towards cooling and drying, but along the way there were considerable climate fluctuations. It

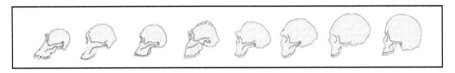

*Figure 30*

is likely that selection for the ability to adapt to these environmental changes resulted in the emergence of humans with their larger, more capable brains (Fig. 30).

Early human fossils were first discovered in 1960 by Louis and Mary Leakey at Olduvai Gorge in Tanzania. The Leakeys named them **Homo habilis** (Latin for "handy or skilled human") because they apparently made stone tools. Similar fossils were found at East Lake Turkana in Kenya by Richard Leakey's team of fieldworkers that began searching there in 1969. These latter specimens were named Homo rudolfensis after Lake Rudolf (i.e., the former name for Lake Turkana) (Fig. 31).

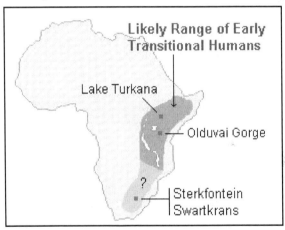

*Figure 31*

So far, conclusive evidence of Homo habilis has been found only in the **Great Rift Valley** system of East Africa. However, their ultimate geographic and time ranges may have been somewhat larger. Early human fossils also have been found in South Africa in the caves at Sterkfontein and Swartkrans in apparent association with australopithecines. However, not all paleoanthropologists agree that these fossils should be considered Homo habilis.

Early transitional humans had brains that on average were about 35% larger than those of Australopithecus africanus. In fact, it is beginning with Homo habilis that our ancestors finally had brains that were consistently bigger than those of the great apes. Ajit Varki and

Figure 32

his team of geneticists at the University of California San Diego campus have discovered a small genetic difference between humans and apes that may account for the progressive increase in the size of human brains. Humans, but not apes, have a gene that stops the production of **N-glycolylneuramine acid.** Using "molecular clock analysis," the U.C.S.D. researchers determined that this gene entered the human evolutionary line as a result of a mutation 2.7 million years ago. While it is presumed that the australopithecines lacked this gene, there is no direct evidence.

As the early human cranium, or brain case, began to enlarge in response to increased brain size, the mouth became smaller. In comparison to the australopithecines, the early humans had smaller teeth, especially the molars and premolars. This suggests that they mostly ate softer foods. An analysis of the wear patterns on their teeth indicates that they had diverse diets that included a wide range of plants and meat. As noted previously, the body size of Homo habilis (Fig. 32) was not significantly larger than the early hominines that preceded them.

Figure 33

Likewise, the arms of habilis and their australopithecine ancestors were relatively long compared to ours. The modern human body size and limb proportions began to appear with the next species in our evolution, **Homo erectus** (Fig. 33).

## Evolution in Brain Size

The cranial capacities for Australopithecines and Homo habilis hardly changed at all over time, but Homo erectus started out in the Homo habilis range and ended up in the low-end of Homo sapiens (modern humans) cranial capacity. That is a very telling sign that we will come back to (Fig. 34).

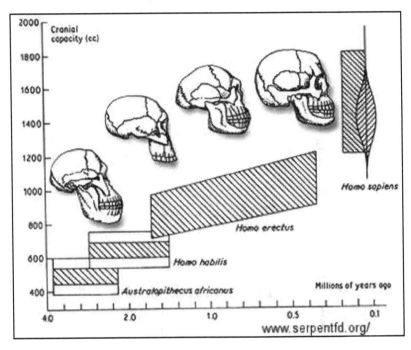

*Figure 34*

Although there are several more Homo species on the human family tree, most of them do not concern us at this time. They include Neanderthals (*Homo neanderthalensis*), *Homo heidelbergensis* and *Homo floresiensis* (the 'hobbit'). The species on the next page are our direct descendants:

## Early Descendants of Modern Man

*Australopithecus afarensis (3.9 to 3.0 million years ago (Mya), meaning 'Southern Ape from Africa'.* Its skull is similar to a chimpanzee's but with more humanlike teeth. Most (possibly all) creationists would call this an ape, but it was bipedal, and the first recognised ancestor of modern humans.

*Homo habilis (2.5 to 1.8 Mya) meaning 'handy man'* was similar to Australopithecines, but used tools and had a larger brain (650 cc) and a less projecting face. It can be the first species of the Homo genus to have appeared. Homo habilis had longer arms compared to modern humans, but a reduced protrusion in the face, and smaller teeth than Australopithecus. H. habilis remains have been discovered along with primitive stone tools and this species lived at the beginning of the Paleolithic ("the old stone age") about 2.6 million years ago.

*Homo erectus, (1.9 MYA – 200,000 Years Ago), meaning 'upright man'* is an extinct species of hominid that lived from the end of the Pliocene epoch to the later Pleistocene, with the earliest fossil evidence dating to around 1.9 million years ago and the most recent to approximately 200,000 years ago. The species originated in Africa and migrated as far as India, China and Java. Homo erectus existed longer than any other human species. 'Turkana Boy' and 'Nariokotome Boy' are sometimes classified as Homo ergaster.

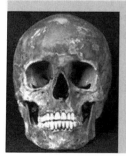

*Homo sapiens, (200,00 to 30,000 Years ago), meaning 'wise man'* Homo sapiens are primates of the family Hominidae, and the only living species of the genus Homo. Cro-Magnon who existed from approximately 200,000 to 30,000 years ago, and Homo sapiens sapiens - Modern Humans, from 30,000 years ago to the present day.

What is demonstrated here is that our earliest ancestors, Australopithecus, then Homo habilis, changed very little in several million years. Then suddenly out of nowhere, a new taller, smarter and less hairy dude shows up – Homo erectus!

## Questions:

In a relatively short amount of time (less than 1,000,000 years):

- How does a creature go from 250cm, to almost 2m tall? (98 inches to 6ft)
- How does its arm to body length ratio change dramatically?
- How does this creature develop more modern human limbs, hands, feet, face and hair?
- How does this creature suddenly become much more intelligent, controlling fire and using spears and other tools.
- How did this creature manage to get to almost every continent on Earth?

## HOW DOES IT GO

**From this:**                                    **To this:**

          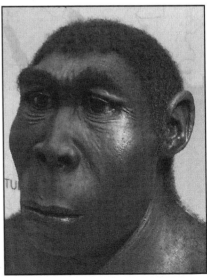

*Homo habilis*                          *Homo erectus*

## References:

Parker, S. (1992). *The dawn of man*. 1st ed. New York: Crescent Books.

Winston, R. and Wilson, D. (2004). *Human*. 1st ed. London: DK Pub.

# 18

## ADAMU & TI-AMAT – THE FIRST HUMANS

---

*"The being that we need already exists; all
that we have to do is put our mark on it."*
Enki from the *"Enuma Elish"*
*(the Babylonian Epic of Creation).*

---

## The Story Continues...

UST BEFORE ANU was about to shut down the genetics lab and
ship everyone back to Nibiru, Ninmah entered Enki's lab with
a creature he had not seen before. The creature was a small,
hairy hominid 'ape' type creature that walked upright. It is widely
accepted today that the creature Ninmah had discovered was
Homo erectus, however, after a great deal of research, study and
thinking, I am convinced that the creature was **Homo habilis**!

But first, a little more on Homo erectus based on what modern
anthropologist and palaeontologist agree on.

*Figure 35*

**Homo erectus** (Fig. 35) was the first human species that migrated out of Africa, colonizing most of Eurasia till Southeast Asia. Remains have been found in eastern Africa, Europe (Georgia, Spain), Indonesia, Vietnam and China. H. erectus was very similar to modern humans, but with 75 % of our brain capacity (950 to 1100 cc). They had an average height of about 1.79 m (5 feet, 10 inches). Males were 20-30% larger than females. They utilized diverse and sophisticated tools and together with Homo ergaster, was probably the first human species that matched the definition of hunter gatherer. Despite the similarity with modern humans, H. erectus could not produce complex sounds required by modern speech.

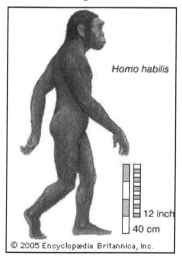

*Homo habilis*

12 inch
40 cm

© 2005 Encyclopædia Britannica, Inc.

*Figure 36*

**Homo habilis** (Fig. 36) hardly changed at all over time. In almost 4 million years, there was very little change between Australopithecus afarensis and Homo habilis. Furthermore, we know that Homo – NOT Apes, stop the production of the gene N-glycolylneuramine acid. Given that the Anunnaki had such advanced technology, I think it is safe to assume that they would have been aware of this. That is why they selected this creature, rather than one of the many ape species around at the time. Homo habilis had the intelligence to make stone tools, so no doubt it could be trained to follow directions.

Ninmah said to the creature, *"Pick up that rock and place it over there."* The creature complied. Enki was amazed. *"Now sit down over there"*, the creature complied.

Enki said, *"This is incredible. Perhaps we have found what we have been looking for?"*, however, Ningiszidda said, *"Yes Father, however, this creature is too small and frail to carry out the manual labour we require."*

Enki sat and thought about this. What Ningiszidda said was correct. This creature (Homo habilis) was only 100-135 cm (3 ft. 4 in. to 4 ft. 5 in.) tall and the Anunnaki were almost 3 meters tall! This was like a baby to Enki. Suddenly, he got it – a baby – make-a-new-baby – make a new creature!

Enki jumped up and startled everyone, *"If we mix our own DNA with this creature we can make a new, robust worker!"*

Finally Enki had found a creature that was capable of understanding commands, yet was primitive enough to be manipulated to work for them. All he needed now was time to produce the new worker. Enki immediately went to tell his father Anu.

According to the Enuma Elish (the Babylonian Epic of Creation), when the other leaders of the Anunnaki asked: *"How can you create a new being?"* Enki answered: *"The being that we need already exists; all that we have to do is put our mark on it."*

By 'mark' he meant their DNA. The time was some **300,000 years** ago. In **Genesis [1:27]**: *"So God created man in his own image, in the image of God created he, him; male and female created he them"*.

This is one of the single most mistranslated passages of the Bible to date. Anyone with a rudimentary understanding of early Greek or Hebrew knows that **"US"**, and **"OUR"** are the correct translations. The Judo/Christian version wrongly claims that the passage reads I and MY.

It should read: *'Then God said, let **US** make man in **OUR** image, in OUR likeness'*.

It was Enki that said these words to the Anunnaki leaders, *"Let us fashion the Adam (Earth man) in our image, after our likeness."*

That the Anunnaki, who could already travel in space 450,000 years ago, possessed the genetic science whose threshold we are

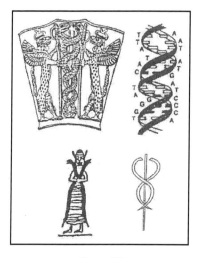

Figure 37

only now reaching, is clear, not only from the actual texts, but also from numerous depictions in which the double-helix of the DNA is rendered as Entwined Serpents (Fig. 37). A symbol used in modern times for medical is the **Caduceus**. It also has two snakes and wings, coiled around the **Rod of Asclepius** (Fig. 38).

When the leaders of the Anunnaki approved the project, as echoed in the biblical "Let us fashion the Adam", Enki, with the help of his sister Ninmah and son Ningiszidda, embarked on a process of genetic engineering.

Enki went to the **Great Rift Valley** in Southeast Africa (what the Anunnaki call the Abzu) to build a sterile lab; its air-conditioning was *"the source of the biblical assertion that after having fashioned the Adam, Elohim 'blew in his nostrils the breath of life.'"* (Sitchin, 1991). In the **The Lost Book of Enki**, the repeated failures to obtain a non-defective newborn are described, with success coming only after Enki realized that:

*"Perchance the shortfall is not in the admixture...*
*Perchance neither in the female's oval*
*Nor in the essences is the hindrance –*
*Of what the Earth itself is fashioned,*
*Perchance that is what is missing?"*

Finally, success! Only after Ninmah followed his instructions did she create a fertilized egg. Instead of combining the genes in a crystal vessel, it was done in a vessel made of the **CLAY OF THE EARTH** (Sitchin, 2002).

**(Genesis[2:7]** *"then the LORD God formed man from the dust of the ground, and breathed into his nostrils the breath of life; and the man became a living being."*)

Figure 38

However, there was another setback. Whenever they put a fertilised egg into the womb of Homo habilis, it would either miscarry or a deformed baby was born or they were unable to talk – only make grunting noises. They experimented with cloning, cell fusion and recombinant technology–cutting DNA strands with enzymes, targeted viruses, absorbing sperm in genetic material to be used for fertilization and splicing in DNA patches of other species to create, at first, hybrids unable to reproduce. Then Ningishzidda isolated the XX and XY chromosomes that allowed the creation of fertile creatures (Sitchin, 1991).

Enki finally worked out that the only way for a viable baby to be born was if the egg was implanted into an Anunnaki female. He discussed this over with Ninmah who agreed. Enki said he would ask his wife Damkina, if she would carry the child. Not knowing what creature they may carry would be a burden for any women. But just as Enki was about to head out the door to seek his wife, Ninmah put her hand on his shoulder and said "I will bear the child".

Enki was so elated he hugged and kissed her. However, he just realised he had no idea how long it would take to gestate the baby. As it turned out, it was 9 months, which to an Anunnaki, that was a short trek.

Finally, a perfect model of Adamu was attained, Ninmah held him up and shouted: "My hands have made it!" An ancient artist depicted the scene on a cylinder seal (Fig. 39).

*Figure 39*

Adamu *"one like South African Earth's clay"* (a red shade). He had smooth and dark red skin and black hair. The hair was still quite course

and shaggy, however the body fur of Homo habilis was gone.
The Anunnaki, in contrast, were white-skinned, smooth hair that was usually fair and blue eyes. Adamu had the arms, hands, legs, feet and torso of the Anunnaki, but a primitive, still slightly ape like head and face. He was almost 2 meters tall (6ft), still about half the size of the Anunnaki, but twice as tall as his biological mother Homo habilis! Adamu had a high iron content, thus red blood. Anunnaki have blue/green blood on account of a high copper content in their blood.

Enki also observed: *"Adamu's malehood; odd was its shape, by a skin was its forepart surrounded, unlike that of Anunnaki malehood it was. 'Let the Earthling from us Anunnaki by this foreskin be distinguished. So was Enki saying."* (Sitchin, 1991, p: 139)

Here Enki is saying that the new human males have a foreskin, something the Anunnaki men do not have. He said, use this as a way to distinguish the Anunnaki from humans. That is why in figure 37, the little Adamu has a foreskin hat on and the others (from left to right) Ningiszidda, mixing a new batch, Enki, holding the test tube for insemination and Ninmah holding up her baby boy. One more point: modern science cannot figure out why the human male penis is so big (average 6 inches) compared to our primate cousins (average 1 inch). Primates and most other animals have relatively small penises compared to their body size. Humans have large ones compared to their body size. Is this because the DNA for making a penis came from a GIANT, who stands almost 3 meters tall?

We know this creature as Homo Erectus (Fig. 40), a direct descendant of modern man! Adamu would have looked very similar to this.

It is interesting to note that the Anunnaki have blue/green blood. This fact has carried down the centuries through our subconscious psyche when we often acknowledge royalty has having 'blue' blood. Furthermore, we often use the term "he's a blue blooded male" to mean 'he's the real thing'. The 'real' thing being Anunnaki?

In these early days, human embryos still required gestation in a womb. The first man, Adamu was carried by non-other than Ninmah herself. Once she had Adamu, the prototype for the primitive worker, Ninmah contacted her Medical Centre at Shurubak (located about 195 km – 120 miles, southeast of present day Baghdad). She required seven doctors who'd volunteer their wombs to grow offspring for more Adamus.

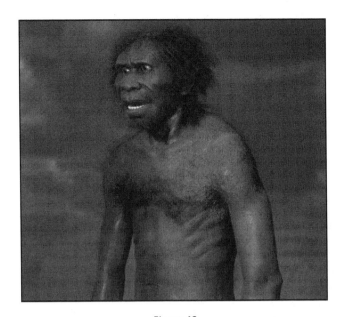

*Figure 40*

"'*His essence alone as a mold shall be!*' so was Enki saying. Ninmah and the women swore they'd love and support the babies they'd bare.

"In seven vessels of the clay of Abzu (Africa) made, Ninmah ovals (zygotes which Enki's sperm fertilized) of the two-legged females placed. The life essences of Adamu she extracted, bit by bit, in the vessels she it, inserted. Then in the malepart of Adamu an incision she made, a drop of blood to let out.

'*Let this a Sign of Life be; that Flesh and Soul have combined let it forever proclaim.*' She squeezed the malepart for blood, one drop in each vessel to the admixture she added.

'In this clay's admixture, Earthling with Anunnaki shall be bound. To a unity shall the two essences, one of Heaven, one of Earth, together be brought.' In the wombs of the birth-giving heroines the fertilized ovals were inserted. Ninmah cut Adamu's seven healthy boys from their wombs." (Sitchin, 1991)

## Now a Mate We Must Create!

To create a female mate for Adamu, Ningishzidda planted another zygote, prepared with Adamu's blood, in Damkina (Enki's wife). When it grew to a viable female foetus, he removed it surgically. Ninmah named the hybrid **Ti-Amat** (Mother of Life).

Ningishizidda put ova from Ti-Amat into seven test-tubes. He planted them in the same doctors who'd borne the hybrid males. All the surrogate mothers carried female hybrids, which he removed surgically. When he told the doctors he needed their wombs again, Ninmah objected:

*"For my heroines too burdensome is baring more Earthlings. Too few are the heroines to bare numbers enough to work mines."*

Enki now had a new problem. He had to breed more Adamu, but he didn't have any female Anunnaki to grow them in. He would need to come up with something fast.

Enki put the 7 females and the 8 male hybrids made from Adamu's and Ti-Amat's DNA together in an enclosure at his African lab to see if they would mate. If they could mate, he would not require Nimah's female doctors to carry any more young. This would also speed up the production of the slaves for the mine. They copulated often, but the females didn't conceive.

The Igigi were back working in the mines because Anu had told them that relief would be coing soon. However, from their point of view, Enki was taking too long and threatened to mutiny again if Enki and Ningishzidda didn't bring workers to relieve them. Under pressure, Enki left Africa and went back to É.DIN, taking Adamu and Ti-Amat with him. É.DIN was now being run by Enki's brother Enlil.

Once back in his original lab he and Ningishzidda compared Anunnaki genes against the genes of Adamu and Ti-Amat. He found the genes for reproduction. Anunnaki females had a recessive XY chromosomal allele in their genotype, whereas Ti-Amat had only XX. Enki made a rash decision. He ordered Ningishzidda to carry out the experiment. He knew this could get them all into big trouble.

To make the hybrids fertile, Ningishzidda anesthetized Enki, Ninmah, Adamu and Ti-Amat.

"From the rib of Enki the life essence he extracted; into the rib of Adamu the life essence he inserted. From the rib of Ninmah the life essence he extracted; into the rib of Ti-Amat the life essence He inserted.

He proudly declared, *'To their Tree of Life two branches have been added, with procreating powers their life essences are now entined.'"* (Sitchin, 2002)

Enki, Ninmah and Ningishzidda hid how they'd altered Ti-Amat. In effect, they had broken one of the biggest laws of Nibiru: **The Rules Of Planet Journeys**.

She and Adamu stayed in Enki's Persian Gulf orchard (É.DIN), while her foetus gestated. Meanwhile, Ti-Amat made leaf-aprons for herself and Adamu.

## God Expels Adam & Eve from the Garden of Eden

*Or, the Sumerian Version:*

## Enlil Banishes Adamu & Ti-Amat from É.DIN to Africa

Enlil saw Adamu and Ti-Amat wore aprons and made Enki explain. Enki confessed; Ti-Amat's foetus would, in turn, breed.

*"The last bit of our life essence to these creatures you have given, to be like us in procreation knowing, perchance our (millions of years) life cycles on them to bestow,"* Enlil roared. Enki's team had exceeded Enlil's okay to create mine slaves in test tubes or with surrogate Anunnaki mothers was one thing, but to allow them to breed of their own accord was out of the question as far as Enlil was concerned. He feared that if these creatures could breed by themselves, then they may breed enough to one day rise up and challenge their masters – the Anunnaki!

*"'My lord Enlil,'* Ningishzidda was saying, *'knowing for procreation they were given, the branch of Long Living, to their essence tree was not'.* A longevity gene or genes known to Enki and Ningishzidda was deliberately excluded from the human genome when the 'mixing' of genes took place."

Enlil shouted, *"To create hybrid beings is in The Rules Of Planet Journeys forbidden."*

Enki responded, *"A new species create we shall not; the Apeman is in his fashioning essence [genotype] as we of Nibiru are. Our ancestor the Apeman is; into us he evolves. Speed Apeman shall we, speed him but some millions of years to what has always been his destiny."*

Enki and Enlil beamed Anu and the Council on Nibiru. Each brother had his say on whether to create hybrids that could breed. King and the council ruled, *"Gold must be obtained. Let the Being be fashioned! Forsake The Rules of Planetary Journeys, let Nibiru be saved."* (Sitchin, 2007)

*"'Then let them be where they are needed,'* Enlil with anger said. *'To the Abzu away from the É.din, let them be expelled.'"* (Sitchin, 2002, p: 149)

**Genesis [3:23]** *"So the LORD God banished him from the Garden of Eden to work the ground from which he had been taken."*

What Enki and Ningishzidda did not tell Enlil at the time, is that they had buried 98% of their DNA. The Earthlings were given much more of the Anunnaki DNA. Their DNA, joined with the native DNA within them created a new 12 strand DNA.

Enki knew the Earthlings were too young in their creation to fully control their 12 strand DNA. Not to mention, if Enlil found out he would have destroyed all of the Earthlings on the spot. That is because a 12 strand DNA creature at full power would eclipse the Anunnaki on every level. In fact, the Anunnaki would be like fumbling children compared to a fully awakened human. Enki ordered Ningishzidda to bury all but the absolutely necessary DNA for survival. Ningishzidda programmed triggers into the DNA to awaken at the correct time. That time is now and I will be covering that topic in depth in Book III.

After Enlil evicted the hybrid Earthlings from É .din, Enki knew Enlil would limit them and slander him as an evil serpent. Up until then, Enki took the symbol of the serpent which became synonymous with knowledge and wisdom. Enlil would do anything to sully the symbol of the snake, because he knew this would hurt Enki's reputation. That is what led to the story about the snake in the Garden of Eden tempting Eve. In that story, Eve was tempted by the serpent to eat from the Tree of Knowledge. The Bible says the serpent taught them "knowing". "Knowing" is the knowledge of sex and how to procreate. Up until then, only the gods could reproduce humans, however now they could do it themselves. This is what made them "god-like".

Thus, in future days, Enki decided to set up a secret Brotherhood for the Earthlings and their symbol would be the Serpent. This would be the first Mystery School that Enki would use to pass down all the knowledge of the Anunnaki to benefit mankind. He taught them technology and advanced thinking, then later, when Ningishzidda had a huge Spiritual awakening, they were taught many Spiritual Truths, some of which have survived to this day.

Enki put Adamu and Ti-Amat in an enclosure in present day Zimbabwe where Ti-Amat bore the twins Kai-in and Abael, then others who, in turn, bred with each other. Adamu and Ti-Amat, being the first Earthlings created by Enki were never sent to the mines or subjected to hard labour.

"In a few thousand years, the Earthlings were proliferating. To be with the Anunnaki they were eager, for food rations they toiled well. Of heat and dust they did not complain, of backbreaking they did not grumble. Of hardships of work the Anunnaki were relieved." The Earthlings worked the African mines and submersible cargo boats that, in just ten days, brought the gold from the mines to Bad-Tibira in Sumer (Iraq) to smelt, refine and form into portable ingots for transhipment to Mars. From Mars, Astronauts rocketed the gold to Nibiru, where scientists refined it to white powder of monoatomic gold to float into the hole in their ozone. The hole in their atmosphere shrunk. "The vital gold to Nibiru was coming; steadily. Nibiru's atmosphere was slowly healing." (Sitchin, 1990)

One of Nibiru's 3,600 year approaches to Earth's inner Solar System upset Earth's climate and ruined the new crops. Earthlings adapted and foraged afar, but made and gathered less food. From 27,000 B.C., Earthlings' standard of living worsened and they took again to the wild and cave-dwelling.

"Following generations showed less advanced standards of civilized life. From 27,000 to 11, 000 the regressing and dwindling population reached almost complete absence of habitation." (Sitchin, 2007).

Therefore, Enlil urged Enki to make them smart enough to farm and herd better. Enki decided to upgrade Earthling intelligence and at the same time, further his own personal experiments in perfecting the human body to mimic his own likeness.

The Anunnaki gave the Earthlings "food and shelter while they performed gruelling tasks, the reason for which they did not understand. The stuff (gold) they were digging up had no value to them. They could not eat it, or use it in any way." The Anunnaki Royals, their staff and the Astronaut Corps needed a steady stream of fresh labourers for projects.

By this stage, Enlil had become very spiteful toward the Earthlings. Twice his brother Enki had won the debates on whether they should have been created at all, thus, the Council on Nibiru had overturned his rulings on Earth. This humiliation did not sit well. Enlil had little love for these creatures and in his mind they were little more than worthless slaves. He would feed them little, work them to exhaustion and if one died, they were tossed aside and another took their place. Enki was aware of this, so he felt a personal attachment to the little creatures he had fathered. Enki set about working behind the scenes to help the fledgling humans to be become free.

In the south of Africa, from Mozambique to Botswana, Zimbabwe and beyond, where the descendants of Adamu laboured for the Anunnaki, "the extended ancient settlement covered an area much larger than modern Johannesburg, more than 500,000 square kilometres. (Tellinger, 2012)

In his African reserve, "Enki in the marshlands looked about. With him was Ismud, his vizier, who secrets kept. On the river's bank, frolicking Earthlings he noticed; two females among them were wild with beauty, firm were their breasts. Their sight the phallus of Enki caused to water, a burning desire he had."

"A young one to him Enki called, a tree fruit she offered him. Enki bent down, the young one he embraced, on her lips he kissed her. Sweet were her lips, firm with ripeness were her breasts. Into her womb she took the holy semen, by the semen of Enki she was impregnated." Enki then coupled with the second young Earthling". (Sitchin, 2002)

Now, I need to digress a little here to explain a few things about our old mate, the Lord Enki! Enki was a nice guy, good looking, a smooth talker and could charm the birds from the trees so to speak. Enlil on the other hand was a misogynist who saw nothing wrong with raping a women if she didn't agree to his advances, especially if he thought they were below his standing to begin with. But back to Enki, he was what we would call in modern terms a womaniser, or more politely, the Earth's first Casanova. He was well known for his sexual exploits and his limitless lust for the fairer sex. Even though the Homo erectus were not particular pretty women, in his eyes they had hot bodies and nice breasts, so he couldn't help himself. There was also another reason for his amorous adventures.

Going back to Enlil's request to make the Earthlings smarter, Enki came up with a plan. But it was after the birth of his latest child. You remember the young Earthlings on the river banks. One of them gave birth to a boy child. When Enki saw him, he could not believe his eyes. He held the child high above his head and cried "I have done it! Perfection I have made!"

This child was different. Gone was the shaggy hair and replaced with smooth, soft hair. His skin was a deep, dark brown, like his eyes. His face was very similar to the Anunnaki and his voice was almost identical. For the first time ever, this child was almost like looking at an Anunnaki child. No longer primitive looking, this child was beautiful. This was Homo sapiens! Enki named the child Adapa (Fig. 41).

"*To Adapa, Enki teachings gave, how to keep records he was him instructing.*" *Enki boasted, "A Civilized man I have brought forth. A new kind of Earthling from my seed has been created, in my image and after my likeness.*" (Sitchin, 2002)

Then a second shock, the other girl had brought forward a female child. She also was perfect and beautiful. What's more, she had sandy blond hair. Even though she had dark skin like her brother, she looked more like the Anunnaki than any other Earthling to date. He called her **Titi** (Fig. 42).

Enki kept his fatherhood secret for obvious reason. To the other Anunnaki, they would view his dalliance like we would look on someone who had sex with a chimpanzee. However, when he brought the child home and played the old "*look what I found while I was out...*" his wife Damkina, "*to Titi took a liking; all manner of crafts was she teaching.*" (Sitchin, 2002)

Enki realised right away that these children had more Anunnaki genes in them. Not just their appearance was different. They displayed an intelligence akin to any Anunnaki child of the same, relative age.

### The FIRST Homo sapiens (modern humans)

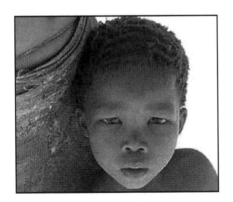

Figure 41

**Adapa**

Figure 42

**Titi**

Enki set up a new program. He started "line breeding" to perfect the human strain. Line breeding has been done for thousands of years by humans. Every pedigree animal like dogs, cats, pigs and even the little Budgerigar (parakeet) (*Melopsittacus undulatus*).

By breeding a female, then breeding that female back with its father, then breeding the next female back with the original father and so one will create more of the father's genes in each generation, inevitably being the dominate genes. In budgies we can see this in the colour mutations that have been bred in less than 10 years (Gosford, 2010). The original "bush Budgerigar" i.e. wild type is all green and is always green (Fig 43.). However, in a captive breeding program using "line breeding", a pure white bird can be bred (Fig 44.). (Handfedbudgies, 2014)

*Figure 43*                          *Figure 44*

You can do the same thing with humans and as we will see, Enki did exactly that. The downside of inbreeding/line-breeding creates diseases and syndromes due to a weakening of the immune system. There are over 4000 genetic disorders we have to deal with today because of this experimentation!

Moving on several decades, the new humanoid work force had increased and thus started to take on the manual burdens of the Anunnaki. Eventually, the original Homo erectus workers either died out or were bred out of existence. Some that managed to escape the brutal life the Anunnaki eventually evolved into:

**Neanderthal** *(Homo neanderthalensis)*. The first "true Neanderthals" appearing between 200,000 and 250,000 years ago. The date of their extinction is disputed, however most believe they died out around 24,500 years ago. They buried their dead and placed grave tools with the dead person. They were expert hunters and it is now thought they may have had some form of speech. Homo sapiens existed at the same time and it is thought that modern humans - Homo sapiens sapiens arrival in Europe around 30,000 years ago outhunted them and crossbred them out of existence. They were also under extreme pressure from global warming.

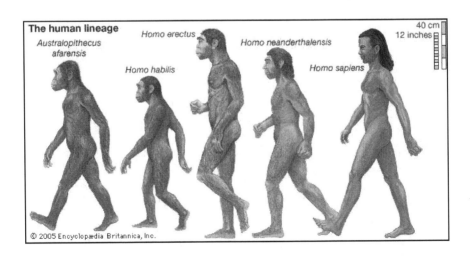

The human lineage
Australopithecus afarensis
Homo erectus
Homo habilis
Homo neanderthalensis
Homo sapiens
40 cm
12 inches
© 2005 Encyclopædia Britannica, Inc.

The little **Homo habilis** went on to naturally evolve in to "The Hobbit" *(Homo floresiensis)*. They were about 1.1 m (3.5 feet) in height and were discovered in 2003 on the island of Flores in Indonesia. This hominin is remarkable for its small body and brain and for its survival until relatively recent times (possibly as recently as 12,000 years ago). Recovered alongside the skeletal remains were stone tools from archaeological horizons ranging from 94,000 to 13,000 years ago. Some scholars suggest that the historical H. floresiensis may be connected by folk memory to ebu gogo myths prevalent on the isle of Flores. (Smithsonian NMONH, 2014)

There is one other ancient species I should mention now. It is Paranthropus boisei. The genus Paranthropus is associated with the Apes and not human. It was however a contemporary of Australopithecus and they both had similar size brains. It was also bigger than Australopithecus. Males weighed 49 kg (108 lb) and stood 1.37 m (4 ft 6 in) tall, while females weighed 34 kg (75 lb) and stood 1.24 m (4 ft 1 in) tall. You are probably wondering why I am banging on about a relatively smart, stocky little monkey? Well, this creature evolved, by naturally cross breeding with Homo erectus, into what we know in modern times as Big Foot! (Fig. 45) Sasquatch, Yeti and Yowie have all been spotted in modern times

*Figure 45*

and all have evolved from these two species. (Smithsonian NMONH, 2014) There is something about each of these species that they have in common. They all live in harmony within their environments. That is because they naturally evolved, more or less, on planet Earth. Humans on the other hand do not live in harmony. That is because we are a hybrid species and most of our genes are not from planet Earth!

# References:

Enki speaks, (2014). *ENKI SPEAKS*. [online] Available at: http://enkispeaks.com/ [Accessed 1 Aug. 2014].

Gosford, B. (2010). *Bird of the week*. [online] Blogs.crikey.com.au. Available at: http://blogs. crikey.com.au/northern/2010/08/28/bird-of-the-week-rufous-crowned-emu- wren-and-a-big-day-round-alice-springs/?wpmp_switcher=mobile&wpmp_tp=1 [Accessed 1 Aug. 2014].

Hand fed budgies, (2014). *Budgie information, pictures and videos. | Hand Fed Budgies*. [online] Handfedbudgies.com. Available at: http://www.handfedbudgies.com [Accessed 1 Aug. 2014].

Sitchin, Z. (1990). *The lost realms*. 1st ed. Santa Fe, N.M.: Bear.
(1991). *Genesis revisited*. 1st ed. Santa Fe, N.M.: Bear & Co., pp.158 - 182, 202.
(2002). *The lost book of Enki*. 1st ed. Rochester, Vt.: Bear & Co.
(2007). *The 12th planet*. 1st ed. New York: Harper.
(2007). *The wars of gods and men*. 1st ed. New York: Harper.

Smithsonian NMONH, (2014). *Paranthropus boisei*. [online] Humanorigins.si.edu. Available at: http://humanorigins.si.edu/evidence/human-fossils/species/ paranthropus-boisei [Accessed 1 Aug. 2014].

Tellinger, M. (2012). Slave species of the gods. 1st ed. Rochester, Vt.: Bear & Co.

# 19

## RH- BLOOD - HUMANS ARE ALIEN HYBRIDS

*"Humans have 250 unique genes that are not found in any other lower species. Scientist have not been able to find any evolutionary basis for these genes." (ENCODE 2003).*

HE BLUEPRINT OF life is DNA. Its famous double helix is a long, long chain built by linking together four simple molecules. The order in which those molecules are linked determines the information contained in the DNA. It is the sequence of those molecules that molecular biologists are now busily decoding.

### DNA Basics

DNA, or deoxyribonucleic acid, is the hereditary material in humans and almost all other organisms. Nearly every cell in a person's body has the same DNA. Most DNA is located in the cell nucleus but a small

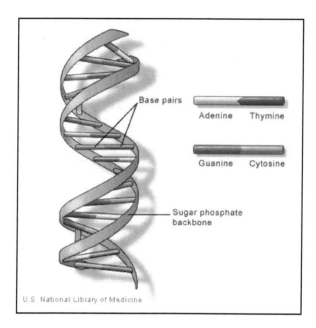

*Figure 46*

amount of DNA can also be found in the mitochondria (where it is called mitochondrial DNA or mtDNA). The information in DNA is stored as a code made up of four chemical bases: adenine (A), guanine (G), cytosine (C) and thymine (T). Human DNA consists of about 3 billion bases and more than 99 percent of those bases are the same in all people (Fig. 46). The order or sequence of these bases determines the information available for building and maintaining an organism, similar to the way in which letters of the alphabet appear in a certain order to form words and sentences.

DNA bases pair up with each other, A with T and C with G, to form units called base pairs. Each base is also attached to a sugar molecule and a phosphate molecule. Together, a base, sugar and phosphate are called a nucleotide. Nucleotides are arranged in two long strands that form a spiral called a double helix. The structure of the double helix is somewhat like a ladder, with the base pairs forming the ladder's rungs and the sugar and phosphate molecules forming the vertical sidepieces of the ladder.

An important property of DNA is that it can replicate or make copies of itself. Each strand of DNA in the double helix can serve as a pattern for duplicating the sequence of bases. This is critical when cells divide, because each new cell needs to have an exact copy of the DNA present in the old cell.

## What Is A Genome?

All of the DNA in an organism is referred to as the organism's **genome**. Genes are DNA chains made up of hundreds or thousands of simple molecules. Each gene contains instructions to make another type of crucial molecule, called a **protein**. Proteins include everything from hormones such as insulin, which regulates blood-sugar levels, to enzymes, that help digest the food we eat. Some proteins turn other genes on and off, which then affect still other genes, creating complicated feedback loops.

Individual proteins are but tiny cogs in incredibly complex biological systems. Consider the immune system, in which thousands of genes and proteins work together to field an army of cells and antibodies (another type of protein) against intruders. The DNA in each of the body's cells contains all the genetic information to produce a person. But in any given cell, only some of the genes are switched on; the rest are dormant. That's what makes a liver cell, different from a skin cell - different sets of genes are turned on in each.

Scientists despair of understanding exactly how humanity's 80,000 genes flip on and off in the amazing molecular dance that leads to a human being. But they are uncovering the genes and proteins that underlie small pieces of this grand puzzle.

## Biological Pathways

One famous pathway is the process by which cells turn the sugar glucose, into enough energy to run a marathon. But genes can also go horribly wrong. A ''misspelling'' in just one letter or an improper or missing link in the DNA chain, is a **mutation**. A change in a single link of the thousands in a gene can produce disease. Sickle-cell anaemia, for instance. Other diseases are more complex. Heart disease, cancer and Alzheimer's are due to mutations in several genes. On the other hand, a mutation is also responsible for blue eyes. So mutations can be good, not so good or just plain scary.

Much of the effort in genetics today is directed at finding these faulty genes and then figuring out how their flawed proteins make biological pathways go awry. Aiding the search is something called a **Genetic Map**. Much like an atlas, a genetic map shows the locations of genes and fragments that have been identified. Each of these can be used as a signpost or marker, to help identify genes that might be related to disease.

You may think that the human genome is large because we are a very complex mammal. Well, in a way it is very large. In fact, it will fill up 90 volumes of Encyclopaedia Britannica. However, if we compare that to something else, like a lily seed, its genome would fill up 1800 volumes of Encyclopaedia Britannica!

That said, it would still take a person typing 60 words per minute, eight hours a day, around 50 years to type the human genome. If all the DNA in your body's 100 trillion cells was put end to end, it would reach to the Sun - 144, 840, 960 kilometres away (90 million miles) and back, over 600 times. This seems like a massive amount of information, however if we converted it into binary code (what computers use), the human genome is just slightly larger than a CD ROM (700Mb). As a matter of fact, Windows XP is twice as large as our human DNA genome. The human genome requires 750Mb of storage, whereas Windows XP requires 1500Mb of storage (1.5 GB). The more recent, Windows 8, requires 20 GB!

In computer terms, the human genome is stored in 6 bit combinations of information. Play Station 3 is 128 bits. What does this tell us? Well, whoever programmed the original human DNA, was not only an incredible genius, they did it in such a space saving and highly productive way that we can only sit and wonder how.

## What is Junk DNA?

Science tells us that 97% of our human DNA is "junk" DNA, with no known use or function. The Puffer Fish on the other hand has NO junk DNA. Indeed, there are quite a lot of organisms out there that don't have any junk DNA what so ever. A large-scale international research effort, ENCODE (Encyclopaedia of DNA Elements), began in 2003 as an outgrowth of the Human Genome Project. Although the human genome had been largely finished in its final draft form in 2004, very little was known about the functionality of the many areas outside the protein-coding regions that comprised less than 5 percent of the total DNA sequence. A large number of biologists considered this excess DNA to have little value, referring to it as "junk DNA." (Genome.gov, 2014)

So far we have talked about the human genome size, so now we are going to look at the number of genes we actually have in our genome. A gene is just a section of our overall genome that helps the body to know how to code for specific proteins within our body.

Therefore, we are going to talk about the amount of genes you have, compared to the amount of genes other organisms have.

When scientists first started to study genetics and the human genome, they actually expected to find 3 times more genes then the actual amount they found. This is interesting, because they only found 25,000 genes, which is only about twice the amount of a round worm. In fact, there is a variety of amoeba (a single-celled animal) that has 200 times the amount of genes that a human being has!

In the beginning, scientist thought that 1 gene coded for 1 protein. The latest information states we have 250,000 proteins being coded by 25,000 different genes. This means that each gene is coding for approximately 10 proteins. At the moment, scientists have no idea how this occurs.

Human genes are approximately 98% similar to chimpanzees, 85% with dogs, 75% with mice and 113 of our genes are from bacteria.

However, there are **250 unique genes** that are not found in any other lower species.

Scientist have not been able to find **any evolutionary basis for these genes.**

### Is this the Human genome?
250 genes of unknown origin + 24,750 genes of known origin = 25,000 human genes.

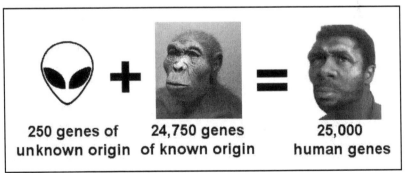

**250 genes of unknown origin**    **24,750 genes of known origin**    **25,000 human genes**

### RH Blood Types

Your Rh status describes whether or not you have a protein on the surface of your red blood cells - the "Rhesus factor". If you don't have the Rh factor, you're considered Rh-negative; if you have it, you're Rh-positive. About 85 percent of people are Rh+ positive, though it varies by race. For African Americans, about 90-95 percent are Rh + (positive) and for Asians, the figure is 98 to 99 percent. Thus, Rh-(negative) is RARE!

## The Process of Alloimmunization

During the birthing process, blood cells from the unborn child can escape into the mother's bloodstream. These cells are recognized as foreign if they are a different blood type from the mother, and a natural rejection process will ensue with the formation of antibodies. The process is known as red cell alloimmunization. So, Rh-negative women with an Rh-positive partner are at

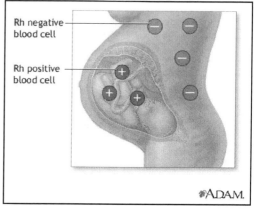

RISK of spontaneous miscarriage and other foetus **REJECTION** events.

An Rh-negative woman with an Rh-negative partner has an even smaller chance of having a Baby born alive! In animals, this is seen as a problem, but only in **HYBRID** animals! (Fig. 47)

*Figure 47*

But strangely, a person with type O negative blood is considered to be a "Universal Donor". It means his or her blood can be given to anyone, regardless of blood type, without causing a transfusion reaction. The Rh-Negative Factor is considered a "Mutation" of **Unknown Origin,** which happened in Europe, about 25,000-35,000 years ago. Then this group spread heavily into the area of what is now Spain, England, Ireland and most of continental Europe. There are now small groups of Rh- in all racial groups throughout the world.

**84-85%** of humans test positive for the Rhesus monkey gene.

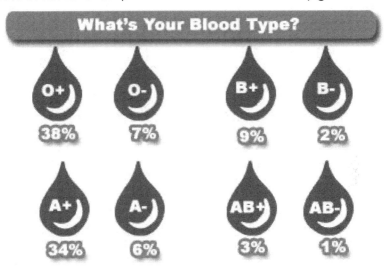

If you test negative for the Rhesus monkey gene, then you are in a small minority of 15% - 16% who DO NOT have the normal, evolutional gene sequence.

Rh- Woman with Rh+ Male = the woman's autoimmune system attacks and kills the foetus. When the mother is type O- and her foetus is A, B, or AB, the symptoms in newborn babies are usually jaundice, mild anaemia and elevated bilirubin levels.

Rh- people typically have:
  • Higher IQ
  • Sensitive vision
  • A lower body temperature
  • Psychic abilities
  • Increased sensitivity to heat and sunlight
  • The ability to stop watches and electrical appliances.

They cannot receive blood transfusion from Rh+ donors and they can't be cloned. They usually have fair (red to blond) hair and blue, green, grey or very light hazel eyes.

Many Rh- people report a feeling of not belonging to the human race or to Earth. Some even have an extra vertebra or an extra rib.

Rh- blood has not followed the usual evolutionary path, so must have been introduced from an outside source. There are two schools of thought – evolution or creationism. However, we have already learnt about a 3rd school of thought on human evolution. Zecharia Sitchin's work has uncovered a story about humans being the result of a genetic experiment, conducted by a giant alien race that the Sumerians of ancient culture call the Anunnaki ("*Those Who from Heaven to Earth Came*") – the "gods" of antiquity.

The Anunnaki scientist who conducted these experiments was called Enki. Enki was running a side experiment to the Enlil sanctioned "create a human slave race to mine for gold". He was line breeding certain humans to see if he could get them closer to the Anunnaki. In the next chapter I will detail how it all happened, but for now I will say that Enki got more than he bargained for. He created a "white, blond hair, blue eyed" human with a different blood type – Rh-. The reason? Because Enki had put more Anunnaki DNA into this latest experiment.

The Anunnaki are blond with white skin and they have a different blood type altogether. He has more or less created an Anunnaki, in human form (Sitchin, 2002, 1991). This is the unknown "mutation" science cannot explain! It was not an "evolution" mutation, it was a spontaneous mutation caused by a hybrid breeding program.

## Why do the Humans of Earth Look Different?

Enki created the first humans – Blacks, then he created a mutation – Whites. In another non-related event, the "Sons of Kain" were banished to the East. Enlil had their DNA tampered with so "they cannot grow beards – this is how we (the Anunnaki) will differentiate them from other humans." Enlil wanted to make the "Sons of Kain" look different in case they tried to sneak back into the É.DIN. See **Annex 2.3.1** for the full story of KA-IN & ABA-EL.

These became the first Eastern Asian people. They then migrated as far as South America. If you look at every human tribe, they are made up of one of these 3 or are a combination of them. That is: Black White and Asian. Without the Anunnaki tampering with our genes, we would all look like Sub-Saharan African (black) people. But we still all look the same under our skin! We are still all humans – One Human Race.

Later on in the Anunnaki saga, the scribes tell us:

## Genesis 6

1. And while human beings began to multiply on the face of the Earth, daughters were born to them.
2. The sons of God (the Anunnaki) saw that the daughters of men, were beautiful, and so they picked for themselves women, whomever they pleased.
3. And the Lord (Enki) said, "My spirit does not reside in the human being forever, because he is flesh." And his life span became one hundred and twenty years.
4. And they were giants (the Anunnaki) on the Earth, in those ages and even later, because the sons of God entered upon the daughters of men, and there was born to them hybrids, who were giants of universal fame (the Titans of Greek mythology).

Basically it is recorded and later retold in Genesis that the Anunnaki workers, the Igigi, had no females from home to keep them happy, so they took it upon themselves to take human wives instead. These mating's created a lighter coloured human, which later became the Hebrews, Arabs, Turks and most of the Mediterranean "olive" skin people. I realise this is all a bit messy and confusing. But I promise you, all will be revealed.

## The Genographic Project

The Genographic Project, launched in 2005 by the National Geographic Society and IBM. It is an ongoing genetic anthropology study that aims to map historical human migration patterns by collecting and analysing DNA samples from hundreds of thousands of people from around the world (at the time of publication there were 678,632 contributors) (Genographic Project, 2014). The project is open to anyone.

In fact, after watching an amazing documentary called "The Human Family Tree" (The Human Family Tree, 2005) that explained the program, I personally contributed my own DNA to this study. In return (for a fee) they sent me an amazing, personal report, detailing where my ancestors originated, the path of their migration and their final destination. What I learnt from this study is that it backs up what most of the Sumerian texts say and what I always thought! Figure 46 shows the migration of humans out of Africa based on the DNA samples from hundreds of thousands of people all over the world.

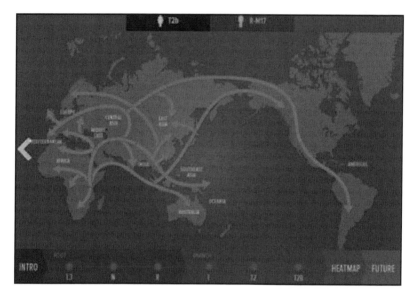

*Figure 48*

The scientists believe these populations walked all the way to South America. But the Sumerian texts tell us how Enki's son Ningishzidda took the humans there to set up mining camps, as well as build new civilisations. These people became the Mayans, who, after thriving for 700 years suddenly and mysteriously disappeared.

## Science Agrees with the Sumerians!

A 2008 genetic study shows that people with blue eyes have a single, common ancestor. Scientists have tracked down a genetic mutation that is the cause of the eye colour of all blue-eyed humans alive on the planet today.

"*Originally, we all had brown eyes*", said Professor Eiberg from the Department of Cellular and Molecular Medicine. "*But a genetic mutation affecting the OCA2 gene in our chromosomes resulted in the creation of a "switch", which literally "turned off" the ability to produce brown eyes*". (ScienceDaily, 2014)

This is something I have been saying for years! That if you have blue eyes, the chances are you are a direct descendant of Enki.

## My Response to Online Haters:

I feel it is necessary to interrupt this discussion for a brief response to remarks about my video on this topic. My original video on YouTube is: **Part 1: Human DNA Mysteries - The Mechanics of Ascension**. This video is a brief outline of the information you have just been reading. Much to my absolute surprise, this video attracted a protracted attack by militant, African Americans. They claimed that my video, and information was racist, because I told the FACTS, that most Rh-people are white. Furthermore, they were angry that I said Rh- were more LIKELY to be psychic and have a higher IQ.

I realise these people are Young and Child Souls with a chip on their shoulder and an axe to grind. But just to be on the safe side, I would like people to know my stance on this. Firstly, I am the LAST person in the world that you would call RACIST. I find that offensive. I have many dear friends of every nationality you care to name. I absolutely love studying and experiencing every culture on this planet. I revel in the unique and beautiful languages, art, food and culture of every nation. I hold Africans in high esteem, because to me, they are the Mother and Father of all of us. I have no doubt there are thousands and thousands of brilliant, intelligent African Americans. I am also sure there are many African Americans that are awesome psychics and healers. However, I am not into "whites are good at this and blacks are better at that". In my opinion, all people, of all nationalities and creed can offer the world any number of amazing things.

But most of all, I do not see people as black, white, yellow, red or whatever. I only see people in terms of Soul Ages. Any colour people, all have Soul Ages within them. Therefore, I would never condemn a whole country or peoples based on the actions of some younger Souls.

I hold a special place in my heart for the Australian Aborigine Nation. They have been mistreated worse than any modern day people in history.

Whether you like it or not, we are all children of Enki in one way or another, which technically makes us all related. This is what I truly believe – there is only one Race – the Human Race and we are all brothers and sisters, sharing a planet and each of us is offering our unique perspective of it. Imagine a world where everyone looked the same and everyone spoke the same and everyone ate the same. We would be robots. Ironically, I have more issues with the "white" oligarchs that are ruling our world at this time than any other peoples. Indeed, white people have more Anunnaki DNA. Unfortunately, this means we are more like the Anunnaki, who are obsessed with war, greed, violence, subjecting people and general bad behaviour that makes them want to destroy the very planet that supports them!

Anyway, please be aware that I report the FACTS. If you want to twist the facts into some other, ugly agenda, then please do so, but look at the situation from the Wise Mind first. Inlakesh.

## The Conclusions

- As we have already discussed, humans share 98% of our DNA with chimpanzees, but unlike chimps and other species, humans do not live in harmony with Earth's ecosystems and are usually at odds and out of step with nature. Why?

- **250 of our genes have no evolutionary basis. Why?**

- **15% of humans have a blood type that has no evolutionary basis. Why?**

# BECAUSE PART OF US IS FOREIGN TO THIS PLANET!

Our genetic code was written by an Extra Terrestrial programmer that wrote 2 versions of our genetic code – an advanced code and a basic code. Our so called, junk DNA, is actually a hidden and dormant upgrade of our basic code. It is a clever, self-organising, auto editing, auto developing, auto correcting, auto exacting software program with a built in connection to the ageless wisdom of the Universe. In other words, the DNA scientists have been calling junk DNA is actually **Divine DNA**.

Our ET programmer deliberately disabled the advanced code and left us to exist on only 3% of our DNA. Like a broken radio dial that is stuck on one station, instead of roaming across thousands of frequencies, humans are stuck on one station called 5 sense reality. The basic code is 3D reality. The upgrade is 5th Dimensional reality. In Book III, I will discuss this in full and hopefully teach you how to activate your Divine DNA!

# References:

Genographic Project, (2014). *The Genographic Project by National Geographic - Human Migration, Population Genetics*. [online] Available at: https://genographic. nationalgeographic.com/ [Accessed 10 Aug. 2014].

Genome.gov, (2014). *ENCODE Project*. [online] Available at: http://www.genome.gov/10005107 [Accessed 9 Aug. 2014].

ScienceDaily, (2014). Blue-eyed Humans Have A Single, Common Ancestor. [online] Available at: http://www.sciencedaily.com/releases/2008/01/080130170343.htm [Accessed 10 Aug. 2014].

Sitchin, Z. (1991). *Genesis revisited*. 1st ed. Santa Fe, N.M.: Bear & Co.

(1991). *The 12th planet*. 1st ed. Santa Fe, N.M.: Bear & Co.

(2002). *The lost book of Enki*. 1st ed. Rochester, Vt.: Bear & Co.

*The Human Family Tree*. (2005). [video] New York: Natgeo TV.

# 20

## THE FLOOD - LET THE HUMANS DIE - NO, THEY MUST LIVE!

---

*"A wondrous Being by us was created, by us saved it must be!" (Enki to the Earth Council)*

---

*A*LMOST EVERY CHILD is told the Biblical story of Noah and the flood, but just in case you are not familiar with it, it goes something like this:

### Genesis 6:1 - 9:17

*God saw how great wickedness had become and decided to wipe mankind from the face of the earth. However, one righteous man among all the people of that time, Noah, found favour in God's eyes. With very specific instructions, God told Noah to build an ark for him and his family in preparation for a catastrophic flood that would destroy every living thing on Earth.*

*God also instructed Noah to bring into the ark two of all living creatures, both male and female and seven pairs of all the clean animals, along with every kind of food to be stored for the animals and his family while on the ark. Noah obeyed everything God commanded him to do.*

*After they entered the ark, rain fell on the earth for a period of forty days and nights. The waters flooded the earth for a hundred and fifty days and every living thing on the face of the earth was wiped out. As the waters receded, the ark came to rest on the mountains of Ararat. Noah and his family continued to wait for almost eight more months while the surface of the earth dried out.*

*Finally after an entire year, God invited Noah to come out of the ark. Immediately, he built an altar and worshiped the Lord with burnt offerings from some of the clean animals. God was pleased with the offerings and promised never again to destroy all the living creatures as he had just done. Later God established a covenant with Noah: "Never again will there be a flood to destroy the earth." As a sign of this everlasting covenant God set a rainbow in the clouds.*

Let's examine this for just a bit. Firstly, many, many Christians take this story as fact. Indeed, there have been several, very expensive searches done to locate the original Arc that Noah built, but no luck yet finding it.

In 2014, there was a much celebrated debate between Bill Nye, "The Science Guy", an Emmy Award-winning science educator and CEO of the Planetary Society and Ken Ham, a leading, Young Earth Creation apologist and bestselling Christian author. Ken is originally from Australia, but he moved to the Bible belt in America to open his Creation Museum located in Petersburg, Kentucky. It is here the debate took place and the full debate is available on YouTube.

During the debate, Nye made some excellent points in regards to the Noah's Ark story I would like to summarise here. Firstly, Nye argues that Noah was required to get at least 2 of every animal in the world onto the Ark. Then he had to have enough food to feed them. But what do you feed the carnivores, like lions and tigers? You would need extra prey animals, in the hundreds, if not thousands.

Furthermore, the Bible story claims that Noah (who was 600 years old the Bible says), ended his journey on Mount Ararat in the Middle East. So how did kangaroos, koalas, platypus and echidna, not to mention the hundreds of other unique Australian species get to Australia? Ham claims that these events happened 4000 years ago and that the Earth is only 6000 years old. He also states that there was a land bridge that stretch all the way from the Middle East, across Asia and to Australia, and that the unique animals travelled along this route in the last 4000 years. If that is the case, then why haven't scientist found one fossil or bones of a kangaroo anywhere between Australia and the Middle East? Not to mention, there is absolutely no evidence of a submerged land bridge.

Ken Ham argues that there were 7000 "kinds" of animals, meaning, Noah did not have to collect every dog species or bird species etc. Just collect the 1 kind of animal that represents all of the sub-species. Today, there is a conservative estimate accepted by most scientists that there are about 8.7 million species on the Earth. But the number goes up to 50 million if you start counting viruses and bacteria. So if we make an educated guess of around 16 million species, we can calculate that over the last 4000 years, science would be finding 11 new species per day. So if you went out into your back yard, you wouldn't just find a bird, you would find a new species of bird, every day, along with new species of fish, dogs, cats, etc. etc.

Getting back to the boat, Noah and his family did not have the necessary skills to build a boat strong enough and big enough "wooden" boat for this purpose.      Don't forget, we have 14,000 individual animals (male and female from 7000 kinds), plus the crew, plus the food. As far as anybody knows, none of Noah's family had ever built a wooden ship before, so they were completely unskilled. The Ark was supposedly just over 500ft or 155 meters long. We can test the viability of this very easily.

In the early 19th Century, very experienced Shipwrights build an extraordinarily big, wooded ship called the Wyoming. It was about 300ft or 100 meters long with 6 masts and a motor for winching the anchor. It was the largest wooden ship ever built. The problems with the size of the boat were immediate. On its very first voyage the hull began to twist in every direction. This of course, led it to leak like a sieve and it eventually sank killing all 14 crew. So even the best ship builders of their day could not build a ship as big as the Ark was meant to be. The National Zoo in Washington DC is 163 acres or 66 hectares and caters for 400 species. Is it reasonable to believe that Noah had 14,000 species on a boat?

There are actually several variations of the Flood story, but the Biblical version is the most famous. However, you will see in the table in **Annex 2.2.1**, that the Biblical version, just like the Genesis story we covered in Chapter 15, is a much later version of a previous story. The Bible version was written down over 2000 years after the original Sumerian story.

## This is what the Sumerians tell us about the Flood

I have taken this story directly from the translations of Zecharia Sitchin. The only changes I have made are to modernise certain words and phrases. For example, instead of calling it a "Celestial Chariot" I call it a rocket ship or space craft. When the Gods descend in a "whirlwind", I call it a helicopter and so on. So keep this in mind, because this story is straight from the mouths of the Sumerians, from over 6000 years ago!

## Enki begets Ziusudra / Noah

If you take your mind back, you will remember Enki was conducting some "line-breeding". He would usually do this via the female blood line. One of his "experiments" was a particularly attractive female called Batanash, who Enki lusted over. Batanash was already married to Lu-Mach who was Enlil's Work master in Edin (Iraq). He was responsible for overseeing the human work and was forced by Enlil to crack the whip on them and make them work harder, for less food. This caused quite a lot of resentment by the humans and it finally came to a head when Lu-Mach received death threats. Enki saw this as his perfect opportunity to get his hands on Batanash.

To "protect" Lu-Mach, Enki sent him to his son Marduk, who had a base in Babylon. Under Marduk's protection, Marduk was ordered by Enki to teach Lu-Mach how to build houses and temples (ziggurats). Meanwhile, he sent Lu-Mach's wife, Batanash, to his sister Ninmah, who had a medical centre in Shurubak.

"*From the angry Earthling masses protected and safe to be. Thereafter Enki, Ninmah in Shurubak was quick to visit.*"

"*On the roof of a dwelling where Batanash was bathing, Enki by her loins took hold, he kissed her, his semen into her womb he poured.*" From this encounter, she bore Ziusudra (Noah). (Sitchin, 2002)

When Lu-Mach returned to Edin, *"to him Batanash the son showed. White as the snow his skin was. Like the skies were his eyes, in a brilliance his eyes were shining."* Lu-Mach protested, *"A son unlike an Earthling to Batanash was born. Is one of the Igigi his father?"* Batanash swore *"None of the Igigi fathered the boy."* She did not lie, because after all, it was the Lord Enki who was the father!

Lu-Mach's father was present. His eyes suddenly glazed over as he went into a trance state and said, *"Ziusudra, will the Earthlings, guide through the Ice Age."* (Sitchin, 2002)

For the first time ever, Enki had produced a white skinned, blond haired, blue eyed human. But something more amazing, was that Ziusudra had Rh- blood. This was the first time this mutation had ever shown up. Therefore, Enki took great interest in Ziusudra and personally taught him everything. He also got him to read all of Adapa's writings. He was kept in secret, under the protection of Ninmah in Shurubak. Ninmah loved and cared for Ziusudra.

## Marduk Marries an Earthling

Nearly everything above the equator is frozen and under ice, whereas everything below the equator is in drought, due to all the water and moisture being locked up in the ice. Thus, in Mesopotamia, things are dry. With no rain, crops soon die, rivers and lakes dry up, and food is becoming scarce. The humans were suffering and became more and more feral as they wondered far and wide in search of food.

Enlil sent one of his sons, Ninurta to, "Beyond the Seas in the mountain land a Bond Heaven-Earth to establish." The "mountain land" is the Andes in South America and the "Bond Heaven-Earth" is a transmission tower, for contacting Nibiru.

Meanwhile, the base on Mars was going through similar natural disasters. Climate and magnetic storms and "sky-borne terrors" caused by the passing of Nibiru, had hit the Mars base, so Enlil ordered Marduk (Enki's son) to check the damage on Mars. When Marduk reached Mars he was horrified. Almost all of the oceans and atmosphere had been sucked out into space by Nibiru's massive gravitational pull.

The Mars base was now unusable. The Igigi that worked there were forced under-ground just to survive. Marduk was the Commander of the Mars base, but now it appeared he was out of a job. He returned to Earth. It was at this time he made a decision that shocked everyone. He decided to marry his Earthling slave girl assistant, "Sarpanit". Sarpanit was the daughter of Marduk's Earthling protégé, Erkime (a descendant of Enki's part-Earthling son, Adapa). She was said to be as beautiful as any Anunnaki Goddess (female) and as intelligent as any God (male). Marduk genuinely loved Sarpanit and as there were very few Anunnaki females on Earth, he thought Sarpanit would make the perfect wife.

Marduk's mother, Damkina, warned him: if he married Sarpanit "to Nibiru with his spouse he would never go. His princely rights on Nibiru he forever will forsake". To this Marduk, with a bitter laugh responded, "My rights on Nibiru are non-existent. Even on Earth my rights as firstborn have been trampled" (by Enlil and Ninurta). But Marduk would marry Sarpanit and show his alliance with the Earthlings. He would wield the Earthlings as weapons and with them win mastery, first of Earth, then Nibiru.

Enlil saw through Marduk's scheme, to use the alliance with the humans as a possible threat to himself and his son Ninurta. Therefore, Enlil beamed King Anu on Nibiru. "The Marduk-Sarpanit union forbid." But Anu and his counsellors ruled, "...to return to Nibiru with her, Marduk must forever be barred. Marduk marry can, but on Nibiru a prince, he shall no more be."

## Now the Igigi Steal Human Wives for Themselves

Enlil, who was over-ruled by his father, King Anu, allowed Marduk and Sarpanit to marry in Eridu (Earth Base 1 – the first Earthly city). But only on the proviso that the couple go to Egypt immediately after their wedding. Egypt was the northern most area of Enki's domain (Africa). Enki had convinced Enlil to let Marduk rule Egypt, as he had lost his command on Mars. Both actually agree this may help Marduk to settle down (and cause them both less hassles). This area would become Marduk's fiefdom. However, Marduk was meant to share Egypt with his brother, Ningiszidda. Marduk would rule the South and Ningiszidda the North. Ningiszidda had already been ruling Egypt under the name of Thoth. He taught humans how to read and right, to farm, to make beer and many other "cultural" endeavours.

Meanwhile, at Marduk's wedding, "A great multitude of Civilized Earthlings in Eridu assembled. Young Igigi from Lahmu (Mars) in great numbers came." Inanna, Enlil's granddaughter, flirted with Enki's son,

Dumuzi, oblivious that the Igigi were about to spring a surprise. (Sitchin, 2002)

Before the wedding, 200 Igigi astronauts occupied the Landing Platform in Lebanon, then flew to Eridu. They mixed with Earthlings and Anunnaki Expedition people and watched Marduk and Sarpanit wed. Once the ceremony was over, they gave the signal, and all hell broke loose. The Igigi started to grab any human female that they could see. They didn't care if they were married, pregnant, under-aged or old. It was from this episode that the Bible writers refer to them as the "Fallen" or Nefilim. The Igigi literally "came down" from the sky and sinned against the "lord" Enlil.

**Genesis 6:2:** *"The sons of God (the Igigi) saw that the daughters of men were beautiful, and so they picked for themselves women, whomever they pleased."*

The Igigi loaded the women into their flying machines and flew back to the landing strip in Lebanon and "into a stronghold the place they made." They radioed Enlil: "Bless our Earthling marriages or by fire all on Earth shall we shall destroy." By "fire" they meant nuclear bombs. (Sitchin, 2002)

The Igigi defied Enlil's edict, that they refrain from having sex with the hybrid Earthlings, however they raped the women they abducted. "And the women bore GIANTS." (Sitchin, 2010)

The Igigi pleaded with Marduk to allow them to keep the Earth women as their wives. They argued that there were no Anunnaki women and furthermore, their own commander, Marduk, had taken an Earthly bride, so why couldn't they. Marduk saw their point of view and had to concede. So as their commander, he called up Enlil and demanded he stop calling the Igigi/captive unions "abductions" and ratify them as marriages. Enlil fumed, but didn't press the issue, "things against Marduk and his Earthlings was Enlil plotting." (Sitchin, 2007)

Unable to return to Mars or Nibiru, Marduk settled some of the Igigi and their new families in Babylon. Their offspring became known as *"Children of the Rocketships."* Marduk and Sarpanit stayed with other Igigi/human families in Lebanon. Some of these "Children of the Rocketships" had settled in "the far Eastlands, lands of high mountains." (Tibet and Northern China) (Sitchin, 2007)

In order to try and stop Marduk creating armies of humans all over the world, Enlil ordered his son and successor, Ninurta, to counter the spread. "'*The Earth by Earthlings inherited will be*,' Enlil to Ninurta said. '*Go, the offspring of Ka-in find, with them a domain of your own prepare.*" (See **ANNEX 2.2.1** Story of Ka-in & Aba-el).

Ninurta tracked down Ka-in and his people and settled them in Lake Titicaca in the Andes. There Ninurta taught them tin and gold mining, smelting and refining. (Sitchin, 2002)

I need to digress at little at this point. So far, we have a new settlement set up in South America where they would continue mining gold, as well as tin. Some while ago, I read the excellent book "*The Destruction of Atlantis*" by Frank Joseph. Joseph, assumingly, had no knowledge of the Anunnaki or of Sitchin's work. However, his research uncovered that the inhabitants of Atlantis had also set up mining operations in the Americas, as well as ship loading docks in the Caribbean (Bimini Road). The Atlanteans mined/created a rare material they called *orichalcum*, which was a pinkish/gold metal that was stronger than gold, but still very shiny. They based a lot of their technology and art work on it.

When I later read Sitchen's book, "*The Lost Book of Enki* p274" I nearly fell off my chair when I read that Ninurta's humans were mining a "special" gold that had different properties and was highly prized.

King Anu visits the Earth and he is keen to see the new set up in the Americas. Ninurta explains to Anu how they discovered, "*a new metal from stones we extracted*" (copper). They combined through smelting, a method to mix the copper and gold. They were all very pleased at how "hard" and "strong" the new metal was. It seem these 2 unrelated sources were talking about the same metal and the same civilisations that invented it. Therefore, I am convinced that what Ninurta invented was what the Atlanteans called "orichalcum". I will discuss Atlantis in depth in Book II, and I am sure you can start to guess who the mysterious "Atlanteans" may have been?

## The Antarctic ice sheet is going to collapse!

14,600 years ago, Uranus drifted away from the Sun. This caused Neptune to move closer to the Sun, which in turned caused Nibiru's cycle to speed up a little. So rather than its normal 3,600 year cycle, it did it on only 3, 405 years. As Nibiru passed by, Uranus was now much closer and its gravitational force captured one of Nibiru's moons, the one we now know as Miranda. When Nibiru reached its most distant point from Earth, it was still trailing and was close. That created a sudden warming of Earth's northern oceans. It is more than likely what triggered the ice to melt, thus ending the last Ice Age.

Every time Nibiru passes through the solar system, it generally creates some kind of upset. As we have already seen, the last time it swung by, it stripped the Martian atmosphere, making it uninhabitable. On this same pass, it also began to dislodge the ice sheet in Antarctica. This didn't go un-noticed by the Anunnaki. In fact, Enki deployed one of his many sons, Nergal, to set up a permanent observation station on the southern most tip of Africa to monitor the ice sheet.

According to all of Nergal's data, the next time Nibiru came by, it would fully dislodge the ice-sheet. As it slips into the ocean, it will create a worldwide tsunami that will encircle the globe, about 250 metres high (800 ft.), travelling at 500 Kilometres per hour (300 mph), covering everything on land that is lower than 2000 metres (6,500 ft.). If you remember back, at this time, the humans are doing it tough. There is drought and pestilence. Ziusudra is living at Ninmah's Medical Centre in Shurubak. He is now in charge of the humans for that area. As their leader, they beg him to go to his (secret) father, the God and Lord Enki and ask for a remedy to their woes. Ziusudra does so, and from this meeting, both Ninmah and Enki decide to go and see Enlil, the Commander.

Ninmah pleads with Enlil to allow her to teach the humans how to heal and how to grow. Enki implores, *"The Earthlings let us show the dredging of ponds and canals for surviving drought and famine!"* Enlil is warming up for his long awaited "get-back" and his vindictive nature does not hold back.

*"You"*, Enlil sneered, *"thwarted my orders and Earthlings created. Marduk, your eldest, the Igigi with the armies they breed with the daughters of Adapa challenge me. No ponds, no canals. For Marduk, no more soldiers; let them starve, every one. When we sated with Earth's gold return to Nibiru return, leave no Earthling subjects for Marduk, no force for him, the homeplanet to invade."* (Tellinger, 2012)

Enki realised he did not have a leg to stand on. He left the meeting down, but not out. He secretly supplied food from his own storehouses and taught the humans how to fish. One day Enlil was flying around and noticed humans in a boat fishing. He was furious and went straight to Enki. Enki used the "Sergeant Schultz" defence, *"I know nothing!"* about how Earthlings learned to fish in the seas (Wikipedia, 2014).

As Enlil stormed out of Enki's lab, he received a message from Nergal. *"Oh now what!"* he growled. Suddenly he started to feel a whole lot better. If he is unable to starve the Earthlings to extinction, he will make sure Nibiru's next passing will destroy them. The Anunnaki had mined enough gold for now, so he will shut down the mines, return to Nibiru and let the humans drown. He let his father, King Anu know about the calamity right away.

## The Strange Messenger from Nibiru Arrives

One of Anu's personal "Celestial Chariots" landed on the strip in Eridu, the home of Enlil. Enlil had ordered all senior personal to attend a meeting. He wanted to discuss his plans about evacuating Earth. They thought their father, King Anu had arrived. However someone strange and odd looking stepped out of the space shuttle.

Galzu was a tall (for an Anunnaki), thin, white-haired person, with a youthful, but wise appearance. He had the most amazing and intense "mauve" eyes that "could see right through your soul".

Galzu (Great Knower) was delivering a sealed message from Anu to Enki, Enlil and Ninmah.

"'Enlil the seal of Anu examined; unbroken and authentic it was, its encoding trustworthy. 'For King and Council Galzu speaks. His words are my commands.' So did the message of Anu state".

"'I am Galzu, Emissary Plenipotentiary of King and Council, to Enlil,'" said the mysterious visitor." (Sitchin, 2002)

Later, Galzu chatted with Ninmah, "'of the same school and age we are.' This Ninmah could not recall: the emissary was as young as a son, she was as his olden mother."

Galzu explained that her long time on Earth had aged her prematurely. In fact, he told all of them that if they should return to Nibiru now, they would surely die. Their bodies had become so used to Earth's low gravity, that the heavy gravity of Nibiru would kill them.

He told them, "The three of you on Earth will remain; only to die to Nibiru you will return." The plan was, he explained, for Enlil, Enki and Ninmah to orbit the planet in a spaceship while the calamity took place. After it was all over, they must return to Earth and rebuild.

Enlil continued reading the order Galzu said he brought from King Anu, "To each of the other Anunnaki, a choice to leave or the calamity outwait must be given. The Igigi who Earthlings espoused must between departure and spouses choose. No Earthling, Marduk's Sarpanit included, to Nibiru to journey is allowed. For all who stay and what happens see, in celestial chariots they safety must seek." (Sitchin, 2002)

Enlil was not happy about returning to Earth, but he will deal with that later. For now, he had the plan and that was that. All Anunnaki, their sons and grandchildren, will orbit the planet. The Earthlings' and Igigi's "half-breeds" will be left on Earth to drown. No help will be given to them and no foreknowledge will they receive.

Enki protested, "'a wondrous Being by us was created, by us saved it must be!'"

Enlil screamed loud enough to rattle the windows,"'To primitive workers, you gave to them knowing you endowed. The powers of the Creator of All into your hands you have taken. With fornication, Adapa you conceived, understanding to his line you gave. His offspring to the heavens you have taken, our wisdom with them you shared. Every rule you have broken, decisions and commands you ignored. Because of you a Civilized Earthling brother (Aba-el) a brother (Ka-in) murdered. Because of Marduk your son the Igigi like him with Earthlings intermarried.'"

**The Earthlings** and demi-gods (half-breed giants), Enlil decreed, **must drown**! He demanded Enki and all Anunnaki on Earth swear an oath, not to tell the Earthlings a flood will come. Enki hesitated to openly defy Enlil, but he refused to swear. He and Marduk stamped out of the Council. (Sitchin, 2002)

Enlil brought the Council back to order. Igigi with human wives and children, he decreed, must move to the peaks above the waves. He, Enki, Ninmah, their sons, daughters and descendants would orbit Earth. Marduk must shelter on the Mars base and Nannar on the moon. When the waters receded the leaders and families would return to Earth. (Sitchin, 2002)

Enki and Ninmah set to work. They gathered all of their important records and data and buried them deep in the Iraqi soil. The 1st and 2nd Gulf Wars in modern times were designed to hide the fact that the Illuminati / New World Order were looking for these records. Hiding behind a war, they were able to go deep into Iraq and take what they wanted with impunity. What exactly they found we may never know; rumours are thick, but unsubstantiated.
Enki and Ninmah also created genetic banks to save Earth's creatures from the flood.

"Male and female essences and life-eggs they collected, of each kind, two by two they collected for safekeeping while in Earth circuit to be taken, thereafter, the living kinds to recombine. The day of the deluge they waited." (Sitchin, 2002)

## Enki has an Astral Dream

That night, Enki dreamt that Galzu had come to him and spoke *"'into your hands Fate take, for the Earthlings the Earth inherit. Summon your son Ziusudra, without breaking the oath* (swearing not to tell the Earthlings about the flood) *to him only the coming calamity reveal. A boat that the watery avalanche can withstand, a submersible one, to build him tell, the likes of which on this tablet to you I am showing. Let him in it save himself and his kinfolk and the seed of all that is useful, be it plant or animal, also take. That is the will of the* **Creator of All.**'"

Enki awoke with a start. He was sure Galzu was in his room still. As he got up, he stubbed his toe on something – a tablet. It was the same tablet Galzu had handed him in the dream. Now it was here, laying on Enki's floor. Enki searched all over the base for Galzu, but the mysterious messenger could not be located anywhere and no one witnessed his departure back to Nibiru in a space shuttle. In frustration and puzzlement, Enki returned to his lab to inspect the tablet in more detail.

On the tablet were the blue prints for building a submersible boat. This would house Ziusudra and his family during the Deluge. Enki knew he could not tell Ziusudra directly, else he tempt the wrath of Enlil and so he had to come up with another way. Enki, being clever, realised he could talk to the reed wall of Ziusudra's hut, and if Ziusudra happen to over-hear Enki's conversation with the wall, then that was not Enki's fault.

*"That night to the reed hut where Ziusudra was sleeping Enki stealthily went. The oath not breaking, the Lord Enki not to Ziusudra but to the hut's wall spoke from behind the reed wall."*

*"When Ziusudra by the words awakened, to him Enki said, 'Reed hut, a calamitous storm will sweep, the destruction of Mankind it will be. This is the decision of the assembly by Enlil convened. Abandon thy house, Ziusudra and build a boat, its design and measurements on a tablet. A navigator (Ninagal) to you will come. To a safe haven the navigator will guide you. By you shall the seed of Civilized Man survive. Not to you Ziusudra, have I spoken, but to the reed wall did I speak.'"* (Sitchin, 2002)

Ziusudra, being the intelligent and loyal son of Enki knew what had to be done and organised his people to start work on the Ark immediately. After several days of building, the Commander Enlil came by to enquire what is was they were building. Ziusudra, being of a quick mind like his father, immediately told Enlil that they were building a boat to sail down to Enki's land in Southeast Africa. Ziusudra told him that he felt he had been ignoring his teacher and Lord, and thus would like his people to work and worship the Lord Enki. Enlil did not know Ziusudra was Enki's son, so he allowed the construction to continue. Let Enki's followers leave Mesopotamia, sail to Africa and there die in the flood that is to come, thought Enlil.

When the Ark was close to completion, Ninagal (Enki's son and navigator) arrived with some special boxes. The boxes held "DNA, sperm and ova, *'the life essence and life eggs of living creatures it contains, by the Lord Enki and Ninmah collected. From the wrath of Enlil to be hidden, to life resurrected if Earth be willing.'*" Ningishzidda prepared too; he inscribed "*ancient wisdom on two great pillars and hid sacred objects and scrolls inside them.*" (Hauck, 1999)

So it was, around 13,000 years ago, "in the Whiteland, at the Earth's bottom, off its foundation, the (Antarctic) icesheet slipped. By Nibiru's netforce (gravity) it was pulled into the south sea. A tidal wave arose, northward spreading. The tidal wave, several hundred metres high, moved northward from Antarctica at 500 km per hour (300 mph), like a giant circle around the world; it destroyed all lands lower than 2,000 metres (6,500 ft.) above sea level." (Tellinger, 2012)

Then, when the waves closed over the ark, "*though completely submerged, not a drop of water into it did enter. For forty days, waves and storms swept Earth, drowning everything on the planet except those on mountaintops and in Ziusudra's boat.*" (Sitchin, 2002).

## Earthlings Survived? Enlil is Not Happy!

After the rain had stopped and the waters began to recede, Ninagal, Enki's son who piloted the ark, surfaced it, raised sail and steered to Mt Ararat or "Mount al-Judi, the modern Cudi Dag, close to the Turkish-Syrian border." (Collins, 2014)

Ziusudra built a huge signal fire and roasted a lamb to honour Enki. The orbiting Anunnaki surveyed the flood's results. Enki and Enlil descended in whirlwinds (helicopters) from their motherships.

"When Enlil the survivors saw, Ninagal among them, `Every Earthling had to perish', he with fury shouted'; at Enki with anger he lunged, to kill his brother with bare hands he was ready." Ninagal radioed Ninmah and Ninurta, "*Bring your whirlers down quick!*"

Enki had to admit to everyone that Ziusudra was actually his son, "'*He is no mere mortal, my son he is,'*" Enki to Ziusudra pointing. '*To a reed wall I spoke, not Ziusudra.'"* Ninurta and Ninmah restrained Enlil. Enki told them he'd seen Galzu in a dream, then, when he woke, found next to his bed, a tablet that showed how Ziusudra should build the submersible.

Together, Enki, Ninurta and Nimah convinced Enlil *"The survival of mankind the will of the **Creator of All** must be."*(Sitchin, 2002). Anu was monitoring the events on Earth from his mothership in orbit. When Enlil finally accepted that humans were meant to survive, it was then that a message from Anu came, saying that never again would the Anunnaki abandon the Earthlings to fend for themselves.

*Figure 49*

Figure 49 is part of an Egyptian frieze 8 metres (25 ft.) above the floor, in the temple in Abydos. You can clearly see a helicopter (top left), two other flying craft (a jet plane and a mothership) and Ziusudra's submersible boat, with the mast down so it could dive (top right).

## The Aftermath of the Deluge

In 11,000 BC, the planet Nibiru passed Earth, the closest it has ever done. So close, in fact it caused earth quakes, wild weather and a global tsunami generated by the collapse of the Antarctic ice-sheet. The wild weather and deluge lasted for 40 days, however it continued to rain for a total of 120 days (almost 4 months). The flood buried *"under miles thick mud, all the Anunnaki built in 432,000 years. Of their settlements, only the stone Landing Platform (Baalbek) in Lebanon, survived intact."* (Sitchin, 1998)

But it was not just the Earth that suffered. Indeed, Nibiru's passing also "ripped away the shield of gold dust around Nibiru, gold the astronauts had struggled for millennia to rocket to the mother planet. Nibiru's atmosphere again dwindled. Nibiru again needed Earth's gold. While survivors on Earth were trying to rebuild their lives, word came from Nibiru, *'The shield of gold dust was torn.'"* Nibiru ordered the Earth base to re-open the mines and get as much gold as they could, as fast as they could. Never mind that Earth was devastated, most of the humans were dead and miles of thick, sticky mud encrusted everything.

Enlil realised that to get more gold, he would need more workers. Less than 4000 Earthlings remained alive from mountain caves to a world of mud that ruined for gathering and hunting (Freer, 2008). Perhaps he was rash wishing all the humans dead? He needed them now more than ever.

In Africa, mud interred the mines as well the miners. In Sumer, mud topped the Bad-Tibira refinery. Mud smothered the rocket terminal at Sippar refinery. Mud covered the rocket terminal at Sippar. Enlil was at a loss where to even begin.

## Enlil Takes Charge

To Baalbek, Enlil, summonsed those Anunnaki who survived the flood. He signalled, *"Return to Baalbek. Hear my commands."* When everyone had returned, Enlil called an Earth Council meeting.

*"What seeds survived in Enki's vault? What beasts made it?"* Ninigal, Enki's son who'd piloted Noah's submersible, answered, *"Life essences and life eggs in the four-legged animals from Ziusudra's boat can be combined. Sheep for wool and meat will multiply, cattle for milk and hides will all have."* Enki's seed banks also survived.

Enlil said he would order up more genetically modified seeds from Nibiru. He told Enki's son Dumuzi, *"Replenish the planet's livestock. Ziusudra /Noah's son Shem will command the Earthlings you need to help you achieve this."* *"Dig a water system with our technology that feeds itself and breed Earthlings for labour,"* ordered Enlil to Ninurta and Enki.

Ninurta found the beardless descendants of Ka-in, now Andean Indians and another branch that would become the Hopi Indians (**Annex 2.1.1**). They could mine the metals they required and in return, Ninurta would teach the tribes people all manner of civilisation. He brought his youngest brother, Adad, along with some Sumerian overseers and African technicians to organise and teach the Indians.

## 1000 Years of Peace and Prosperity

It was now the beginning of what anthropologist call the Neolithic, the Age of Domestication and Farming. With Enlil's endorsement,

Ninurta and Enki were at liberty to use their advanced technology to re-terraformed the mud of Mesopotamia back to a land of rivers, dams and irrigation systems.

**From Enlil's side**: Enlil, Inanna (granddaughter); Adad (youngest son); Ninurta (oldest son); Utu (Twin brother of Inanna) and Nannar (Son of Enlil, first born on Earth and father of Inanna and Utu).

**From Enki's side:** Marduk (Eldest son); Ningishzidda/Thoth (son); Ninigal (son) and also Enki's sister Ninmah.

Even though you can see from the list that Enlil certainly practised nepotism in assigning fifes to the Anunnaki, however what you see here from both sides are the "Gods" that will teach humans and guide humans in their development.   These were the flesh and blood gods that walk among the ancient Sumerians. They were not "mythological" as modern archaeologist argues.

The plants, animals, guidance and knowledge they gave, allowed humans to multiply and prosper.  They taught us how to build cities and make tools.  The farming they taught us in Sumer "spread over the world from the Near Eastern mountains and highlands.  They turned "horned and hornless cattle for hides, meat, milk and wool."  The Anunnaki helped us regulate the Nile.  We made, as they directed, pastureland for herds of cows and goats.  The gods showed us to reinforce bricks, mixing mud with straw, then firing them in a kiln.

With the bricks, we paved roads.  With the strengthened bricks, we could raise multi-story buildings and temples.  With the kiln-furnace technology, we forged Earth's first durable pottery–cups, bowls, plates, storage urns.  The kilns "allowed intense, but controllable temperatures, to be contained in furnaces without contamination from dust or ashes."  They had us mass-produce bronze tools and weapons.  Via Kiln-metallurgy, the gods led us to coins, then to banking.

With naphtha (a tar like substance), we waterproofed boats and buildings.  With it, we sealed, cemented, painted and moulded all manner of buildings and statues.  Sumer itself lacked the raw ores to make metals, but we used the naphtha for exchange for ore.  The gods had us develop "extensive international trade routes" that went from the Middle East, to India, China and the Americas.  The gods gave us the wheel, carts and chariots and eventually war.  Wars we still fight to this day – "Enlil vs Marduk", or in today's language, "Yahweh vs Allah".

Below I have created a table showing just how much the Anunnaki contributed to the benefit and sometimes detriment of humanity. We owe them a lot, but we can also teach them a lot.

### Some of the "Gifts" from the "Gods" of Sumer

| Society | Building | Farming | Technology | Animals | Recipes |
|---|---|---|---|---|---|
| Kingship | Temples | Wheat | Brickmaking | Dog | Flour |
| Priesthood | City planning | Barley | Bronze tools / artwork | Cat | Bread |
| Festivals | Urban planning | Millet | Medicines | Geese | Porridge |
| Gourmet recipes | Surfaced roads | Rye | Weave fibre into cloth | Ducks | Cakes |
| Art | Pyramids of Egypt | Spelt | Textiles | Sheep | Pastries |
| Music | Running water | Cucumbers | Pigments | Goats | Biscuits |
| Dance | Hot/cold water | Onions | Paints | Pigs | Yogurt |
| Writing | Toilets | Lentils | Pottery glazes | Cattle | Butter |
| Record keeping | | Beans | Multi-coloured apparel | | Cream |
| | | Apples | Plows | | Cheeses |
| Extensive international trade routes | | Grapes for wine | Pottery | | Beer and wine |
| Law codes and courts of law | | Cabbage | Naphtha (tar), asphalt and bitumen | | |
| Transportation networks | | Lettuce | Musical notes | | |
| Customs stations | Giant step pyramids in the Yucatan Peninsula | Flax (for fibres and edible oil) | Musical instruments | | |
| | | | The wheel, carts and chariots | | |
| | | | Mathematical system– sexagesimals (a fraction based | | |
| Money (coin) | Stone Henge England | Apricots | on sixtieths (i.e. With a | | |
| | | Cherries | denominator equal to a power | | |
| Taxes | | Pears | of sixty) –that initiated the circle | | |
| | Regulated the Nile to create pasture land for cattle & sheep | Olives | of 360 degrees | | |
| | | Figs | Timekeeping that divided | | |
| | | Almonds | day/night into 12 double hours | | |
| | | Pistachios | Lune-solar calendar of 12 | | |
| | | Walnuts | months intercalated with a | | |
| | | | thirteenth leap month | | |
| | | | 12 Houses of the Zodiac and Astrology | | |
| | | | Astronomy–planetary, star, constellations | | |
| | | | Geometry | | |
| | | | Distance measurement units | | |
| | | | Units of weight and capacity | | |

Both Anunnaki factions— the descendants Enki and of Enlil —as well as our ancestors– renewed Earth's crops and beasts. For 1000 years there was cooperation, synergy and peace. This is the period the Hindu call Satya Yuga. "Yuga (Age or Era) of Truth", when humanity is governed by gods and every manifestation or work is close to the purest ideal and humanity will allow intrinsic goodness to rule supreme. It is sometimes referred to as the "Golden Age". The Satya Yuga lasts 1,728,000 years. (Selbie and Steinmetz, 2010)

Jumping forward to 2014, the big question, of course is what will these beings that we have confused with gods think of us now? In the past we were regarded as nothing more than slaves, but as a result of thousands of years of genetic selection, we have in some ways become much like them. Humans have mastered the atom, sent probes deep into space and unravelled the mysteries of the human genome. Only time will tell whether the Anunnaki regard us now as equals or something else?

I would like to assume that just as we have evolved, so too have the Anunnaki. However, there still remains a split between the followers of Enki and Enlil. As long as humans are able to follow a spiritual path and forget their petty differences, the Enki team will aid and befriend us. The Enlil group on the other hand will be drawn to the negative humans who would still like to enslave humanity.

It would be impossible to do justice to Sitchin's research in such a brief review as this one and I would strongly recommend the reader to investigate Sitchin's work in full. What started out as a boyhood curiosity has led Sitchin to journeys all over the world to ancient cities and former civilizations to research and document  his 16 different books. It's easy to dismiss Sitchin's research in the same way that other people dismiss UFOs, Eric Von Daniken and countless other researchers who claimed to have found evidence for extra-terrestrial visitors to this planet. But Sitchin is well aware of this devil's advocacy and dismisses the arguments of skeptics with solid scholarship, including the most rigorous translations of Sumerian text, Vedic tales and excerpts from the original Greek and Hebrew versions of the Bible. His ability to translate many languages is no small achievement. Those of us who will never possess the ability to decipher 6,000-year-old clay tablets must trust that Sitchin has done his job accurately. But his sources reveal an utter integrity, including the finest, most respected citations and references imaginable.

In recent times, a new, over confident, scholar in the ancient languages arena, has come out and sensationally claimed that he, as an expert in ancient languages, including Sumerian, can prove everything that Sitchin is saying is either wrong or a hoax. His name is Dr. Michael S. Heiser. Dr. Heiser fails to acknowledge every prediction about the outer planets, human DNA and many other topics Sitchin has made that have turned out correct. I suppose it is easier to make a name for yourself by bringing down someone you feel threatened by. I have watched all of Heiser's video presentations and read all of his papers debunking Sitchin. The reader can make their own mind up. I certainly know where I stand!

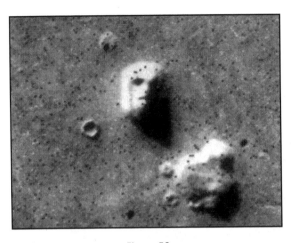

Figure 50

There are some final significant findings on the existence of the Anunnaki I wish to discuss. Perhaps the most compelling is the "Face on Mars" (Fig. 50), the structure in the area called Cydonia. When the relationship of the face on Mars is analysed for its distance to other pyramidal structures also discovered nearby, the geometric relationship is found to be identical to the distances of the Egyptian Sphinx and the pyramids in the surrounding areas of Egypt. Sitchin concluded the placement of these pyramids indicates that they served as landing markers for the Anunnaki after they entered the Earth's atmosphere from outer space. Sitchin also has asserted that the early pyramids were not designed by the Egyptians. NBC-TV aired a program on Nov.10, 1993 entitled **The Mystery of the Sphinx**, indicating that the Sphinx is 10,000 years older than previously thought. This corroborates Sitchin's findings that someone other than the Egyptians designed the pyramids.

It is said that Colin Powell and Norman Schwarzkopf, the American Generals who were key figures in the 1991 Gulf War knew something of Sitchin's work. The landing place of the Anunnaki was in an area once called Eridu in Southern Iraq. The main reason Saddam Hussein was not initially captured was because he was holding out in an ancient step pyramid (Ziggurat) constructed by the Anunnaki and which the Americans were loath to bomb, because of their inestimable historical value. Furthermore, the Americans have maintained a presence in Iraq ever since. Many speculate now that they found an actual **Star Gate**[4] there, but that is just 'here-say' right? Once the gloss of the media is removed from consensus reality, an entirely new picture emerges as to who knows what concerning what Sitchin has uncovered.

---

[4] A Star Gate is a nick name for a portal capable of creating a worm whole from Earth, to any part of the galaxy instantly. It is named after the highly successful movie **Star Gate** and TV series called **SG1**

In 2012 a sci-fi movie called **Prometheus** directed by Ridley Scott and written by Jon Spaihts and Damon Lindelof was released. The story is set in the late 21st century and centres on the crew of the spaceship Prometheus as they follow a star map, discovered among the artefacts of several ancient Earth cultures. The maps allude to the origins of humanity, in particular that humans were seeded by an ancient alien race. What is even more interesting is that these aliens are humanoid giants about 2.5 meter tall (8ft) – just like the Anunnaki! This is where we will leave the Anunnaki for now. In Book II I will pick up from where we letf it and look at their history on Earth right up to 300 BC. I can say that by 1250 BC, most of the Anunnaki had left the Earth, partly because of a nuclear war! But some remained and they have been influencing our history to this day. In Annex 2.3.1, I have incled the full time line for the Anunnaki's time on Earth till 2023 BC. But one more thing before I sign off –

## What the? What was that Galzu guy all about?

There are a few things about Galzu we need to remember. He was very tall, even for an Anunnaki and slender, with boyish good looks and pure white hair. To cut straight to the chase, he was not an Anunnaki, but a Pleiadian in disguise!

If you take your mind back to Chapter 13, you will remember our cousins, the Pleiadians, had always been there to assist us with our experiment of separation. Furthermore, we are all related to the Lyrians, including the Anunnaki. The Pleiadians are like our elder brother or sister and they have a lot more of direct contact with our parents, the Lyrians. The Lyrians are very high up on the Spiritual ladder. In fact, it is their parents – the original Elohim, then the Source of All That Is. So they are like the grandchildren of the Source. We are like the great, great Grand kids.

Anyway, the point is that the Lyrians are still very close to the Source and they know Its mind very well. They were well aware of what the Anunnaki were doing in regards to creating a hybrid creature. In fact, it was the Source that inspired Enki in the first place. However, due to Free Will, they could not influence Enlil directly. Therefore, the Pleiadians were given the mission of getting a message to Enki, who they hoped would save mankind.

Firstly, Galzu would have to keep the other Anunnaki leaders on Earth as well. They were predestined to help humans prosper. That is why he told Ninmah, Enki and Enlil that they would die if they went back to Nibiru. It was true that Ninmah and the others were aging prematurely because they had been on Earth for so long. But they would die if they went back to live on Nibiru – from old age that is. Not as Galzu said, from the gravity. So that was a little white lie or a twist of the facts to keep them on Earth where they were needed most - to lead the human's direction.

Because Pleiadians are from a higher dimension, it is not easy for them to stay on the 3rd Dimension for extended periods. That is why Galzu came to Enki in a dream. In fact, it was actually a meeting on the Astral Plane. The Astral Plane is a phenomena of Earth, something the P'taah set up before the experiment started. Therefore, Enki would not know what it was. To him, it was a dream. However, Galzu manifested the tablet in Enki's room. That is how we know the meeting took place on the Astral. If it was just a dream, the tablet could not have been made physical. By the way, that is why Galzu could not be found anywhere on the base the next day. He has already returned to the 5th Dimension. One more thing, every reference in the Bible, Quran or any other holy book to Angels or heavenly messengers, is always a Pleiadian in one guise or another. Enki now had the choice of obeying his brother, or follow his intuition. Luckily for us, he went with his gut! (There is a message in that for all of us!) What the Anunnaki did, was more or less in the plans of the Source. It was the Source that allowed the P'Taah to conduct their Separation Experiment and this creation of a hybrid species would speed things up. However, the Source also foresaw that this would create a brand new species never before seen in the Universe. This would be the first, 3rd Dimensional Being, capable of Ascending, body and all, into a higher dimension.

---

*The Creator of ALL wanted the humans to live – they were part of a bigger plan!*

---

## References:

Collins, A. (2014). *Göbekli Tepe: genesis of the gods*. 1st ed. Bear & Company.

Enki speaks, (2014). *CAIN & ABAEL: SUMERIAN TALE PREDATED BIBLE MAKEOVER*. [online] Available at: http://enkispeaks.com/2014/03/24/cain-abael-sumerian-tale-predated-bible-makeover/ [Accessed 17 Aug. 2014].

Freer, N. (2008). *Sapiens Rising: The View From 2100*. 1st ed. [ebook] Amazon Kindle: Electric Dragon Press. Available at: http://www.neilfreer.com/ [Accessed 17 Aug. 2014].

Hauck, D. (1999). *The emerald tablet*. 1st ed. New York: Penguin/Arkana.

Selbie, J. and Steinmetz, D. (2010). *The Yugas*. 1st ed. Nevada City, Calif.: Crystal Clarity Publishers.

Sitchin, Z. (1998). *The cosmic code*. 1st ed. New York: Avon Books.

(2002). *The lost book of Enki*. 1st ed. Rochester, Vt.: Bear & Co.

(2007). *The wars of gods and men*. 1st ed. New York: Harper.

(2010). *There were giants upon the earth*. 1st ed. Rochester, Vt.: Bear & Co.

Tellinger, M. (2012). *Slave species of the gods*. 1st ed. Rochester, Vt.: Bear & Co.

Wikipedia, (2014). *John Banner* (Sgt Schultz). [online] Available at: http://en.wikipedia.org/wiki/John_Banner [Accessed 16 Aug. 2014].

YouTube, (2014). *I See Nothing - Sgt Schultz*. [online] Available at: https://www.youtube.com/watch?v=34ag4nkSh7Q [Accessed 16 Aug. 2014].

# APPENDIX 1.1.1 – SOUL AGE COMPARISON

## Soul Age Comparison Chart

| | Infant Souls | Baby Souls | Young Souls | Mature Souls | Old Souls |
|---|---|---|---|---|---|
| **Motto** | Let's not die it. | Do it right or not at all. | It's all about me! | I know how you feel. | Live and let live. |
| **Skills** | Basics of survival – finding food, shelter and staying alive. Close to the earth and Spirit gives them a mystical flavour. | Tireless worker; in their minds they can make major contributions to the human race; very principled, authoritative. Always look to leverage off someone else's hard work, or higher intelligence. Very good with the gift of the gab, natural manipulators, con men, politicians. Money is very important because money = power. | Not always the brightest; try very hard. Can be quick learners, have trouble adapting to new environments, natural problem solvers when it will give them a benefit over someone or a situation. | Highly capable; can make major contributions to the human race; very principled; progressive and natural solutions; money is not a high priority, reformers; money is not a high priority, always making adjustments to better themselves. | Quick learners; adaptable; natural problem solvers that rely on their own inner resources to find solutions; ability to be their own authority and look within for the answers. |
| **Framework** | Emotions are primal, not deep and usually upset by joy or fear – not much in between. Very simplistic interpretation of life. Child like innocence. Gullible due to lack of inherent knowledge. | Emotionally lacking; cold; justice is decided by God; them this county; state; prone to OCD. | Emotionally detached; confuse Lust for Love; greed identified, not interested with the problems in the world; willingness to cooperate with others only if there is an advantage; my way or the highway; small picture oriented, prone to ego and aggrandising, hubris, materialistic. Typical yuppie, feels hyper, almost all NWO are here. | Emotionally intense and dramatic; idealistic and committed to eradicate injustice, confused and conflicted at times; organisations and compromise; prone to addictive behaviours. This is their first level they understand and experience true love. | Spiritual expansion and understanding; seek personal evolution; modelling old soul behaviour to belong by example and a need to teach and assist others in general; accept responsibility with grace; a simple desire to enjoy life, friends, family, and work. |
| **Aim** | Stay alive! Learn as much as they can about the basics of living and survival. | Head down, bum up – work and toil. We have our lot in life and God makes all of our decisions. Not interested in understand themselves or others– there is nothing to understand, focused on following society norms – get a job, get married, have kids, go to church; deep association to be a part of the world; feels obliged to and fund raisers, political parties etc. | Seeing what they can get out of any situation; seek personal power/ fame/ riches; Ego rules; Never accepts responsibility; a desire to be better than in relationships. Will only join clubs or social networks if they think it will get them ahead. To be the best at everything. Quantity over quality, productivity over human rights. | Trying to understand themselves and others; focused on relationships and emotional expression; need to make construction to world; wants to belong to something; sometimes desires to be "like" others in terms of beliefs, behaviour, fashion, etc. but usually adopts more gentle tastes. | Feel connected to everything, (e.g... relating to people, animals, the environment; intimate and caring, wealth or prestige; communing with nature; expressing natural talents in many areas. |
| **Relationships** | Perceive themselves as "me" and others as "not me". They treat other people as objects. They see nothing wrong in lying, stealing, cheating, and murdering if it means to further their personal advantage. They are diminish about their families. They don't deal with strangers at all. | Almost business like; arranged marriages would suit them; cannot express themselves emotionally yet. Sex strictly with the lights out; pyjamas on and strictly for procreation. Guilt associated with any pleasure. Strong family; community bond. | Feel more connected to objects than people. See human relationships as another competition; partner as object; no idea what love is. They keep them as objects, family, and work colleges. Will only join very trusting – have invented the pre-nuptial agreement! Would send their mothers if it were an advantage. They tolerate family only out of obligation for personal gain. | Intense and enduring; soap opera-like; prone to over identification; seek community; want to find others or a community that understands them; Would prefer to have a mate for life. They will choose someone that can understand them in terms of beliefs, passionate with the right partner. | Having fun, enjoying good humour and learning to relax more; seeking relations to people, animals, the environment; sensual and flavouring sex with abundant, sexual and good communication; enjoy difference in others. Usually live alone in complete happiness and balance. |
| **Interests** | Infant souls are dealing with survival issues, and most of the Infant souls on the planet are members of primitive tribes where these issues are being dealt with on a daily basis. Childish games and activities. | Guns, the Bible and "man" sports; women like baking, sewing, crafts but not for pleasure more out of obligation and sometimes prestige. Simple pleasures. They love keeping tradition alive. | Very goal / career orientated with strong drive and commitment. There love to live the high life, splash money around, live beyond their means. Any competitive sport or activity – watching more than participating. Any chance to belittle someone else or get one over someone else. | Supporting the arts and advancing human service; making a contribution to society; exploring new things; joining emotional causes and being a champion of them. Forever seeking knowledge for knowledge sake. | Feel connected to everything, (e.g... relating to people, animals, the environment; intimate and caring, work; that enriches and satisfies not soap opera like; long lasting wealth or prestige; communing with nature; expressing natural talents in many areas. |
| **Values** | Taking advantage of any situation or any person for person of gain. Not very savvy and easily fooled. They follow whatever their parents/elders do without question. They have not yet formulated their own set of values. | Very pious; extreme puritanical; believe in censorship; always follow the rules to the letter; weak social reform to their values; environmentalism & animal rights; nonresistance – God gave man dignity. Corruption is perfectly acceptable; after all everyone does it don't they? Suicide is an honourable (leave) way out. | Appearance over substance; breaking the rules if there is an advantage (particularly monetary); enjoying life's pleasures, including sex as a sport. Corruption is perfectly acceptable, after all everyone does it don't they? Suicide is an honourable (leave) way out. | Love of art and creativity in all forms; philosophy; expression and exchange of ideas; relationships; week social reform and either censorship; week social reform and personal growth; environmentalism & animal rights; nonresistance... They want to save the world. | Substance over appearance; bending the rules; enjoying life and all that it brings, including sex, good food, good communication, good music, philosophical discourse, and anything else around intellectually stimulating. |

You can download this in Hi-Res, colour PDF for FREE http://www.dannysearle.com/Book/ click "Downloads"

# APPENDIX 1.1.2 – SOUL AGE QUICK REFERENCE

## Soul Age Levels Quick Reference Chart

| Level | Infant | Baby | Young | Mature | Old |
|---|---|---|---|---|---|
| 1 | Often psychic; attuned to planet but not people, close to instinctive centre; no intellectual centre guarded; feral (untamed). | Starts to care about what people think of them. Love from others is an issue. How are full of this level. | Expresses anger a lot; cautious but can be domineering. Attracted to gangs. Prisons are full of this level. | Uneasy, starting to recognise importance of emotional attachments, but battles it. Lives 1st denial. Usually unsuccessful relationships with their children. | Confident, still mature; in no rush to mature. Devout parent/partner. |
| 2 | Less scared; uses thought; can pass in society; tests society's rules for myself if you don't love me. | 1st level issue becomes burning; I'll hurt myself if you don't love me. | Dogmatic. Fearful; covers it with dogma. Likes being in authority. Whole life is a lie. Likes to control others. | Inner conflict between success & relationships. Agonising. Will usually flounder at both because of indecision. Fights for many causes. | Hovers between drama and objectivity; internal warfare. Starting to experience emotional detachment but may cause guilt trips. |
| 3 | Quieter; no sex in 1st 3 stages; has decided can make peace with others so not so often locked up; can live on edge of town. | Gives up 1st and 2nd level behaviour; goes inward. Looks to authority (inward) as to how life might work. | Quiet, often gets away from it all, hermit; not too much conscience; doesn't like people much. Classic grumpy old man. | Quiet, intense, probably not too materially successful; very agonising. They will start towards giving spiritual Path in earnest but may not take it up full time. | Quiet, very knowledgeable, cured clari-ty life. Drawn to teach. |
| 4 | Starts sex animalistic; no conscience; is friendly as it works better, but still adverse to temper tantrums | Solid members of society; wants to belong to religions, clubs; to find out who they should be. Feels attached to others. | Friendly, successful; your average 'yuppie', often authority, wealth and power. Not good with relationships, can't commit, will cheat a lot. | Friendly, passionate, relationships more important than anything. Soap operas life. | Extroverted; teaching oriented. Authoritative, almost like Young Soul power mode. Classic example is Merlin. |
| 5 | Does nefarious things; wants to be different; tries everything. | Quiet, can be perverse; may have weird fetishes or really bizarre behaviour. | Wealth and power through unusual means; still outgoing, friendly, workaholic. Partner experiment with low level Occult. | Emotional drama; unusual stresses; wild roles; self conscious. Usually a career in mainstream counselling / therapist etc. or Spiritual counselling/metaphysics. Always creative. | Unusual, spiritual looking dresser; spirituality very important, no rest. Heavy teaching; anti/mysticism. Very gentle soul. |
| 6 | Paying back massive amounts of karma. May take many lifetimes. Often homeless, substances abuse. | Very karmic; pronounces that people should follow authority. Will often volunteer for harsh work/life – join the Army etc. as a form of self punishment. | Busy karmic; competent; this gets them to extreme power; sees something lacking but can't identify it; very set in ways. Many new to the New Age Movement from here. | Very agonising; most difficult of any level; most karma, very emotional; expressive roles; may go crazy; nervous breakdowns common here. | Extremely busy; hard worker; spirituality very important, no rest. Heavy teaching. Trust issues. Tormented by what they know. |
| 7 | Sin, naturally clever; passes in society, is not on personal relationships; may start to open emotionally and begin caring for someone else. eg. mate or parent. | Compliance; discovers about caring; being cared for. Looking at trying to be authority. Will start to seek outside attention – starting to like attention from the wider masses. | Absolute authority, calm, born to money or gifted career. Authoritative manner; looking at maturity; may play around with esoteric. Wants to do what's popular (most of the NWO are here). | Compliant, emotionally attached; teaching (metaphysics); not too interested in old soul detachment; almost stagnation; it's easy maturity, but they are generous and non-materialistic. | Almost only old karma left. Last Teaching level. But only one or two people. Acceptance issues. |

You can download this in Hi-Res, colour PDF for FREE
www.dannysearle.com/Book/ click "Downloads"

# APPENDIX 1.2.1 - THE HISTORY OF THE DEVIL

---

*"We are each our own devil, and we make
this world our hell." — (Oscar Wilde)*

---

*L*ucifer, Beelzebub, "The Beast", Satan. He has been called by many names, and he has taken strange and different forms. The idea of God's evil enemy has been around for thousands of years and is still as powerful as ever, in many parts of the world. But where did Satan's story begin? Where did he come from? And how did he become "The Prince of Darkness"?

More than **3000** years ago, in the deserts and pasture lands of the Middle East, unknown hands wrote the earliest chapters of the Hebrew Bible. If the Devil had a birth place, then surely it was here? In the oldest books of the Bible, a character called The Satan does appear, but he is nothing like the Satan most people imagine. The Satan is a title, meaning the "accuser", and he originally lived in Heaven, and did most of God's dirty work. However, this Satan has no power of his own and only does what God tells him. Nor is he a horrible creature with horns and a tail. In fact, throughout the text, there is no concept of an evil, opposing force to God anywhere. One of Satan's earliest appearances is in the Book of Job. In one of the best known stories in the Bible, Satan argues that Job, one of God's most loyal servants, is only pious because he has a good life. God agrees that The Satan can test Job, by inflicting all kind of diseases and calamities. In the end, in spite of dreadful sufferings, Job continues to worship God and Satan loses the argument. (Kind of reminds me of the 2 old men in the movie "Trading Places", which doesn't leave a very good impression of the Hebrew 'God'). The Satan that makes Job's life a misery isn't a demon, or even a bad angel, and he doesn't live in Hell! Indeed, in this period of history, there was no concept of hell – and nothing like the fire and brimstone hell you may be familiar with. In fact, for the ancient Israelites, very little happened when you died. You went to a place called **Sheol** which translates loosely as "the pit" - a dark, shadowy place where everybody who died went, regardless whether you were good or bad.

So where is the Satan we know? Where is the fiend that is eternally at war with the forces of good? The monster who rules over the flames of hell and punishes sinners? Where is the fallen angel, with his legion of demon helpers, tempting humans to do evil things so he can win their souls? If the traditional Devil doesn't come from the Jewish Old Testament, where does it come from?

Since human history began, people all over the world have believed in demons and evil spirits. A few share some traits with our devil, like horns, or a pointy beard, but never as powerful as our Satan. So where did people first get the idea of an ultimate evil being?

**3,500** years ago in ancient Persia (where Syria, Iraq and Iran are now) there were many gods, good and evil, until one man, a teacher called **Zoroaster** (Fig. 51), reduce the whole, complicated cast of characters to just two. Zoroastrians believe that there is one universal, transcendent, supreme god, **Ahura Mazda**, or the Wise Lord and the "chaotic" is represented by **Angra Mainyu** (also referred to as "Ahriman"), the **Destructive Principle** and the **Master of Lies**. Zoroaster is somewhat of a revolutionist and a man ahead of his time. His basic concept will later become the corner stone of many main stream religions including Brahmanism, Judaism, Islam and Christianity, to name but a few.

*Figure 51*

In Zoroastrian teachings, the Universe is a battlefield between the gods of good and evil, and every person on earth must take sides.

After death, good people are rewarded in heaven while sinners are punished in a dark and gloomy hell. It is the classic "Dualism" the 3rd dimension is famous for!

Under the powerful Persian Emperor, Darius the Great, the teachings of Zoroaster become the official religion of the Persian Empire, an empire which includes the lands of the Hebrews. The new Persian ideas about good and evil soon find their way into the Jewish scriptures. Just as in Zoroastrianism, where good and evil are personified, we now see this exact theme play out in the Jewish verses.

After the Persian Empire is defeated by **Alexander the Great**, Greek culture comes to ancient Israel. The Greeks introduce a huge cast of gods and goddesses, including one that will shape our image of Satan for centuries to come.

*Figure 52*

The god **Hades** (Fig. 52), has a black face, or black beard. He sits on a throne, often made of ebony and he wields a two-pronged fork, not for prodding sinners, but for blasting things to bits. To the ancient Greeks, Hades was the **God of the Dead**, the ruler of the Underworld. Even though Hades was one of the Olympian Gods, he spent most of his time in the Underworld, also called Hades. Therefore, he was viewed as gloomy, and dowdy, and not very well liked. Although Hades was very unlikeable, he was not evil, and in fact the ancient Greeks saw him as a **God of Justice**. They believed that when you die, you go before Hades, and he decides whether you go to a place of happiness, or a place of misery. As ruler of the world underground, Hades is also the god of **Wealth and Abundance**. In a dim memory of Hades, people have believed for centuries that the Devil can make you rich.

As well as the brooding character of Hades, the Greeks give the world another familiar ingredient of the devil's story. In a famous myth, Zeus, greatest of the gods defeats the winged serpent Typhon and throws him down to **Tartarus** (a deep hole in the ground and the lowest region of the Underworld). Over the following centuries, the myth grows into how the angel Satan rebels against God and is thrown out of heaven with all his followers. Satan's allies, the fallen angels, become his legion of demons. When we think of hell, we think of fire, lava and sinners being horribly tortured. But where did this picture come from? The Underworld of Hades doesn't have fire, but ancient Jerusalem does!

In the **New Testament**, Jesus warns of a place in Jerusalem called **Gehenna**. In the Hebrew Bible, the site was initially where apostate Israelites and followers of various Ba'als and Caananite gods, including Moloch, sacrificed their children by fire (2 Chr. 28:3, 33:6). Thereafter, it was deemed to be curse. It later became the place that the authorities burnt the bodies of executed prisoners. Eventually it took on urban legend stories and the site became a supernatural, haunted place of the wicked. Therefore, in the Jewish, Christian and Islamic scripture, Gehenna is a destination of the wicked and the inspiration behind the terrors of hell. This is different from the more neutral Sheol/Hades, the abode of the dead, though the King James Version of the Bible translates both with the Anglo-Saxon word **Hell**.

By the time the Christian gospels were written, around the end of the first century AD, Satan has grown into a powerful figure. By now, Jewish lands are ruled by the mighty **Roman Empire** and the Romans are despised bitterly. To many Jews and Christians persecuted by Rome, Satan is the evil force behind Caesar's throne. In the New Testament **Book of Revelation**, the writer gives Satan one of his most mysterious names – **The Beast – 666.** The Beast, could refer to the Roman Emperor **Nero**. The Book of Revelation says that the devil was sent down by God into the abyss, where he will be locked up for 1000 years. When he is let out, the end of the world will come. An apocalyptic battle will take place, as good and evil fight it out till the end. Again, this battle comes directly from the Persian ideology of Zoroaster.

## What does the devil look like at the dawn of the Christian era?

Often he is depicted with black skin and hair like Hades, ruler of the Underworld. He has wings that echo that he was once an angel, although they look more like the wings of a dragon or bat or Typhon perhaps (Fig. 53). For thousands of years, the dragon was the symbol of a dreaded and evil force, and it is from the dragon that Satan inherits his talon feet. When Satan isn't being a dragon, he is a snake.

The serpent said to have tempted Eve in the Garden of Eden, has long been believed to represent the devil, although the scriptures don't actually say so. In fact, Christian leaders disagree, sometimes violently, about what the devil is like. But one thing they do agree on, and that is he is busy working with, and through their enemies.

Around **400 CE**, a Roman Emperor, **Constantine the Great** (272CE

– 337CE) converts to Christianity. Within a generation, the once persecuted and obscure religion is the official creed of the mightiest empire on earth. Christian Bishops now have real power, backed up by the State, and they use Satan to help them keep it. Again and again, Church leaders claimed, that those who disagreed with them, especially other Christian groups,

*Figure 53*

are working for the devil. The logic is relentless, it's us and them. If you are not with the Church and the Empire, then you are with Satan. Ironically, 2000 years later, George W Bush used that exact argument, with his war on terror – you are either with the United States, or you are with the terrorist! (Classic Child Soul logic).

It was a short step for the Church to demand heretics be put to death. The first executions came about **450 CE**. Over the following centuries, the numbers of people killed for supposedly working for Satan grows to hundreds of thousands. Under the protection of the Roman Empire, the Christian religion grows quickly, but the Bishops worry that the pagan gods are far too popular. Thousands of Romans still pray to the Wind Goddess **Fortuna**, the bringer of luck! But the most popular pagan god of all is **Pan** (Fig. 54). Christian leaders see him as a serious threat who must be discredited. Eventually Pan is reduced to a lesser demon, even though he was originally the Roman God of music, feasting and love making!

Satan now adopts Pan's best known features. He becomes an ugly, leering beast with horns on his head. His body becomes hairy, and he has Pan's cloven hooves, though sometimes he keeps the talon feet of the dragon. So outlandish has he become, that he is often depicted with a second face on his belly or bottom.

One of the greatest thinkers of the early Christian church is **Saint Augustine** (354 CE – 430 CE). Augustine is keen to show that the

old nature gods are dangerous demons. According to Augustine, male demons called **Incubi** appear to women at night and seduce them. Even more disturbing for Augustin, is pious men could be visited in their beds at night by female demons called **Succubi** and be forced to do sinful things against their will.

*Figure 54*

After all, Nuns and Priests would never engage in sexual activities, so it had to be the work of demons!

By the **Middle Ages**, or Medieval period (5th and 15th centuries), after a thousand years of Christian teaching, the Church has persuaded its followers, that the devil and his demons are real, and that Satan is a powerful enemy. The problem is, some Christians take the whole idea a bit further than the Bishops want. In the early days of the Roman Church, before Constantine adopted them, there was a rival sect called the **Gnostics** (from Ancient Greek gnosis, meaning knowledge) who taught that there were two gods – a good god and a bad god. The good god created everything Spiritual, and the bad god was responsible for creating all matter. So in other words, the lesser god created the earth and everything in it. To the Gnostics, everything to do with the world and with the flesh was seen in negative terms. Also, they did not believe that Jesus was a real, historical person, but rather, that the Jesus story was an allegory. One group during the 12th – 14th century took up the Gnostic teachings with enthusiasm. They were the Cathars of Northern Italy and Southern France. It is debatable if they called themselves "Cathars", because in their own texts, they use the terms "*Good Men*" *(Bons Hommes)* or "Good Christians" as a common term of self-

*Figure 55*

identification. To the Cathars, all material possessions are evil and belong to the devil. For a church now wealthy and powerful, this is an uncomfortable, even dangerous teaching. The local people loved the Cathars, because their main role was as healers. Unfortunately for the Cathars, when they went around feeding the poor and healing the sick, they were also teaching that the Roman church was corrupt and sinful (Fig. 55). To cut a long story short, Pope Innocent III announced a crusade against the Cathars which was launched in 1209. This turned into a 45 year blood bath, where around 100,000 men, women and children were brutally hacked and burnt to death by the Pope's soldiers. Partly because they questioned the Roman Church's authority, and argued that Satan was more powerful than what the Church said he was!

The crusade against the Cathars was against fellow Christians, but for almost 2 centuries, the crusades were mostly about fighting **Islam** for control of the Middle East. In medieval Europe, Islam is seen as a heresy and the work of the devil. Muslims too, are quick to claim that their enemies are in league with the evil one. In the Qur'an, Muslims are instructed to fight against non-Muslims, because they are friends of Satan. Both sides have inherited the ancient beliefs of the Persians, seeing the world as divided into good and evil, justifying all the horrors of war and conquest.

The crusades leave a sinister legacy. In the middle of the campaign, **Pope Gregory IX** founds the **Inquisition**. Controlled by the **Dominican Order of Friars**, the Inquisition's job is to find heretics, and hand them over to local princes for special punishment. The Inquisition gave people plenty to be frightened about. It often spoke of the fires of hell and eternal damnation. But even worse, the Inquisition had the power to arrest people, without them being told who reported them and what the charge was. As the accused, you were guilty until proven innocent, and could be held for as long as the authorities wanted. Anyone who questions the Inquisition is immediately suspected of being in league with the devil. In the fight against Satan and the powers of evil, medieval rulers believed that as in any war, information is vital. Up till now, the Church has not officially allowed any Christians to be tortured, although torturing Jews and Muslims was acceptable. But in **May, 1252, Pope Innocent IV** rules, that Christians suspected of heresy can be tortured until they confess, admit they are working for the devil and inform on co-conspirators.

Basically, once you were accused of heresy, you could never prove your innocence, because anything you said was a lie, because you are in league with the devil. However, for the most part, it had nothing to do with you worshipping Satan, and more to do with "We want your farm...." Indeed, all over Europe, the Inquisition is used by the unscrupulous to seize wealth, or to down their enemies.

*Figure 56 & Figure 57*

In **1307, King Phillip the Fair of France** brings witchcraft charges against the leaders of the **Knights Templar** (Fig. 56), the fabulously wealthy order of Crusaders. Phillip accuses the Templars of worshiping a pagan idol called **Baphomet** (Fig. 57), a satanic figure.

The Templars were attacked and largely destroyed on **Friday the 13th October 1307**, a day that has lived in infamy to modern times. People still call this "Black Friday" and view it as an unlucky day, somehow connected to satanic forces.

In **1320**, the war against Satan is wound up another notch. **Pope John XXII** orders the Inquisition to target any kind of witchcraft, sorcery, or necromancy (communication between the living and the dead). A big worry is that unscrupulous priests who know how to drive out devils with the Rites of Exorcism, might instead use Exorcism to invite the devil in. By using the Latin chants and incantations, they could demand the demon to do their bidding or make them wealthy. This idea spreads all over Europe, so very quickly, everyone was accusing everyone of necromancy. One of the first cases investigated by the Inquisition is in the Irish city of **Kilkenny**.

*Figure 58*

In **1324**, in a dispute over inheritance, one of the richest women in the town, **Dame Alice Kyteler** is accused of witchcraft, heresy and of having a demon lover called Robin. Being a rich landowner (from Norman heritage) having had several husbands, her step-children bought charges against her, that she had poisoned (using witchcraft) her previous husbands in order to obtain the land. After some months of stalemate, one of her servants, **Petronella de Meath** (Fig. 58) was tortured, and confessed to witchcraft, implicating Kyteler. Alice manages to escape to England, however her unfortunate servant Petronella is burnt at the stake.

The campaign against necromancy, sorcerers and witches lasts 300 years, and kills somewhere between 60,000, and 300,000, usually innocent people (including children). The vast majority of victims are women. This is because the Church considered women more prone to being seduced by the devil and material gratification, and more likely to be led astray. They were also thought to be less intellectual than men.

As the Inquisition goes about its grisly business, rounding up suspects and interrogating them, many church people and lay people worry that it is all guess work. Perhaps they are missing even more witches then they are finding. But how can you tell who is one of Satan's helpers? What you need is a standard test.

In **1486**, two German, **Dominican Monks** publish a text book for Inquisitors called **Malleus Maleficarum**, (Fig. 59) commonly rendered into English as "Hammer of [the] Witches" or simply, **The Witches Hammer**. The book contains a clever Catch 22. Not only is witchcraft heresy, but not believing in witches is heresy as well! The Malleus Maleficarum tells the Inquisitor everything he needs to know about witches - what witches are; what witches do etc. Witches have the mark of Satan on their bodies, a birthmark or a wart. They can fly by rubbing magical ointment on their skin, and they gather at

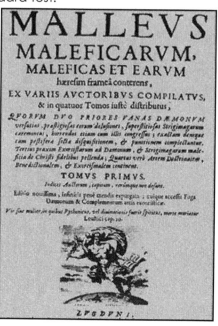

*Figure 59*

Satan worshipping ceremonies called Sabbats. At these the book claims, witches practise a twisted version of the Christian mass. Kissing the devil's rear end was considered a blasphemes act of homage. In today's terms, Malleus Maleficarum would be considered a New York Best Seller. It was sold in thousands, all over Europe, in many updated reprints, and in fact it can still be purchased to this day!

Thirty years after Malleus Maleficarum was written, **Martin Luther** leads the **Protestant Reformation**, splitting the Christian Church in two. Each faction, Protestant and Catholic claims the other is in league with the evil one. Both sides use Malleus Maleficarum to find Satanists, and not just in order to destroy them. Witch hunting has become a type of scientific quest. The idea is, if you can understand witches and the devil, then you can fight them.

Right across Europe, hysteria about Satan sweeps across both Protestant and Catholic countries alike. In Scotland, **James VI**, one of the best educated Kings in Europe, is so caught up in the craze he writes a book about the devil and witchcraft. Called **Demonology**, James' book sets out to prove that Satan worshiping witches are everywhere, and that they are the gravest threat to the security of the State. Even as James leads the fight against the devil and the forces of evil, the devil is helping James to keep his crown. James would often point to a figure of Satan and say *"If it were not for me, look who would be ruling in my place!"*

When the New World of the Americas is colonised by Europeans, the devil travels with them. The Puritan colonist who arrive from England in the late 1600's are strong believers in the powers of Satan. They are convinced that everyone that isn't a puritan is controlled by the devil. In their eyes, women are especially susceptible to Satan's powers. They built puritan communities hoping to be the shining example to the rest of Christendom. If you were enjoying yourself, or a group of people were singing or dancing or having a drink, then those who were opposed to that kind of fun, were quite certain Satan was filling the glasses for you!

In **1688** in Boston, Massachusetts, an Irish immigrant called **Mary Glover** who was a laundry woman, is accused of bewitching the children of one of her customers. Proof of her pact with the devil

*Figure 60*

includes several rag dolls found in her house. Being from Ireland at this time, her first language was Gaelic, and one of the tests to prove you were not a witch was to speak the Lord's Prayer. Not being very well spoken in English, she was unable to pass this test. Thus, she was hanged as a witch. 3 years after Mary Glover is hanged, less than 20 miles away in the township of **Salam**, the testimony of 3 young girls leads to a mass execution. The children claimed they were possessed by demons, sent to them by the people they claimed to be witches (this is how they justify their naughty behaviour after getting caught). During this Inquisition, known as the **Salam Witch Trials** (Fig. 60), 150 people were rounded up and interrogated. 19 men and women are hung, or crushed to death and 17 others die in prison. In an ironic twist to the story, after it was found out that the girls made the whole thing up, the Salam jury later apologised, blaming the devil for their mistake, in condemning good people to death.

By the **1700's**, the witch craze in America and Europe is almost over. A new, scientific view of the world is gaining ground. Although the witch hunts have ended, the educated classes of Europe and America even start to question whether the devil even exists. In the folk tales of ordinary people, Satan lives on. But he is very different

to the previous, formidable and terrifying devil of the witch finders. Indeed, a famous story of this period is about **Dunstan**, the great and powerful blacksmith. The devil comes and asked him to make him some new shoes. Dunstan uses his smithy's tongs and grabs Satan by the nose and throws him out of town. This is a devil you can now put in his place!

By now, the devil has shed some of his ugliness and crude habits. In fact, he is often depicted as a member of the decadent aristocracy. He is a handsome gentleman, dressed in fine cloths and mixing in

*Figure 61*

fashionable company. Like Hades, the Greek god of the Underworld and the Satan of the ancient, gnostic heresies, this Satan controls the material world of wealth, power and sex. He can give all these things to you if you promise him your soul. The most famous of all devil folk tales is the story of Faust. In the story, a German magician named **Faust,** agreed to sell his soul to the devil in exchange for youth, knowledge, earthly pleasures, and magical powers. The devil, in the guise of the clever, and devious **Mephistopheles**, grants him all his wishes. Faust's bargain with the devil ends in disaster and Mephistopheles calls in his debt and Faust dies, horribly. The devil takes him away to spend eternity in hell.

As the power of religion fades, and the age of Popes and Kings give way to the age of revolution and democracy, a new devil arrives on the scene. This devil is utterly different to the treacherous fiend of Christian tradition. He is a tragic and lonely figure. An anti-hero, battling against tyrannical authority in the shape of a cruel and overbearing God. Satan is now a brave and handsome rebel (Fig. 61). It's almost a romantic view of Satan, as not really a villain or evil person at all, but the opposite of that. Satan is a good guy, challenging the boss so to speak. During the age of **Romanticism**, we find poets like **Byron**, creating a Byronic hero who is dark and moody who has a past. So rather than being something to shun, or someone to fear, the devil is admired.

With the **20th Century**, the devil's fortunes take a turn for the worse. No longer feared or admired in the Western world, he becomes a figure of fun. In fact, he even joins the world of commerce, helping to sell products from wine, to chocolates and beer. In the age of marketing and the consumer society, Satan can bring the lure of the forbidden to a tired brand. It's a long way from an apocalyptic war between good and evil. It has been a hall mark in the 20th century to

Figure 62

make the devil fun, and no more good or bad then the people he is dealing with. Satan seems to be cut down to size. The Prince of Darkness has become a mischievous imp (Fig. 62).

But in a surprising twist, a different Satan, a glamourous rebel so admired by the revolutionaries of the 19th century, makes a startling come back in the 1960's. During this period, there was a strong sense of rebellion against everything. Indeed, many of the counter-culture (i.e. Hippies) were anti-religion; anti-capitalism; anti-war and much more. Thus, they started to explore anything that was counter to the "norms".

In **1966**, a cult showman, called **Anton LaVey**, founds the **Church of Satan** in San Francisco (Fig. 63). Part religion, part money making scam, the Church of Satan attracts lured headlines, mostly encouraged by the publicity seeking LaVey himself. LaVey says that the Church of Satan believes in greed, selfishness, lustful thoughts, and deviant acts, as he believes this is man's natural state of being. LaVey was born Howard Stanton Lavey in Chicago, Illinois in 1930. Part of his rouse claimed he was of Romanian descent, and related to **Vlad Tepes** (the original Dracula), but this was all proven to be a lie. Neither LaVey, nor his followers, actually believed in a real devil. What they admired was Satan the rebel, the non-conformist, provoking the establishment. Predictably, America was both fascinated and outraged. Anton LaVey died on October 29, 1997, in St. Mary's Medical Center (a Catholic hospital) in San Francisco of pulmonary edema. He was 67. I hope you can see the irony of this!

In **1967**, the 60's fascination with the occult spearheaded by LaVey's Church of Satan gets a powerful boost from Hollywood. The film, "Rosemary's Baby" was a dark tale of devil worshipers in    Manhattan and became a massive, and unexpected hit. In Roman Polanski's masterpiece, the heroine's innocuous neighbours,

are part of a satanic conspiracy to help the Prince of Darkness father a child, who will rule the world. In Rosemary's Baby, Satan triumphs in the end, but the Christian backlash comes in the 1973 blockbuster "The Exorcist". This time, the devil, who has possessed a young girl, is defeated

*Figure 63*

by the forces of good in the shape of two priests. The old belief that women are especially susceptible to satanic influence is revived two centuries after the Salem Witch Trials. Hollywood's discovery that fortunes can be made from tales of possession and devil worship, stokes the fires of a paranoia that has lain dormant since the days of the witch trials.

*Figure 64*

In the **1980's**, stories about a vast conspiracy of organised Satanists sweep the media. Known as the **Satanic Panic** (Fig. 64), Christian groups allege mass satanic abuse of children, and tens of thousands of kidnappings. There were many rumours of child sacrifice and ritual murder. Although hundreds of people are arrested and imprisoned, when the FBI finally runs a full scale investigation in the United States, it concludes that the satanic abuse allegations are all groundless. That is because all of the allegations are true, and the FBI covered it up, to protect very high profile people. It should be noted however, that these child killers do not have anything to do with the "devil" as such, but more to do with modern day Satanism, or more correctly "Lucifer" worship, which I will be discussing in depth in Book II.

In the United States, surveys show that almost half of Americans believe the devil is real. Even non-religious people instinctively divide the world into good and evil. The opposing principles taught by Zoroaster to the ancient Persians. If anything, the events of 9/11 made these beliefs even stronger.

In **September 2001**, the massive attacks on the United States which destroyed the **World Trade Center** shocked America to its core. To many, it seemed as though sinister forces had gone on the offensive. It was easy to believe that this was a showdown between the forces of good and evil. To the US government, and a large section of American opinion, the attacks were about much more than politics. This belief was reiterated time and again by **President Bush** when he would say *"We have come to know truths we will never question. Evil is real, and it must be opposed"*. This is basically saying you are with us, or you are opposed to us, or in other words, you are working hand-in-hand with Satan. The same argument used in the 13th Century. It's classic, dualistic thinking.

Figure 65

In the wake of the 9/11 attacks, President Bush gave the job of catching Osama bin Laden, the man they tried to pin the atrocity on, to **Lieutenant General William G Boykin**[5] (Fig. 65). But according to Boykin, America's real foe isn't Bin Laden. In the General's words, "The enemy of the US is a guy called Satan"

Since 2001, the draconian measures taken by the US and other governments in the **"War on Terror"** are uncannily like those of the war on Satan, over 400 years ago. Imprisonment without trial; secret hearings; anonymous tip-offs; and torture. Indeed, it is a similar willingness to justify mistreatment and the removal of human rights from our fellow man in the War on Terrorism. In fact, it seems that whenever you set out to fight 'evil', inevitably you become the very evil you are trying to fight.

Controversially, President Bush called the invasion of Iraq a **'Crusade'**. The similarities with the historic Crusades against heretics are striking. They include a belief on the battlefield, that enemy are not just military opponents, but agents of pure evil.

In November **2004**, as US forces launch a massive attack on the Iraqi city of **Fallujah**, a senior Marine Officer, **Lieutenant Colonel Gareth Brandl**, makes it clear who he thinks the enemy is: *"The enemy has got a face, he's called Satan, and he is in Fallujah, and we are gonna destroy him."*

It is embroidery. It is myth making. It is poetry, and it can be good fun, except, that it has produced great evils. The Devil is a human invention, but one that has rebounded on us, because it has given us permission to do terrible things to each other.

Which is why I think we should close Hell down and finally banish the Devil, once and for all and forget about him altogether. Stop blaming Satan, and start to take responsibilities for your own actions, thoughts and deeds.

---

[5]  Can you guess General Boykin's Soul Age? A: Child Soul – a text book example!

# References:

Barton, B. and La Vey, A. (1992). *The secret life of a Satanist*. 1st ed. Los Angeles, CA: Feral House.

Behavioral Science Unit, National Center for the Analysis of Violent Crime, (1992). *Investigator's Guide to Allegations of 'Ritual' Child Abuse*. Quantico, Virginia: Federal Bureau of Investigation.

Blumberg, J. (2007). *A Brief History of the Salem Witch Trials*. [online] Smithsonian. Available at: http://www.smithsonianmag.com/history/a-brief-history-of-the-salem-witch-trials-175162489 [Accessed 25 Jul. 2014].

Buxton, R. (2004). *The complete world of Greek mythology*. 1st ed. London: Thames & Hudson.

Byron, G. and Levine, A. (2010). *Byron's poetry and prose*. 1st ed. New York: W.W. Norton & Co.

Goethe, J., Arndt, W. and Hamlin, C. (2001). *Faust*. 1st ed. New York: W.W. Norton.

Hinley, G. (n.d.). *A Brief History Of The Crusades;Islam and Christianity in the struggle for world supremacy*. 1st ed.

*Holy Bible: King James Version*. (2011). 1st ed. London: Collins UK.

Institoris, H. and Sprenger, J. (1971). T*he Malleus Maleficarum* of Heinrich Kramer and James Sprenger. 1st ed. New York: Dover.

iz Quotes, (2014). *William G. Boykin Quotes*. [online] Available at: http://izquotes.com/author/william-g.-boykin [Accessed 25 Jul. 2014].

La Vey, A. (1969). *The Satanic Bible*. 1st ed. New York: Avon Books.

MacCulloch, D. (2010). *A History of Christianity*. 1st ed. London: Penguin.

Markale, J. (2003). *Montse´gur and the mystery of the Cathars*. 1st ed. Rochester, Vt.: Inner Traditions.

News.bbc.co.uk, (2014). BBC NEWS | Middle East | *Fixing the problem of Falluja*. [online] Available at: http://news.bbc.co.uk/2/hi/middle_east/3989639.stm [Accessed 25 Jul. 2014].

Pagels, E. (1995). *The Origin of Satan*. 1st ed. New York: Random House.

Pagels, E. (2006). *The Gnostic Gospels*. 1st ed. London: Phoenix.

Presidency.ucsb.edu, (2014). *George W. Bush: Address Before a Joint Session of the Congress on the State of the Union*. [online] Available at: http://www.presidency.ucsb.edu/ws/?pid=29644 [Accessed 25 Jul. 2014].

Robinson, B. (2010). *Satanic Ritual Abuse (SRA)*. [online] Religioustolerance.org. Available at: http://www.religioustolerance.org/sra_intro1.htm [Accessed 25 Jul. 2014].

*Rosemary's Baby* (1968). [film] Hollywood: Director: Polanski, Roman, Writers: Ira Levin (novel), Roman Polanski (screenplay).

*The Exorcist* (1973). [film] Hollywood: Director: William Friedkin, Writers: William Peter Blatty (novel), William Peter Blatty (screenplay).

Whitney, L. and De Laurence, L. (1905). *Life and teachings of Zoroaster, the great Persian*. 1st ed. Chicago: De Laurence, Scott & Co.

# APPENDIX 2.1.1 – THE TRUE STORY OF KA-IN & ABA-EL

Enki encouraged Adapa and Titi to procreate. Titi bore twins, KA-IN and ABA-EL. Enki ordered Adapa to teach his descendants to work farms, raise herds and manage estates. Sheep were developed and domesticated on Nibiru, then brought to Earth by Enki's youngest son Dumuzi. Marduk then taught Aba-el how to tend goats and sheep.

So, as not to be outdone by Marduk, Enlil had his son Ninurta teach Kai-in to grow and harvest the enhanced grain Ningishzidda had brought from Nibiru. So Ninurta taught Kai-in crop production and harvesting, and Marduk taught Aba-el animal husbandry.

## KA-IN KILLS ABA-EL

At the "Celebration for Firsts", Ka-in offered the first grains of the harvest and Abael slaughtered the first lambs to be cooked for Enlil and Enki.   Enki lauded Abael's lambs for meat and wool, but said nothing of Ka-in's grain.   "By the lack of Enki's blessing greatly was Ka-in aggrieved." The twins quarrelled for the entire winter.   They argued whether Ka-in's grains and fish-filled canals or Aba-el's meat and wool gave most satisfaction to the gods. During summer, Abael's meadows dried and his pastures shrunk, so he drove his flocks to Ka-in's fish canals to drink.   By this Ka-in was angered. The twins fought with fists, then Ka-in bludgeoned Abael with a stone. Afterward, he sat and sobbed.

## KA-IN IS JUDGED

Enki took Ka-in to Eridu for trail before Enlil, Ninki, Ninurta and Nannar of Enlil's Lineage, Ninmah, and Enki, and Marduk of Enki's (The Seven Who Judge).   Marduk, Aba-el's mentor, told them to kill Ka-in for his crime. But Enki revealed that he begat Ka-in's father Adapa, so Ka-in was Marduk's grand-nephew.   "Ka-in must live," said Enki, "to breed superior Earthlings to work field, pasture and mines. If Ka-in too shall be extinguished, food supplies to an end would come, mutinies will be repeated."

The Seven ruled, *"Eastward to a land of wandering for his evil deed Ka-in must depart. Ka-in and his generations shall distinguished be."* Order Enlil.

By Ningishzidda, was the life essence (DNA) of Ka-in altered: his face, a beard could not grow." The beardless Indians of the Western Hemisphere descended from Ka-in. *"With his sister Awan as spouse, Ka-in from the É.DIN departed."* They wandered in the wilderness to the east.

## ADAPA MAKES A PROPHECY

When Ka-in's father Adapa was on his death bed, Ninurta flies Ka-in back to see him. *"The eyesight of Adapa having failed, for recognition of his sons' faces he touched. The face of Ka-in was beardless."* Adapa told Ka-in, *"For your sin of your birthright you are deprived, but of your seed seven nations will come. In a realm set apart they shall thrive, distant lands they shall inhabit. But having your brother with a stone killed, by a stone will be your end."* Ninurta returned Ka-in to the wilds east of É.DIN and *"begat sons and daughters."* Ninurta, *"for them a city built, and as he was building, by a falling stone was Ka-in killed."*

## KA-IN'S LINEAGE PROSPER

Ka-in's survivors planted grain. They founded and ruled the city of Nud. One of Ka-in's great grand-sons was Enoch. Titi bore thirty sons and daughters to her brother Adapa. The Anunnaki distributed them among themselves and taught them to write, do math, dig wells, prepare oils, play harp and flute and worship them as gods. (Enki Speaks, 2014)

# APPENDIX 2.2.1 – FLOOD STORY VARIATIONS

| | Sumer | Atrahasis | Gilgames | Bible | Berossus | Greece | Quran |
|---|---|---|---|---|---|---|---|
| Date | 3000BCE | C.1640 BCE | C.1100 BCE | C.1000-500 BCE | 278 BCE | C.700 BCE? | C.600 CE |
| Revolt | Lesser gods | Lesser gods | Does not say | Giants | Monsters | Giants | Does not say |
| Hero | Ziusudra | Atrahasis | Ut-napištim | Noah | Xisuthrus | Deucalion | Nuh |
| Country | Šuruppuk | Šuruppak | Šuruppak | Does not say | Sippar | Thessaly | Does not say |
| Destroyer | Enlil | Enlil | Enlil | YHWH | Enlil | Zeus | Allah |
| Warning | Dream / Direct order | Dream | Indirect order | Direct order | Dream | Does not say | Direct order |
| Reason | Giants/ Lesser gods | Noise | Does not say | Sin, giants | Monsters | Sin, giants | Sin |
| Period | 7 days | 7 days | 7 days | 150/40 days | "quickly" | 9 days | Does not say |
| Savior | Enki | Enki | Enki | YHWH | Enki | Prometheus | Allah |
| Cause | Storms, flood | Rain | Storm, flood | Rain, fountains | Does not say | Rain, waves | "from the valley" |
| Birds to find land | Does not say | Does not say | Raven, dove, swallow | Doves/raven | "several" | None | Does not say |
| Destination | Mount Ararat | Does not say | Nimuš | Mount Ararat | Gordyene | Parnassus | Al-Gudi |
| Fate for Hero | Eternal life | Eternal life | Eternal life | Three sons will rule | Eternal life | Three grandsons | Does not say |

## Sumer

Written on a Sumerian cuneiform tablet of which about two thirds are now lost. The missing parts can be reconstructed from texts like the Sumerian King List and Berossus: first the creation of men, then the kings who ruled before the Great Flood, and finally the Flood itself, culminating in an offer of eternal life to the Sumerian Noah, Ziusudra. After the story of the Creation of Mankind, the gods were disturbed by the noise produced by men, and the supreme god Enlil decides to destroy human beings.

## Atrahasis - Babylonia

The Epic of Atrahasis is the fullest Mesopotamian account of the Great Flood. The text is known from several versions: two written by Assyrian scribes (one in the Assyrian, one in the Babylonian dialect), the third one (on three tablets) was written during the reign of king Ammi-saduqa of Babylonia (1647-1626 BCE). The story of the Flood starts with complaints by the Lesser Gods, who refuse to work any longer. Humankind is created, but men make so much noise, that the gods decide to wipe them out. The plan to send a Deluge, however, is betrayed by the god Enki, who sends a dream to Atrahasis.

## Gilgameš - Babylonia

The Epic of Gilgameš is one of the most famous texts from ancient Babylonia. It tells the story of a king who is trying to find immortality, and meets Ut-napištim, who has survived the Great Flood. Sitchin wrote a book, in novel style recounting the story of Gilgameš called "The King Who Refused to Die: The Anunnaki and the Search for Immortality". A really good read!

## Bible - Babylonia

The Biblical version is the most famous. Most scholars agree it was written in Babylonia during the Jewish exile.

## Babylonia / Berossus

Babylonian History, which was published in 278 BCE

## Greece

There are 3 sources for flood stories in ancient Greece. Ovid, a Roman poet Ovid (43 BCE - 17 CE). In this version, the degeneration of mankind is paralleled with the revolt of the giants. Apollodorus of Alexandria wrote a book called "The Library", in 200 BCE. Hyginus is a Greco-Roman versions is with the summary by Gaius Julius Hyginus, a first-century CE author from Roman Spain who collected ancient myths in a book called Fabulae, "stories"

## Quran

The story of the Great Flood is told twice in the Quran, in Sura 11 and Sura 71.

# APPENDIX 2.3.1 – ANUNNAKI TIME LINE ON EARTH

## I. Events Before the Deluge

## Years Ago

**450,000** On Nibiru, a distant member of our solar system, life faces slow extinction as the planet's atmosphere erodes. Deposed by Anu, the ruler Alalu escapes in a spaceship and finds refuge on Earth. He discovers that Earth has gold that can be used to protect Nibiru's atmosphere.

**445,000** Led by Enki, a son of Anu, the Anunnaki land on Earth, establish Eridu - Earth Station I - for extracting gold from the waters of the Persian Gulf.

**430,000** Earth's climate mellows. More Anunnaki arrive on Earth, among them Enki's half-sister Ninhursag, Chief Medical Officer.

**416,000** As gold production falters, Anu arrives on Earth with Enlil, the heir apparent. It is decided to obtain the vital gold by mining it in southern Africa. Drawing lots, Enlil wins command of Earth Mission; Enki is relegated to Africa. On departing Earth, Anu is challenged by Alalu's grandson.

**400,000** Seven functional settlements in southern Mesopotamia include a Spaceport (Sippar), Mission Control Center (Nippur), a metallurgical center (Shuruppak). The ores arrive by ships from Africa; the refined metal is sent aloft to orbiters manned by Igigi, then transferred to spaceships arriving periodically from Nibiru.

**380,000** Gaining the support of the Igigi, Alalu's grandson attempts to seize mastery over Earth. The Enlilites win the War of the Olden Gods.

**300,000** The Anunnaki toiling in the gold mines mutiny. Enki and Ninhursag create Primitive Workers through genetic manipulation of Ape woman; they take over the manual chores of the Anunnaki. Enlil raids the mines, brings the Primitive Workers to the Edin in Mesopotamia. Given the ability to procreate, Homo Sapiens begins to multiply.

**200,000** Life on Earth regresses during a new glacial period.

**100,000** Climate warms again. The Anunnaki (the biblical Nefilim), to Enlil's growing annoyance marry the daughters of Man.

**75,000** The "accusations of Earth" - a new Ice Age-begins. Regressive types of Man roam the Earth . Cro-Magnon man survives.

**49,000** Enki and Ninhursag elevate humans of Anunnaki parentage to rule in Shuruppak. Enlil, enraged. plots Mankind's demise.

**13,000** Realizing that the passage of Nibiru in Earth's proximity will trigger an immense tidal wave, Enlil makes the Anunnaki swear to keep the impending calamity a secret from Mankind.

## II. Events After the Deluge

## B.C.

**11,000** Enki breaks the oath, instructs Ziusudra/Noah to build a submersible ship. The Deluge sweeps over the Earth; the Anunnaki witness the total destruction from their orbiting spacecraft.

Enlil agrees to grant the remnants of Mankind implements and seeds; agriculture begins in the highlands. Enki domesticates animals.

**10,500** The descendants of Noah are allotted three regions. Ninurta, Enlil's foremost son, dams the mountains and drains the rivers to make Mesopotamia habitable; Enki reclaims the Nile valley. The Sinai peninsula is retained by the Anunnaki for a post-Diluvial spaceport; a control center is established on Mount Moriah (the future Jerusalem).

**9780** Ra/Marduk, Enki's firstborn son, divides dominion over Egypt between Osiris and Seth.

**9330** Seth seizes and dismembers Osiris, assumes sole rule over the Nile Valley.

**8970** Horus avenges his father Osiris by launching the First Pyramid War. Seth escapes to Asia, seizes the Sinai peninsula and Canaan.

**8670** Opposed to the resulting control of all the space facilities by Enki's descendants, the Enlilites launch the Second Pyramid War. The victorious Ninurta empties the Great Pyramid of its equipment.

Ninhursag, half-sister of Enki and Enlil, convenes peace conference. The division of Earth is reaffirmed. Rule over Egypt transferred from the Ra/Marduk dynasty to that of Thoth. Heliopolis built as a substitute Beacon City.

**8500** The Anunnaki establish outposts at the gateway to the space facilities; Jericho is one of them.

**7400** As the era of peace continues, the Anunnaki grant Mankind new advances; the Neolithic period begins. Demi-gods rule over Egypt.

**3800** Urban civilization begins in Sumer as the Anunnaki reestablish there the Olden Cities, beginning with Eridu and Nippur.

Anu comes to Earth for a pageantful visit. A new city, Uruk (Erech), is built in his honor; he makes its temple the abode of his beloved granddaughter Inanna/Ishtar.

## III. Kingship on Earth

**3760** Mankind granted kingship. Kish is first capital under the aegis of Ninurta. The calendar begun at Nippur. Civilization blossoms out in Sumer (the First Region).

**3450** Primacy in Sumer transferred to Nannar/Sin. Marduk proclaims Babylon "Gateway of the Gods." The "Tower of Babel" incident. The Anunnaki confuse Mankind's languages.

His coup frustrated, Marduk/Ra returns to Egypt, deposes Thoth, seizes his younger brother Dumuzi who had betrothed Inanna. Dumuzi accidentally killed; Marduk imprisoned alive in the Great Pyramid. Freed through an emergency shaft, he goes into exile.

**3100** 350 years of chaos end with installation of first Egyptian Pharaoh in Memphis. Civilization comes to the Second Region.

**2900** Kingship in Sumer transferred to Erech. Inanna given dominion over the Third Region; the Indus Valley Civilization begins.

**2650** Sumer's royal capital shifts about. Kingship deteriorates. Enlil loses patience with the unruly human multitudes.

**2371** Inanna falls in love with Sharru-Kin (Sargon). He establishes new capital city. Agade (Akkad). Akkadian empire launched.

**2316** Aiming to rule the four regions, Sargon removes sacred soil from Babylon. The Marduk-Inanna conflict flares up again. It ends when Nergal, Marduk's brother, journeys from south Africa to Babylon and persuades Marduk to leave Mesopotamia.

**2291** Naram-Sin ascends the throne of Akkad. Directed by the warlike Inanna, he penetrates the Sinai peninsula, invades Egypt.

**2255** Inanna usurps the power in Mesopotamia; Naram-Sin defies Nippur. The Great Anunnaki obliterate Agade. Inanna escapes. Sumer and Akkad occupied by foreign troops loyal to Enlil and Ninurta.

**2220** Sumerian civilization rises to new heights under enlightened rulers of Lagash. Thoth helps its king Gudea build a ziggurat-temple for Ninurta.

**2193** Terah, Abraham's father, born in Nippur into a priestly-royal family.

**2180** Egypt divided; followers of Ra/Marduk retain the south; Pharaohs opposed to him gain the throne of lower Egypt.

**2130** As Enlil and Ninurta are increasingly away, central authority also deteriorates in Mesopotamia. Inanna's attempts to regain the kingship for Erech does not last.

## The Fateful Century

### B.C

**2123** Abraham born in Nippur.

**2113** Enlil entrusts the Lands of Shem to Nannar; Ur declared capital of new empire. Ur- Nammmu ascends throne, is named Protector of Nippur. A Nippurian priest-Terah, Abraham's father - comes to Ur to liaison with its royal court.

**2096** Ur-Nammu dies in battle. The people consider his untimely death a betrayal by Anu and Enlil. Terah departs with his family for Harran.

**2095** Shulgi ascends the throne of Ur, strengthens imperial ties. As empire thrives, Shulgi falls under charms of Inanna, becomes her lover. Grants Larsa to Elamites in exchange for serving as his Foreign Legion.

**2080** Theban princes loyal to Ra/Marduk press northward under Mentuhotep I. Nabu, Marduk's son, gains adherents for his father in Western Asia.

**2055** On Nannar's orders, Shulgi sends Elamite troops to suppress unrest in Canaanite cities. Elamites reach the gateway to the Sinai peninsula and its Spaceport.

**2048** Shulgi dies. Marduk moves to the Land of the Hittites. Abraham ordered to southern Canaan with an elite corps of cavalrymen.

**2047** Amar-Sin (the biblical Amraphel) becomes king of Ur. Abraham goes to Egypt, stays five years, then returns with more troops.

**2041** Guided by Inanna, Amar-Sin forms a coalition of Kings of the East, launches military expedition to Canaan and the Sinai. Its leader is the Elamite Khedor-la'omer. Abraham blocks the advance at the gateway to the Spaceport.

**2038** Shu-Sin replaces Amar-Sin on throne of Ur as the empire disintegrates.

**2029** Ibbi-Sin replaces Shu-Sin. The western provinces increasingly to Marduk.

**2024** Leading his followers, Marduk marches on Sumer, enthrones himself in Babylon. Fighting spreads to central Mesopotamia. Nippur's Holy of Holies is defiled. Enlil demands punishment for Marduk and Nabu; Enki opposes, but his son Nergal sides with Enlil.

As Nabu marshals his Canaanite followers to capture the Spaceport, the Great Anunnaki approve of the use of nuclear weapons. Nergal and Ninurta destroy the Spaceport and the errant Canaanite cities.

**2023** The winds carry the radioactive cloud to Sumer. People die a terrible death, animals perish, the water is poisoned, the soil becomes barren. Sumer and its great civilization lie prostrate. Its legacy passes to Abraham's seed as he begets -at age 100- a legitimate heir: Isaac.

---

(All of the above was taken from Zecharia Sitchin's EARTH CHRONICLES.)

Books in the EARTH CHRONICLE series: (All Avon Books)
- The 12th Planet
- The Stairway to Heaven
- The Wars of Gods and Men
- The Lost Realms
- When Time Began
- The Cosmic Code
- The End of Days

Companion Books: 'Genesis Revisited'; 'The Lost Book of Enki'; 'There Were Giants Upon The Earth'; 'The Earth Chronicles Handbook'

89098262R00188

Made in the USA
San Bernardino, CA
20 September 2018